INTERNATIONAL MONETARY AND FINANCIAL ISSUES FOR THE 1990s

Research papers for the Group of Twenty-Four

VOLUME IX

UNITED NATIONS
New York and Geneva, 1998

Note

Symbols of United Nations documents are composed of capital letters combined with figures. Mention of such a symbol indicates a reference to a United Nations document.

*

*   *

The views expressed in this compendium are those of the authors and do not necessarily reflect the views of the UNCTAD secretariat. The designations employed and the presentation of the material do not imply the expression of any opinion whatsoever on the part of the Secretariat of the United Nations concerning the legal status of any country, territory, city or area, or of its authorities, or concerning the delimitation of its frontiers or boundaries.

*

*   *

Material in this publication may be freely quoted; acknowledgement, however, is requested (including reference to the document number). It would be appreciated if a copy of the publication containing the quotation were sent to the Editorial Assistant, UNCTAD, Division on Globalization and Development Strategies, Palais des Nations, CH-1211 Geneva 10.

UNCTAD/GDS/MDPB/3

Contents

Page

Abbreviations .... *vii*
The authors .... *ix*
Preface .... *xi*

FINANCIAL LIBERALIZATION AND CAPITAL ACCOUNT REGIME: NOTES ON THE EXPERIENCE OF DEVELOPING COUNTRIES

José María Fanelli 1

Abstract 1
   I.   Introduction 2
  II.   Financial liberalization and the capital account: analytical framework and stylized facts 3
       A.   The analytical approach and the empirical and policy-making implications 3
       B.   The transition period as a source of concern 7
 III.   Uncertainty, instability and financial intermediation 8
       A.   Uncertainty, institutions and markets 8
       B.   Some basic financial relationships 10
       C.   The effects of changes in uncertainty 12
       D.   Dollarization 14
  IV.   Conclusions 15
Notes 17
References 17

RESPONDING TO THE AID CRISIS

Tony Killick 19

Abstract 19
   I.   Is there an aid crisis? 20
       A.   Trends in development assistance 20
       B.   Changes in the global context 24
       C.   Evidence on the effectiveness of aid 25
       D.   Models of aid and development 27
       E.   Conclusion: there is a genuine aid crisis 31
  II.   The future 32
       A.   Prospects for the future volume of ODA 32
       B.   Tackling the crisis - A strategy to raise the effectiveness of ODA 33
Appendix 37
Notes 41
References 42

EXTERNAL DEBT, STRUCTURAL ADJUSTMENT AND ECONOMIC GROWTH

Jeffrey D. Sachs 45

Abstract 45
Introduction 46
    I.   External debt and economic growth 46
    II. Mechanisms for providing debt reduction 49
         A.   Standards for judging the sustainability of debt 49
         B.   Efficient debt reduction: a digression on bankruptcy law 50
         C.   Debt-reduction mechanisms for multilateral creditors 53
Conclusions 54
Notes 54
References 55

THE SIGNIFICANCE OF THE EURO FOR DEVELOPING COUNTRIES

Jacques J. Polak 57

Abstract 57
    I.   Introduction 58
    II. The impact of the euro on the international monetary system 58
         A.   What is the euro? 58
         B.   The euro and the international monetary system 59
         C.   The euro: a strong or a weak currency? 60
         D.   Will the euro be a stable currency? 61
         E.   Towards greater stability among the principal currencies? 62
         F.   Implications for the exchange-rate policies of developing countries ... 63
         G.   Implications for foreign reserve management 65
    III. The impact of the euro on the IMF 65
         A.   Structure and governance 65
         B.   The euro and the future of the SDR 67
Conclusions 68
Notes 69
References 69

**THE ROLE OF SPECIAL DRAWING RIGHTS IN THE
INTERNATIONAL MONETARY SYSTEM**

Hannan Ezekiel 71

Abstract 71
    I.   Introduction 72
    II. International capital flows and reserve needs 72
    III. Holding of SDRs by financial market institutions 74
    IV. Voluntary member commitments to hold SDRs 75
    V. SDRs and international payments crises 77
    VI. SDR procedures and practices 78
    VII. Conclusions and recommendations 79
References 80

GOVERNANCE IN INTERNATIONAL ORGANIZATIONS: THE CASE FOR REFORM IN THE BRETTON WOODS INSTITUTIONS

Ngaire Woods 81

Abstract 81
   I.   Introduction 82
  II. Defining governance and good governance 83
 III. Good governance within international organizations 84
      A.   Governance and effectiveness 84
      B.   Alternative voting structures:
           the experience of the regional development banks 85
      C.   Voting versus consensus decision-making:
           the experience of the United Nations Security Council and the GATT 88
      D.   Special voting arrangements and decision-making: the experience of the
           Council of the European Union, the International Fund for Agriculture
           Development, and the Global Environment Facility 91
  IV. Voting and decision-making in the Bretton Woods institutions 95
   V. The case for reform in the Bretton Woods institutions 100
 VI. Conclusions 102
Notes 103
References 103

NON-GOVERNMENTAL ORGANIZATIONS AND THE INTERNATIONAL MONETARY AND FINANCIAL SYSTEM

Charles Abugre and Nancy Alexander 107

Abstract 107
   I.   Non-governmental organizations - An overview of the movement 108
      A.   Definition and typology 108
      B.   International reach of NGOs 109
      C.   The role of Southern NGOs in regional and international fora 110
      D.   Sources of funding 111
  II. Power imbalances among Northern and Southern NGOs and Southern governments 112
      A.   Relations among NGOs 112
      B.   Relations between NGOs and Southern governments 113
 III. NGO opposition to asymmetry in decision-making 114
 IV. NGO advocacy and the international financial institutions 115
      A.   Background 115
      B.   Typical advocacy positions 117
      C.   NGOs and the external debt problem 118
      D.   Structural adjustment and governance 120
      E.   Stakeholder participation 121
   V. Conclusion 122
Notes 124
References 124

THE STATE IN A CHANGING WORLD:
A CRITIQUE OF THE WORLD DEVELOPMENT REPORT 1997

Devesh Kapur 127

Abstract 127
    I.   Introduction 128
    II. Structure and approach of the WDR 1997 128
    III. The World Bank's conception of the State 130
    IV. Underexplored issues 131
        A.   State capability 131
        B.   Property rights 131
        C.   Industrial policy 132
        D.   Corruption 132
        E.   Civil society and participation 133
        F.   International collective action 133
        G.   Anglo-Saxon legal norms 133
        H.   Credibility versus flexibility 134
        I.   Population 134
    V.   Misplaced quantification 135
    VI. Conclusion 137
Notes 137
References 138
Annex I 139
Annex II 140

Abbreviations

ADF	African Development Fund
AfDB	African Development Bank
AsDB	Asian Development Bank
BADEA	Arab Bank for Economic Development in Africa
BIS	Bank for International Settlements
BWIs	Bretton Woods institutions
CFA	Communauté financière africaine
DAC	Development Assistance Committee (of OECD)
DBR	domestically generated budget revenue
DQMs	double-qualified majorities
EBRD	European Bank for Reconstruction and Development
EDI	Economic Development Institute (World Bank)
EMU	European Monetary Union
ESAF	Enhanced Structural Adjustment Facility (IMF)
ESCB	European System of Central Banks
EU	European Union
EUC	European Council
FDI	foreign direct investment
FSO	Fund for Special Operations (IDB)
FY	fiscal year
GAB	General Arrangements to Borrow
GATT	General Agreement on Tariffs and Trade
GDP	gross domestic product
GEF	Global Environment Facility
GNP	gross national product
HIPCs	heavily indebted poor countries
IBRD	International Bank for Reconstruction and Development
ICOR	incremental capital-output ratio
IDA	International Development Association
IDB	Inter-American Development Bank
IFAD	International Fund for Agricultural Development
IFIs	international financial institutions
IMF	International Monetary Fund
IPRs	intellectual property rights
LDCs	least developed countries
LIBOR	London Interbank Offered Rate
MDB	Multilateral Development Bank
MEFMI	Macroeconomic and Financial Management Institute of Eastern and Southern Africa

NAFTA	North American Free Trade Agreement
NEAPs	national environmental action plans
NGOs	non-governmental organizations
NIEs	newly industrializing economies
NPV	net present value
ODA	official development assistance
ODI	Overseas Development Institute
OECD	Organization for Economic Co-operation and Development
OPEC	Organization of Petroleum Exporting Countries
PERs	public expenditure reviews
PPP	purchasing power parity
PV	present value of debt
QMV	qualified majority voting
SAF	Structural Adjustment Facility
SCA-2	Special Contingency Account II
SDR	Special Drawing Right
SILICs	severely indebted low-income countries
SSA	sub-Saharan Africa
TC	technical cooperation
UNDP	United Nations Development Programme
UNEP	United Nations Environment Programme
WDR	World Development Report
WTO	World Trade Organization

The authors

- **Charles Abugre,** Head, African Secretariat, Third World Network, and Executive Director, ISODEC, Accra, Ghana

- **Nancy Alexander,** Development Bank Watchers' Project, Bread for the World Institute, Silver Spring, Maryland

- **Hannan Ezekiel,** Business and Economic Consultant, Alexandria, Virginia (USA)

- **José María Fanelli,** Senior Researcher, Centro de Estudios de Estado y Sociedad, Buenos Aires

- **Devesh Kapur,** Centre for International Affairs, Harvard University, Cambridge, MA

- **Tony Killick,** Senior Research Fellow, Overseas Development Institute, London

- **Jacques J. Polak,** President of the Per Jacobsson Foundation, Washington, D.C.

- **Jeffrey D. Sachs,** Director, Harvard Institute for International Development, and Galen L. Stone Professor of International Trade, Harvard University, Cambridge, MA

- **Ngaire Woods,** Fellow in Politics, University College, Oxford, United Kingdom

Preface

The Intergovernmental Group of Twenty-Four on International Monetary Affairs (G-24) was established in November 1971 to increase the negotiating strength of the developing countries in discussions that were going on at that time in the International Monetary Fund on reform of the international monetary system. Developing countries felt that they should play a meaningful role in decisions about the system, and that the effectiveness of that role would be enhanced if they were to meet regularly as a group, as the developed countries had been doing for some time in the Group of Ten (G-10).

It soon became apparent that the G-24 was in need of technical support and analysis relating to the issues arising for discussion in the Fund and Bank, including the Interim and Development Committees. In response to representations by the Chairman of the G-24 to the Secretary-General of the United Nations Conference on Trade and Development (UNCTAD), and following discussions between UNCTAD and the United Nations Development Programme (UNDP), the latter agreed in 1975 to establish a project to provide the technical support that the G-24 had requested. This was to take the form, principally, of analytical papers prepared by competent experts on issues currently under consideration in the fields of international money and finance.

Mr. Sidney Dell, a former Director in UNCTAD's Money, Finance and Development Division and subsequently Assistant Administrator of UNDP headed the project from its establishment until 1990. During this period, some 60 research papers were prepared by the Group of Twenty-Four. The high quality of this work was recognized by the Deputies and Ministers of the Group and the reports were given wide currency, some being published in five volumes by North-Holland Press and others by the United Nations.

The project work was resumed in 1990 under the direction of Gerry K. Helleiner, Professor of Economics, University of Toronto, Canada. The UNCTAD secretariat provides both substantive and administrative backstopping to the project. Funding is currently being provided by the G-24 countries themselves, the International Development Research Centre of Canada and the Governments of Denmark and the Netherlands. As a result, it has been possible to continue to provide the Group of Twenty-Four with timely and challenging analyses. These studies are being reissued periodically in compendia. This is the ninth volume to be published.

Preface

FINANCIAL LIBERALIZATION AND CAPITAL ACCOUNT REGIME: NOTES ON THE EXPERIENCE OF DEVELOPING COUNTRIES

José María Fanelli

Abstract

The experience of some developing countries such as Mexico, Argentina and Turkey in the present decade has been a source of much concern. The question whether financial markets are dynamically stable in a context of deregulation and absence of capital controls has received particular attention. This paper investigates the linkages between domestic financial markets and the capital account regime in the case of developing countries.

It first analyses some stylized facts which constitute "anomalies" from the analytical perspective of the liberalization approach, but that are relevant to the explanation of the disequilibria and the instability in the interaction between the financial system and the capital account. Examples of such anomalies are the fall in national savings and mounting current-account deficits following the reform, financial crises and speculative attacks. Then a simple analytical framework is developed, to show that the high level of uncertainty created by macroeconomic volatility and institutional flaws is the main cause of financial disintermediation and fragility. The issue of "dollarization" of the financial system is also analysed.

We conclude that finance matters to development because of significant imperfections in the structure of financial markets in developing countries. The main implication for policy-making is that the objective should be to create markets which do not yet exist, and to strengthen existing ones. Therefore, it must be recognized that financial liberalization and the lifting of capital-account controls will foster financial deepening only to the extent that they contribute to removing uncertainty and to improving the institutional infrastructure. We argue that to ensure stability, some degree of market "friendly" financial repression might be necessary in the short run, even if free financial markets are the ultimate objective. Capital controls to restrain capital inflows and to check the expansion of consumption credit during the boom which tends to follow the first stages of financial liberalization are two important examples.

I. Introduction

In the post-war scenario, control over capital account transactions and "financial repression" in domestic markets was the rule, and free convertibility and deregulated financial intermediation were the exception. In the late 1970s, this situation began to change because of the growing number of countries which implemented liberalization initiatives. By the mid-1990s, the process of liberalization of the capital account had concluded and financial intermediation had been strongly deregulated in industrial countries.[1] In the developing world, at present, several countries have introduced full convertibility and many others are following in a swift process to liberalize the capital account.[2] Two main forces (which are still at work) have influenced developing countries to open their capital accounts and increase domestic competition. One was the deregulation of financial markets in developed countries with the concomitant emergence of a new gamut of innovative financial instruments, and the global integration of international capital markets; these factors greatly reduced the effectiveness of capital controls and tended to induce domestic disintermediation because of increased competition from foreign financial centres. The other was the Washington Consensus' (see Williamson, 1990; World Bank, 1991; and Fanelli, Frenkel and Taylor, 1992) recommendations, which promoted the elimination of controls and distortions in the economy as a means of fuelling growth via improvements in the allocation of resources.

In the context of the strong acceleration of liberalization in the 1990s, nonetheless, the experience of some developing countries is a source of much concern. The main reason for this is the question whether financial markets are dynamically stable in a context of deregulation and absence of capital controls. In fact, the concern over the linkages and interactions between domestic financial institutions and foreign investors is fully justified to the extent that these factors have played a crucial role in key financial events in the developing world over the last 15 years. The lack of timing between the opening of the capital account and the liberalization of financial and other markets was a primary cause of the failure of the first attempts at outright liberalization in the Southern Cone of Latin America. Financial crises elsewhere in the 1980s were closely related to capital flight.[3] For many countries, and especially those in Latin America, the debt crisis was definitively overcome only after the surge in capital inflows softened the external constraint, thereby de-activating an important source of macroeconomic and financial disequilibria. The failure of the programmes in Turkey and Mexico and the problems in Argentina in the mid-1990s occurred in a context of increasing liberalization and integration between domestic and foreign financial markets. These latter cases were especially important in fuelling the debate, since Mexico, Argentina and Turkey were seen as examples of the benefits of liberalization in the line of the Washington Consensus.

This paper investigates the linkages between domestic financial markets and the capital account regime in the context of developing countries. Many factors contribute to shaping the features of such linkages: the regulations affecting capital-account transactions and internal financial markets; the composition of capital flows; the exchange-rate regime; the characteristics of monetary and fiscal policies; the structure of financial intermediation; the level of macroeconomic stability; and developments in the international capital markets. Liberalization affects several of these elements and, hence, has important consequences on the interactions between the financial system and capital inflows.

With respect to dynamic stability, the consequences of the reforms on the factors determining the degree of financial fragility and macroeconomic equilibrium are the most relevant. From this point of view, it is not only a problem of choosing the best "sequencing" of reforms but also of ensuring the consistency between economic reform and the existing degree of development in both markets and institutions. For example, one important question for policy-making and sequencing is: should the lifting of controls on capital-account transactions precede or follow the reform of the banking system? Also, is it convenient to liberalize both short- and long-run capital flows at once, or would it be better to liberalize first only long-run flows in order to minimize speculative movements?[4]

An answer cannot be found only by taking into account the question of "speculation" in the foreign exchange markets. The answer depends crucially on whether there is a strong framework for prudential supervision of the banking system to prevent an increase in financial fragility. In turn, to ensure macroeconomic consistency in a more open environment, more reliance on indirect monetary policy instruments will be necessary. However, if the size of bond markets is too small, the attempt to manage the money supply via open-market operations could generate a great deal of instability in the system. Likewise, to guarantee some degree of independence for the monetary authorities to manage the effects of capital movements, the monetization of the fiscal deficit should be strictly limited and, hence, the institutions governing the budgetary process must be changed. Neither capital markets nor institutions can be created or improved overnight, as the experiences in Eastern European transition economies show (Schmidt, 1996). In fact, some experiences of swift liberalization were aborted precisely because they tended to ignore the constraints of the existing market and "institutional" failures. In the presence of such failures, the reform may generate unsustainable levels of financial fragility and macro-economic instability.

Given the complexity of the issue, some clarifications on the scope and characteristics of this paper might be useful. Firstly, this is intended to be a conceptual paper. Its main goal is not to present evidence on countries' liberalization experiences but rather to examine the process of deregulation in terms of stylized facts. The reference to actual experiences is guided more by an analytical interest than by the intention to present a complete systematization of the evidence. The ultimate purpose of our search for new insights into the issue is to draw lessons from the point of view of economic policy-making. Given the influence of the IMF and the World Bank on economic policy-making in developing countries, a reference is made to their recommendations when appropriate.

Secondly, most allusions to particular experiences comprise developing countries, where the issue of the linkages between domestic financial markets and the regime of the external capital account has been most relevant in the 1990s, that is, countries which have received capital inflows and launched important measures to liberalize the financial intermediation process.

Thirdly, the paper focuses on the interactions between the capital-account regime and the banking system, since financial intermediation in developing economies is bank-dominated. Likewise, given the growing importance of internal financial transactions in foreign currency in many developing countries, the issue of "dollarization" receives special attention.

The paper is organized as follows. The first section defines the object of study and presents important stylized facts about the recent experiences of developing countries. The second analyses the structure of financial intermediation in a representative developing country, and indicates a number of characteristics explaining some of the flaws in the design of the packages which aim at financial

deepening and free convertibility. The last section presents policy conclusions, as well as some suggestions for further research.

II. Financial liberalization and the capital account: analytical framework and stylized facts

This section presents the central arguments of the literature on the liberalization of domestic financial markets and the capital account, and analyses some significant gaps between expectations and results observed during the liberalization process in developing countries that have a bearing on the linkages between domestic financial intermediation and the capital account. Finally, there is an analysis of why such gaps or "anomalies" are a cause for concern to economic policy-making and a challenge for economic analysis.

A. *The analytical approach and the empirical and policy-making implications*

Two ideas constitute the core of the financial liberalization approach. The first is that finance matters to development. The second is that the market is the best institution to achieve the maximum efficiency in financial intermediation.

The idea that finance matters could hardly be surprising to any agent involved in the productive process in a developing country. At the analytical level, however, McKinnon's (1973) and Shaw's (1973) approaches were ground-breaking because the role of finance in the growth process had been largely neglected or, at least, overlooked by the mainstream. In the environment of the more closed economies in the early 1970s, the works on financial liberalization focused on the domestic financial markets rather than on cross-border financial transactions and singled out "financial repression"[5] as the most important force restraining the deepening of the financial system.

The policy implications are crystal clear: if financial repression were eliminated, competition would increase the efficiency in the intermediation of funds, thereby simultaneously improving the rate of return to savers and lowering the cost of capital to firms and debtors. The observable consequences which follow from this approach are also clear. After liberalization one should observe: (a) a fall in the spread between borrowing and lending rates in the bank-dominated intermediation process; (b) an improvement in the efficiency of investment; (c) an increase in savings; and (d) greater financial deepening reflected in the upward trend in the ratio of deposits to GDP.

In recent years, the line of research opened by endogenous growth models has given rise to a new trend in the liberalization literature that emphasizes the potential Schumpeterian gains that could be achieved via the liberalization of financial markets. The apparent implication is that there is a positive correlation between growth and financial deepening (King and Levine, 1993a, 1993b).[6]

From the analytical point of view, it does not make a difference if financial intermediation is done by domestic or by foreign agents. Hence, to reap the benefits of liberalization, all government interventions should be eliminated, irrespective of whether they affect financial transactions within the country or across the borders, and irrespective of whether the financial instrument is denominated in foreign or domestic currency. Liberalization should comprise all markets for the intermediation of funds.

Nonetheless, there are "specific" benefits in liberalizing the capital account. It would be welfare-improving because a better allocation of intertemporal consumption and resources in countries with differing preferences and investment opportunities would be possible. Likewise, in the context of the growing importance of international portfolio flows, capital-account liberalization would allow investors to attain the optimum risk-return combination by means of cross-country risk diversification.

An additional benefit, stressed by the IMF, is that an open capital account places a particular premium on appropriate macroeconomic policies. The risk of large capital reversals requires that monetary policy be managed in such a way that interest rates and exchange rates are broadly consistent with underlying fundamentals and market conditions (Quirk and Evans, 1995).

It follows from the conceptual framework that the best policy is to deregulate the banking sector, the capital account of the balance of payments, and the securities and derivative markets. Likewise, the barriers which could limit competition between these different segments of the capital markets should

also be eliminated. The expected benefits would be: (a) an increase in the savings rate; (b) an improvement of investment efficiency and innovation; (c) a reduction in the intermediation spread; (d) greater financial deepening; (e) a better allocation of savings, investment and risks by resorting to international capital markets; and (f) better macroeconomic management.

In general, the results of the financial lib-eralization attempts in developing countries have been mixed. Obviously, it is difficult to isolate and analyse results attributable to the reform, since in most cases reforms were also being undertaken in other areas and there were sizeable exogenous shocks affecting the economy. However, there were many cases in which the discrepancies between expected and observed results were extremely broad. In particular, there were important failures in relatively large developing countries that had implemented radical liberalization packages.

We list below some stylized facts which con-stitute "anomalies" from the analytical perspective of the liberalization approach, but which are relevant to our investigation of the linkages between the financial system and the capital account. Together with each anomaly, we present a brief reference to concrete experiences which we believe are paradigmatic and, hence, useful for highlighting why an anomaly is a cause for concern to policy makers.

(1)   In many countries that have launched financial liberalization programmes the national savings rate has not only failed to increase but has even fallen.

The major factors behind the discrepancy between the results anticipated by the theory and those observed seem to have been the following: (a) sub-stitution effects resulting from the freeing of interest rates were weaker than anticipated; (b) retained corporate profits and public savings are important sources of national savings in developing countries and, while the increment in interest rates redistributes income away from those sectors, it is unclear whether the sectors favoured by the increase in interest rates have a high propensity to save; (c) the expansion in credit that generally follows liberalization softens the liquidity constraints of households and therefore raises consumption.[7]

There is substantial evidence of the importance of these factors. Although Chile had liberalized in the late 1970s, it avoided the collapse of the national savings rate during the debt crisis of the 1980s by increasing public-sector savings (Damill et al., 1994). In the 1990s, there was a remarkable recovery in private savings but the major part is explained by retained earnings in a context of a buoyant investment climate. Between 1985 and 1994 there was an impressive rise of 17.6 percentage points of GDP in the national savings rate, of which 11 points are accounted for by firms and 4.7 by the public sector. In spite of the reform of the social security system, personal savings only increased by 1.9 percentage points of GDP (Solimano, 1996). The negative redistributive effects of interest-rate increases on savings in the case of Turkey's reform in the 1990s is emphasized by Balkan and Yeldan (1996). Another important fact is that the rate of national savings is still very low in Latin America in spite of the liberalization wave of the 1990s (Damill et al., 1994). An interesting case is Uruguay, which has shown no recovery in its savings rate after 20 years of reform. Although there was an increase in financial deepening, it was not the result of a major change in savings. The main effect of the deregulation measures was, instead, a reallocation of the financial portfolio of private agents from the informal curb markets and from assets accumulated abroad through capital flight towards the domestic financial system (Noya et al., 1996).

One piece of evidence regarding liquidity effects on consumption is that the volatility of the consumption rate is much higher in developing countries than in developed ones (IDB, 1995). Argentina and Mexico in the 1990s are examples of consumption booms triggered by relaxation of the credit constraint faced by consumers (Fanelli et al., 1996; Ross, 1996).

(2) In several cases there has been a tendency for a country to generate excessive current-account deficits.

Theory predicts that the opening of the capital account should result in an optimal allocation of consumption, investment and risk. However, the usual outcome of liberalization has been a generation of excessive current-account deficits. This is one of the most important causes for concern among policy makers, and no reliable analytical tools account for this fact. There is no consensus of what an unsustainable current account is (Calvo, 1996). But the fact is that the periodical tightening in developing countries' access to international markets has resulted in their having an excessively volatile evolution of domestic absorption (IDB, 1995).

In the context of increasingly deregulated financial markets and declining control over capital-account transactions in the 1990s, many developing countries have shown a propensity to run a higher current-account disequilibrium. Mexico, Argentina and Turkey have experienced severe macroeconomic crises after rapid increases in their current-account deficits. Mexico shows the sharpest increase: between 1990 and 1994 the current-account deficit rose from 2.7 per cent of GDP to 7.9 per cent (Ross, 1996).

There are several hypotheses on the causes of the current-account deficit. But disregarding causality, an increase in the current account tends to be correlated with a fall in national savings, an increase in the prices of tradable vis-à-vis non-tradable goods, and with an overexpansion of domestic credit (Ffrench Davis and Griffith-Jones, 1995).

(3) Numerous instances have been observed in which the increase in financial deepening was very small and highly dependent on macroeconomic developments. Besides, too many liberalization experiences have resulted in financial crisis.

There are several interesting country experiences on this issue. In the first place, there are countries that have experienced substantial financial deepening at the onset of reform, without, however, reaching the degree of financial deepening characteristic of industrial countries. In Uruguay, for example, financial liberalization and opening of the capital account have been sustained since the 1970s. Since then the country has been through a deep financial crisis (in the mid-1980s); the M3/GDP ratio has only grown from 20 to 39 per cent; dollarization has deepened; and almost 50 per cent of total credit is still generated by public banks (Noya et al., 1996). Chile, on the other hand, which is considered to be the most successful free-market economy in Latin America, has achieved an important degree of deepening. However, the controls on capital movements have not been fully eliminated and the most important force pushing financial deepening was the reform of the social security system, which is based on mandatory savings rather than on financial liberalization. Likewise, according to McKinnon (1991), the maintenance of a certain degree of financial repression has greatly helped financial development in many Asian countries.

(4)   Some countries have undergone an increase in the "dollarization" of the financial system, which the theory had not anticipated.

Uruguay, again, is a good case in point. Peru and Argentina, perhaps the most radical reformers in the Latin American region, have experienced a deepening of the dollarization process since the launching of the reform in the 1990s. In Peru, the dollarized segment represented 56 per cent of total deposits in 1991, when the reform began to be implemented. By 1995, its share had climbed to 61 per cent. In the same period, monetization of the economy rose from 7.6 to 16 per cent of GDP (Romero, 1996; Dancourt, 1996).

In Argentina, the M3/GDP ratio rose from 7 to about 18 per cent during the reform period. The increase in the demand for domestic assets showed a bias in favour of dollar-denominated instruments. The same bias was observed in the credit generated by the system. The banks seem to have been attempting to match dollar-denominated assets and liabilities in their balance sheets in order to avoid taking an excessive devaluation risk. The proportion of dollar-denominated assets rose after the Mexican shock to about 50 per cent of total deposits and is still increasing.

The preference for dollar-denominated assets and liabilities is a significant cause of the persistence of a high degree of financial fragility in the system in both Argentina and Peru. Given the aforementioned behaviour of banks and the impossibility of diversifying away the devaluation risk for the system as a whole, it is the borrower who must bear the devaluation risk, particularly those borrowers producing non-tradables. Under these circumstances, the behaviour of banks matching dollar-denominated assets to dollar-denominated liabilities might not ensure them against the risk of insolvency, because a devaluation could generate a systemic payment crisis.

(5)   There is evidence in a number of countries that efficiency gains may not have been as important and rapid as reformers had expected.

It has often been observed that there has been no clear tendency for the spreads to fall and for market segmentation to disappear. Major differences between the spreads paid by distinct categories of debtors have tended to remain. These differences are huge in many countries. Fry (1995) attributed the lack of success

in reducing spreads to, among other factors, excessive administrative costs, high rates of default and elevated reserve requirements. Market segmentation seems to persist. In the case of Indonesia, Harris et al. (1994) made a positive evaluation of the results of the reform but found that the reform had different effects on establishments with different characteristics. Small establishments benefited from improved access but at substantially higher interest rates. Finance was much cheaper for firms with access to foreign financial markets, namely, large conglomerates that owned banks and enjoyed direct relations with offshore credit markets in Singapore and Hong Kong and exporters with established overseas commercial relations.

*(6)   International capital markets show impor-
        tant imperfections. Developing countries
        have faced serious impediments to reaping
        the benefits of consumption smoothing,
        investment reallocation and risk diver-
        sification that were expected from the
        opening of the capital account and inte-
        gration into the global economy.*

The first relevant imperfection is that the market is highly segmented. Smaller developing countries face tight rationing. The bulk of disposable funds is absorbed by a small number of countries. For example, in the 1990s three quarters of external bond issues by developing countries and economies in transition have been accounted for by four borrowers in Latin America and five in Asia (UNCTAD, 1996). In the second place, the functioning of the market is still far from efficient. Two recent episodes have revealed important anomalies. The tightening of monetary policy in the United States in early 1994 and the Mexican crisis in December 1994 generated strong fluctuations in the availability of funds for developing countries. Particularly important was the volatility of funds flowing into Latin America. At the national level, this caused important variations in key macroeconomic variables. Countries with large current-account deficits and fixed (or heavily managed) exchange rates suffered more from the volatility of capital flows. Another disappointing feature is that the returns on developing countries' securities become increasingly correlated in periods of stress in the financial markets. For example, following the Mexican devaluation the correlations in total returns on Brady bonds in developing countries rose sharply (IMF, 1995). It is very difficult to diversify risk efficiently in a context of instability of return distributions.

(7) There were cases of strong macroeconomic disequilibria following the opening of the capital account and deregulation, which resulted in the abortion of the process.

Independently of the exchange-rate regime chosen, there have been numerous instances of strong domestic currency appreciation followed by an attack on the currency. There are several hypotheses about the direction of causality between financial and capital-account liberalization, on the one hand, and macroeconomic stability, on the other. It is clear, nonetheless, that the beneficial effects of the opening of the capital account on macroeconomic policy making are far from automatic. The most important recent example of perverse interactions between capital inflows, financial distress and economic policy making is undoubtedly Mexico (Calvo, 1996; Roett, 1996; and Ross, 1996).

B. The transition period as a source of concern

Two factors are commonly cited to account for the discrepancies between results and expectations. The first refers to practical issues. Financial repression cannot be eliminated overnight because the distortions affecting distinct markets call for specific treatment and sequencing; the measures affect vested interests which oppose political resistance, etc. The second is the existence of market imperfections which have made the process of resource reallocation more difficult and time-consuming. Under these circumstances, there will be a transitional period of disequilibrium. Hence, it is necessary to carefully design the sequence of the reforms between and within each market to minimize the size and duration of the disequilibria.

The first important studies of the linkages between the financial system and the capital account in the transition period have been provided by the literature on the causes of the failure of the liberalization attempts in the Southern Cone of Latin America in the early 1980s. One significant conclusion attributed these failures to errors in the implementation of the programmes and not necessarily to flaws in the conceptual framework which supported them. From the analysis of the Southern Cone experiences, many practical lessons on the correct sequencing of reforms were drawn.[8] The correct sequence was considered to be the opening of the current account before liberalizing financial markets. Only after these

reforms were firmly established was the capital account of the balance of payments to be deregulated. In the meanwhile, the safest strategy was to maintain capital controls. Another important recommendation on sequencing was the need to achieve a minimum of macroeconomic stability before launching a financial reform package.

Paradoxically, the conclusion that capital controls should be maintained until the achievement of both domestic deregulation and macroeconomic stability was not reached until the 1980s, when controls on capital movements were becoming less and less effective and many developing countries were undergoing their worst period of macroeconomic instability in the post-war period as a consequence of the debt crisis and the breakdown of the socialist system.

In the present decade, the newly invigorated capital flows to developing countries has again posed the question of financial and macroeconomic stability. But no consensus seems to have been reached on what policies would best ensure stability. In fact, recent experience in developing countries shows a varied picture regarding the sequence of reform implementation. While some countries have tried to follow the gradual approach suggested in the literature, others have opted for a shock treatment and liberalized quite rapidly. Obviously, the main determinant of the amplitude, speed and sequencing of the reforms have not been analytical considerations but rather the situation of the economy prior to reforms and the political scenario. This was very clear, for example, in the cases of the transition economies of Eastern Europe, as well as in countries like Bolivia, Peru and Argentina, which underwent episodes of hyperinflation before launching the reforms.

In addition to practical considerations, it seems that a greater degree of understanding of the question of managing the linkages between the financial system and the capital account during the reform could help to avoid failures during the transition period. One important fact that should be taken into account is that the nature of the policy dilemma has changed. In the 1970s the problem facing policy makers was how to adapt the existing capital controls to the deregulation of the domestic financial system. By contrast, the present problem is more how to adapt the domestic financial system to a capital account which tends to be *de facto* (if not *de jure*) free from controls.[9] Under such circumstances, the major cause for concern is that the maintenance of controls tends to generate important costs in terms of domestic financial disintermediation; but their elimination might significantly increase the exposure of the economy to external shocks and financial volatility, in addition to the fact that there would be less autonomy in policy making.

On the one hand, the changes in the international scenario may have eliminated the possibility of resorting to capital controls to defend the domestic economy against shocks and to attenuate volatility. But, on the other hand, the elimination of controls gives rise to a transition process characterized by strong and unstable disequilibria. For example, imagine what would happen in a pessimistic scenario where most of the above-listed anomalies occur after the liberalization process has been launched. Specifically, imagine a transition period of seven years, during which the savings rate falls from 18 per cent of GDP at the beginning of the period to 15.7 per cent; that the current-account deficit increases from 1.4 to 7.9 per cent of GDP; that there is financial deepening and, as a consequence, total outstanding bank loans increase by more than 100 per cent in real terms; and that the country integrates into the international capital market and is considered a leading emerging market. Capital flows, nonetheless, prove to be too volatile. In four years the country receives $91 billion, which represents one fifth of all net inflows to developing countries but, as a result of financial and political problems, in just nine months the country loses $16.4 billion in reserves. Excessive reliance on short-term securities by the government and the increase in the amount of non-performing loans in the banking system results in a speculative attack, devaluation and severe macroeconomic imbalances. One could think that it is too pessimistic to assume that all these anomalies can occur in one country in the same period. Although the example can be considered pessimistic, it is not unrealistic. The figures and stylized facts correspond to the case of Mexico in the 1988-1994 period.

In sum, developing countries are facing mounting pressure from international markets and must find a way to adapt their internal economies to the new environment without jeopardizing growth. A better understanding of this problem can be gained by looking at some structural features of developing countries which the literature has tended to ignore, and that have been overlooked in the World Bank's and the IMF's policy recommendations. We shall examine this question in the following section.

III. Uncertainty, instability and financial intermediation

In Shaw's (1973) seminal work, finance matters to development because the structure of markets for the intermediation of funds is imperfect. According to this author, the most important imperfections characterizing the developing countries' financial structure are market segmentation, the short-term horizon for decision-making, difficulties in the process of information gathering, low factor mobility, narrow capital markets, and difficulties in distinguishing between internal and external debt with respect to the private sector.

In the literature advocating liberalization the primary source of market imperfections is financial repression. If distortions were removed, there would be no major impediment to optimizing the allocation of resources. Research and policy efforts are consequently oriented to analysing and finding solutions to the problems of implementation. Shaw's references to the importance of other sources of market failures and the need to elaborate a "debt intermediation view" to model and analyse the financial structure of developing countries are lost in the subsequent developments of the approach.

We would like to explore here a set of hypotheses which is akin to the initial spirit of Shaw's debt intermediation view. The hypotheses stress the role of financial underdevelopment as an impediment to growth. It is argued that in spite of the negative consequences of some government interventions, the primary causes for the underdevelopment of financial markets are a number of structural characteristics of developing economies. In this view, financial repression is not an exogenous factor but rather an "endogenous" consequence of the rudimentary development of markets.

A.   *Uncertainty, institutions and markets*

The most relevant structural characteristic explaining the underdevelopment of markets in developing countries is the high level of uncertainty. The primary source of excessive uncertainty is the high volatility of key macroeconomic variables.

One way to evaluate the degree of uncertainty that agents face in developing countries is to compare the volatility of key macroeconomic variables of developed countries with those of developing

Table 1

INDICATORS OF VOLATILITY AND INSTABILITY, 1970-1992

(Per cent of standard deviation)

	Latin America	Asian NIEs	South-East Asia	Developed countries
GDP growth rate	4.7	3.0	3.4	2.2
Consumption growth rate	5.6	4.1	5.4	2.1
Investment growth rate	16.1	16.4	11.0	8.3
Real exchange rate	13.4	6.2	n.a.	4.8
Rate of inflation	463.5	6.2	7.9	3.9
Terms of trade (change)	15.1	8.0	7.9	8.9
Capital flows	2.8	1.5	1.1	1.7
Frequency of recessions (years)	2.7	0.7	1.8	2.1
Duration of recessions (years)	1.9	1.0	1.2	1.3
Intensity of recessions (per cent)	-8.0	-1.6	-3.5	-2.0

Source: IDB (1995).

countries. Table 1 shows some valuable evidence of differences these countries have with regard to the degree of uncertainty. In developing countries there is far more built-in noise in the stochastic process governing the evolution of key macroeconomic variables, such as the level of activity and the rate of the investment. Macroeconomic disequilibria show signs of instability in that they tend to be more recurrent, relatively longer lasting and deeper than in industrial countries.

The second important factor impeding the development of financial markets is the flaws in the institutional infrastructure. With non-zero transaction costs institutions matter. In fact, one of the characteristics which differentiates developed from developing countries is that industrial countries found the way to develop the elaborate institutional structure needed for complex and impersonal exchanges to take place at minimum cost. The different institutions which constitute the structure of financial inter-mediation can be conceived of as an arrangement to minimize transaction costs (Fry, 1995). In developing countries, the quality of information and accounting systems is bad; the legal and regulatory framework is typically weak; property rights tend to be more

ambiguous; and guaranteeing the enforcement of financial contracts is more difficult. Consequently, unreliable and inefficient institutions become an independent source of uncertainty.

Macroeconomic and institutional uncertainties are highly corrosive to the structure of financial markets in developing countries. Too much volatility shortens the time horizon and increases credit risk (Rojas-Suarez and Weisbrod, 1995 and 1996). This severely affects markets for long-term borrowing and lending, risk diversification and hedging (Glen, 1993). Likewise, the higher costs of gathering information and designing an optimal contract - taking into account the problems of incentive compatibility and en-forcement - make transaction costs higher, and in many instances prohibitively high. As a result, many transactions are unprofitable and, hence, are not made, so markets become thinner and illiquid or disappear.

These facts significantly contribute to shaping the structure of financial intermediation in developing countries. There are several features of such a structure which merit comment. The first is that functional efficiency tends to be rather low. Illiquid and shallow financial markets imply that it will be very difficult for financial intermediaries to achieve minimum efficient scales and the optimum degree of specialization in the production of some financial services. The lack of specialization and scale push up unit costs. A situation may arise where highly valuable services are not provided just because they are unprofitable on the scale and at the degree of specialization at which they could be produced.

The second feature is that excessive volatility and the difficulties in evaluating credit risk impede the development of numerous markets which exist in industrial countries. In the developing world organized future markets, over-the-counter forwards and option markets either do not exist or are highly rudimentary. Likewise, the markets for long-term credit in domestic currency are very thin and segmented, and, where stock markets exist, their level of capitalization is very low. Besides, risk diversification is very elementary because of the lack of diversity in the gamut of activities in the market, and because only shares of the most representative firms have a liquid and active market. Markets for government bonds are usually more liquid and larger than the markets for private securities, yet they are characterized by a high volatility of returns. On the other hand, there are also markets which exist just because of the high level of uncertainty. A case in point is the market for dollar-denominated deposits, which develops because the public uses foreign exchange as an imperfect hedge against such macroeconomic disequilibria as high inflation and unexpected devaluation.

The third feature is that the banking sector shows two important deficiencies. In the first place, credit rationing is pervasive because of the importance of informational asymmetries and agency costs. The lack of correct information about potential borrowers might result in perverse rules for the allocation of credit which ration out those agents with the projects that yield the highest-return (Cho, 1986). In a situation in which the costs of screening, monitoring and enforcing are too high for certain groups, the market will be segmented, and this segmentation can be highly inefficient. Excessively high interest rates and exchange-rate volatility, on the other hand, not only make organized markets for hedging interest and exchange risk disappear but also cause banks to be highly reluctant to engage in the intermediation of currency denomination and maturity. For the same reason, banks are averse to over-the-counter transactions.

These structural weaknesses in financial markets severely limit the ability of households and firms to attain the optimum risk-return combination in portfolio allocation. Market segmentation tends to discriminate against households, small- and medium-sized enterprises, and innovative entrepreneurs. The expenditure decision of these agents is tightly constrained by liquidity, while investment in credit-constrained firms tends to be financed by retained earnings. As a consequence, "accelerator" variables such as lagged output, sales or cash flow tend to have a great impact on spending (Bernanke and Gertler, 1995).

The capital structure of large firms with access to the credit market tends to show a high leverage. Interlocking between the bank and the firms is common in such cases in order to reduce agency costs and financial fragility. Agency costs exacerbated by institutional problems (such as deficiencies in solving creditors' conflicting claims in case of default) determine the predominance of non-marketable financial claims as well as the existence of thin and illiquid secondary markets for private securities.

These market failures also hinder the conduct of monetary policy. One important problem is the reduced stock of securities vis-à-vis the size of the fiscal deficit and capital inflows. Under such circumstances, the attempt to sterilize capital inflows or to absorb the monetization of the deficit via open-market operations produces huge "jumps" in interest rates, since the flow supply of new bonds is too high with respect to the existing stock. A second problem is that, in a bank-dominated financial system which is prone to credit-rationing and large jumps in rates of return, the ultimate results of monetary actions are very difficult to anticipate.

In sum, it is crucial to take into account that financial liberalization and capital-account decontrol are implemented in a situation in which "institutional" and market failures are pervasive. The essential question, then, is whether liberalization policies help to eliminate the causes of the structural flaws that we have commented on. Before analysing this question, which is the key to economic policy-making, we would like to develop some central aspects of the functioning of an economy with no financial repression or capital controls but where some of the above structural features are present.

B. Some basic financial relationships

We shall use an analytical framework based on the assets and liabilities matrix of a representative developing country exemplifying the interactions

Table 2

MATRIX OF ASSETS AND LIABILITIES OF A REPRESENTATIVE DEVELOPING COUNTRY

	Central bank	Banks	Households	Firms	Rest of the world	Government
R	Rc^d				$-Rw^s$	
H	$-Hc^s$	Hb^d	Hh^d	Hf^d		
D		$-Db^s$	Dh^d	Df^d		
L	Lc^s	Lb^s		$-Lf^d$		$-Lg^d$
F		$-Fb^s$	Fh^d	$-Ff^s$	Fw^d	
B	Bc^d		Bh^d			$-Bg^s$
K				Kf^d		Kg^d
Q	$-Qc$	$-Qb$	$-Qh$	$-Qf$	$-Qw$	$-Qg$

Note: For explanation of symbols see text.

between foreign and domestic investors and assets (table 2).

The rows in the matrix record the financial instruments in the economy while the columns represent the agents. There are seven assets of which six are financial. They are: international reserves (R), the monetary base (H), bank deposits (D), bank loans (L), foreign assets (F), government bonds (B) and physical capital (K). There are six aggregate agents: the central bank (c), the banking sector (b), households (h), firms (f), foreign agents (w) and the government (g). Each cell shows the amount that each agent holds of the corresponding instrument and is denoted by the capital letter corresponding to the instrument. It is followed by a small case letter which stands for the agent holding the instrument, and by a "d" or "s" superscript to signify demand and supply, respectively. In each cell, the variable representing the instrument is preceded by a negative or positive sign depending on whether it represents a liability or an asset for the agent. In this way, for example, Bh^d stands for the households demand for government bonds, which is an asset for the agent, while $(-Ff^s)$ stands for foreign-currency denominated securities issued by firms, which is a liability for them. The last row (Q) records each agent's net worth, which is the difference between the agents' assets and liabilities. It is preceded by a minus sign because the net worth is recorded on the liabilities' side of the balance sheets.

The matrix is quite standard. However, in an effort to simplify the analysis and to highlight structural features of developing countries, some assumptions have been made which merit clarification. Only the government and entrepreneurs are assumed to hold physical capital. Banks supply credit to the private sector (Lb^s) and receive funds from two sources, deposits (Db^s) and foreign financing (Fb^s). Both deposits and credit are short-term. Due to high uncertainty, banks try to reduce to a minimum the mismatch between the maturity of assets and liabilities. The banks can rely on long-term foreign funds (Fb^s) to extend the maturity of credit, but only at the cost of higher exposure to exchange risk. Bank credit received by the government (Lg^d) only comes from the central bank (Lc^s). Under a currency-board-like regime this variable is zero. The bonds issued by firms and the government are of a significantly longer maturity than that of bank credit.

From the matrix, several financial relationships follow which are useful for understanding the linkages between asset markets and the agent's financial position.

Given that each agent's financial asset is another agent's liability, the aggregation of all agents' financial assets and liabilities adds up to zero and, consequently, the aggregate value of the agents' net worth equals the value of aggregate physical capital. For society as a whole the only source of income is real wealth (K).[10] From this perspective, financial instruments can be conceived as contracts that specify how the future income stream generated by K will be shared by the agents under different "states of nature". Under conditions of high volatility, uncertainty will make it hard to define both the states of nature and their probability distribution. Under certain institutional conditions, it will be very difficult to design and enforce contracts because of the difficulties in managing agency problems and information. As a consequence, there will be contracts that are not carried out or that stipulate shorter time periods than would be optimal for financial transactions. Some markets will go missing and others will be very thin and illiquid. But if society is to hold productive assets at all, it is necessary that someone take a "long position" in physical assets. Hence, the greater the public's preference for short-term financial instruments, the higher the risk that someone in the system (i.e. an intermediary or an entrepreneur) must assume.

It is a very well-known rule in safe financial management that agents must set the value of their short-term assets higher than that of their short-term liabilities if they want to avoid liquidity problems. Yet, this does not hold true for the system as a whole. Since one agent's financial asset is another's liability, there must be some agents for whom short-term liabilities exceed short-term assets. The central bank and the banking system play this role; they have a greater amount of liabilities than assets in the short run. In a sense, liquidity is created out of a paradox: under normal conditions, the public perceives the banks as the more liquid agents, when in fact they are highly exposed to liquidity shocks. This system functions well as long as confidence in the central bank and the banking system does not deteriorate. In developing countries, however, the loss of confidence in banks and the central bank is much more frequent than developed countries and, hence, they are far more prone to liquidity shocks, bank runs and speculative attacks than in developed countries.

Each column represents the wealth constraint of one agent. If we sum up all the columns, we obtain the economy's wealth constraint, from which we can deduce the Walras Law:

$$(Rc^d - Rw^s) + (Hb^d + Hh^d + Hf^d - Hc^s)$$
$$+ (Dh^d + Df^d - Db^s) + (Lb^s + Lc^s - Lf^d - Lg^d)$$
$$+ (Fh^d + Fw^d - Fb^s - Ff^s) + (Bc^d + Bh^d - Bg^s)$$
$$+ (Kf^d + Kg^d - Qh - Qf - Qw - Qc - Qb - Qg) = 0$$

(1)

Each parenthesis represents the market of one of the existing financial instruments and the real asset. Two facts must be singled out. First, we have written the supply and demand in each market as the sum of individuals' supply and demand to stress the fact that changes in the agents' balance sheet are readily reflected in changes in the supply or the demand that create a market disequilibrium. And vice versa, if there is a disequilibrium in one market, there will necessarily be adjustments in the individuals' balance sheets. Second, each market disequilibrium affects at least two markets. When the government intervenes in one market, e.g. by establishing capital-account controls, there will be spillover effects on other markets and on the agents' balance sheets. In sum, there is a general interdependence between markets and balance sheets whose (dis)equilibrium values are determined simultaneously. If we aggregate the supply and the demand of individual agents, we obtain the following expression for the Walras Law:

$$(R^d - R^s) + (H^d - H^s) + (D^d - D^s) + (L^s - L^d)$$
$$+ (F^d - F^s) + (B^d - B^s) + (K^d - Q) = 0$$

(2)

We are now ready to use our framework to show the linkages between capital movements, domestic asset demand, the capital-account regime and the structure of the financial system.

C.   *The effects of changes in uncertainty*

Assume that there is an exogenous increment in the level of uncertainty in an economy which has eliminated all capital-account controls and financial repression and, hence, has no impediment to capital flows and portfolio allocation. For example, suppose that there was an increase in volatility which took the form of a widening in the variance of returns. According to the above, the higher the level of uncertainty is, the lower the demand for long-term instruments because of the shrinkage in the planning horizon. In terms of the matrix there will be a fall in the demand for domestic bonds (B^d) and foreign-currency-denominated securities issued by nationals (F^d), which are the instruments with the longest maturity in that economy.

The effect of the fall in B^d and F^d in equation (2) is the creation of an excess supply in the market for bonds and foreign-exchange securities. Two parentheses are negative, and the Walras Law indicates that there must be at least one parenthesis showing a positive sign. What markets will reflect the change? The answer depends on many characteristics of the system, the macroeconomic and international situation, etc. We shall, nonetheless, restrict our analysis to structural phenomena.

Assume that the increase in uncertainty affects the ability of the firms and the government to place direct debt instruments, but that private agents still trust banks. The excess supply for B and F will then produce an excess demand for bank liabilities (D^d) and (with unchanged reserve policies by the banks) an excess supply of loans. The long-term interest rate will rise while the rate for short-term bank credit will fall. The government and the firms can now resort to banks instead of the bond market for credit. The economy will reach a new equilibrium with a wider spread between short- and long-term cost of funds for the business sector.

Indeed, in the new equilibrium, if the level of uncertainty is sufficiently large, the market for long-term securities could disappear. In developing countries, it is very common to find a term structure of interest rates which is steeper than the one in developed countries and that collapses with rates of return of assets with a maturity longer than the medium term. As the term to maturity augments, the premium to be paid over short-term rates for long-term funds rises so fast that it becomes infinite at some point. This means that the market for long-term funds disappears. In this case, the amount of bonds recorded in the matrix would be zero and, *ceteris paribus*, higher uncertainty would mean lower financial deepening. Likewise, in the international market for F instruments, domestic firms and banks would face credit-rationing.

If we take into account the financial relationships implied by the matrix above, it follows that the market disequilibrium will induce changes in balance sheets. It is easy to see why finance matters to the real economy. The bank credit that has replaced bonds as a source of funding is of shorter maturity. Given that firms and the government are the agents with "long positions" in physical assets, they must now finance productive activities with shorter-term debt. The capital structure of firms has changed towards an increase in the level of financial fragility because of the shortening in the creditor's planning horizon. The firms now face a higher interest rate risk and a greater risk of credit-rationing just when debt must be rolled over. They are in a more speculative position and, in the terms of Bernanke and Gertler's (1990) model,

will face a higher premium for external financing. Under these circumstances, the demand for physical capital should fall and the parenthesis corresponding to physical capital in equation (2) would become negative: the demand for physical wealth (K^d) would be lower than existing wealth (Q). This means a lower "Tobin q" and thus a lower investment demand. In sum, the fall in the demand for domestic assets will be partly accommodated by an increase in the external finance premium and partly by a fall in the stock of capital. The effect on the real side will be a lower rate of growth in the long run.

What would happen if agents also mistrusted banks? Not only would F^d and B^d fall but so would D^d. Unlike the previous situation, there will be a reduction in the supply of credit and in the size of the banking system. Now, the only remaining hedge against uncertainty is the money issued by the central bank (H) and foreign assets (F). If agents trust the central bank, when uncertainty increases, there could be a run against banks, but a speculative attack against the currency would not occur. Whether the public will trust the central bank or not depends crucially on the soundness of the public budget. If the financial position of the public sector is weak, it is very likely that people will mistrust the central bank and consider currency a bad hedge. They might expect the deficit to be monetized.

The degree of confidence in the monetary base as a liquidity hedge is crucial in determining the ability of the central bank to act as lender of last resort. Uncertainty regarding the banking sector's health generates an increase in the agents' "liquidity preference". If people trust the central bank there will be an increase in the demand for monetary base. Under these circumstances, the central bank, in principle, could safely act as lender of last resort. The central bank would issue money to sustain private banks and the public would be willing to absorb the money. But if the public mistrust the central bank, then they will still increase their liquidity preference but will use the money issued by other (more reliable) central banks, for example dollars. People would flee from both bank deposits and the monetary base, and would exert pressure not only on deposits but also on the central bank's international reserves. In this scenario, there will be no possibility to offset the forces at work and, consequently, the level of financial fragility caused by a fall in the demand for bonds and deposits will be, *ceteris paribus*, higher.

One fundamental question to economic policy-making is how to stabilize the financial system under these circumstances. If the run against banks and international reserves is sufficiently strong, the authorities could be forced to re-establish temporarily controls over the capital account, to throw sand in the wheels of capital flight and soften the effects on domestic financial fragility.

The IMF does not believe in controls. Their policy recommendation to avoid having to re-establish controls over capital-account transactions is therefore to eliminate the causes of agents' lack of confidence in banks and the central bank. This means improving the banks' prudential regulation and supervision and achieving a strong fiscal position. Although there are numerous examples of problems in the financial sector caused by serious flaws in prudential regulation, we have shown that exogenous changes in uncertainty, *per se,* can cause a crisis. From our point of view, as the recent experience of Argentina and Mexico shows, the system needs a lender of last resort. Consequently, if the central bank does not provide a mechanism to absorb exogenous shocks, such a mechanism must be provided by international institutions. In the recent Mexican and Argentine crises the IMF acted de facto as the lender of last resort.

From the perspective of the efficient allocation of real resources, it is very important to avoid fluctuations in the demand for domestic assets. Sudden increases in liquidity preference and disintermediation have effects on the real economy. If the demand for deposits and the domestic currency fall, banks will not be able to provide liquidity. As was argued above, in such a situation it will be far more difficult for firms to follow the rule of holding more short-term assets than short-term liabilities. Of course, the agents can use dollars or other foreign currency to substitute for the liquidity services of domestic banks. However, this is an imperfect and more expensive substitute. Besides, the counterpart of the disappearance of the demand for money is the vanishing of domestically generated credit. Firms can try to attract funds from abroad, but it is much more likely that small- and medium-sized firms will be rationed in the international markets.

D. *Dollarization*

The above focuses on the analysis of a situation in which there is a generalized loss in the credit-worthiness of domestic debtors which produces a drop in the demand for domestic financial assets. However, the problem is not always a loss in creditworthiness. Another important source of turbulence is the fear of

currency devaluation. To hedge against devaluation, risk agents demand foreign currency. But small investors with no access to international markets will find that the allocation of loanable funds to non-interest bearing foreign currency has an important opportunity cost. Therefore, in situations where domestic debtors enjoy creditworthiness but the value of the currency is unstable, there is room for financial innovation: banks can issue their own dollar-denominated liabilities to satisfy the preference of depositors. In many countries, particularly in Latin America, there has been an important development in the "dollarized" segment of the domestic financial market. Under this system, national banks receive dollar-denominated deposits and supply dollar-denominated credit. In the matrix, we can now interpret the variable Fh^d as household demand for dollar-denominated deposits in the domestic banking system. We also have to take into account that a portion of the domestically generated credit (L) is now in dollars.

In very special situations, dollarization can help to increase financial deepening. In economies where the share of dollar-denominated assets in private-sector portfolios is high because of the effects of "capital flight" fed by uncertainty and exchange-rate instability, dollarization can be a "second best" alternative to recover the capacity of the banking system to generate credit domestically.

Dollarization, nonetheless, has real effects which endogenously limit the expansion of the system. Even under complete dollarization there will be agents with a "long position" in domestic assets: the firms and the government that hold the physical assets of society (K). Consequently, there must be a mismatch for some agents between the liabilities and the asset sides of the balance sheets. In the Latin American experience, banks have tried to avoid exchange-rate risks and, consequently, have tended to supply dollar-denominated credit as a counterpart of dollar deposits. This means that the devaluation risk is borne entirely by debtors. When the cash flow generated by physical assets follows the evolution of the real exchange rate, holding dollar-denominated liabilities is not a great problem for the firm. Obviously, the situation is just the opposite for an enterprise in the non-tradable sector. Given that the risk incurred is higher for the latter, the more closed is the economy, the higher the level of financial fragility in a dollarized economy will be. This fact curbs the expansion of dollarization.

On the other hand, if dollarization occurs without the development of a segment in dollars, financial intermediation in the economy will, de facto, be performed by international intermediaries. The firms and the government could access credit via international banks or institutional investors, etc. However, if there is credit-rationing in the international markets as in the debt crisis, the circuit will collapse. Nationals place their savings abroad, but domestic entrepreneurs are unable to obtain funds to invest.

Dollarization puts constraints on the function of the central bank as lender of last resort because it cannot issue dollars. This means that, *ceteris paribus*, the banks operating in the dollar segment will have to maintain a higher reserve ratio and will hold more capital as a proportion of total assets. All this implies that if banks are prudent, credit will be more expensive since a higher reserve and capital ratio means a higher spread between deposit and lending rates.

In addition, under a dollarized regime, the central bank enjoys much less leverage to manage monetary policy. If there were a surge in capital inflows, for instance, it would be far more costly for the central bank to conduct open-market operations. Under such circumstances, the system, to a certain extent, would become much more dependent on the stability of private demand for domestic financial assets. If this demand is volatile, credit supply will also be volatile and it will tend to induce more volatility in the evolution of aggregate demand.

IV. Conclusions

We have argued that finance matters to development because of the significant imperfections in the structure of financial markets in developing countries. Therefore, the main policy objective should be to create markets which do not yet exist and to strengthen existing ones. We have identified the high level of uncertainty created by macroeconomic volatility and institutional flaws as the main causes of financial market underdevelopment. Therefore, financial liberalization and capital-account decontrol will foster financial deepening only to the extent that they contribute to removing uncertainty and improving the institutional infrastructure. Although the ultimate goal is to develop a financial structure which is as dense and complete as that in developed countries, it does not mean that swift and outright liberalization is the best solution in the short run. In fact, a distinction should be made between those regulations and interventions which are friendly to the development of markets and those which are detrimental to it.

Many countries have resorted, at certain stages in their development, to the building of institutions mimicking the functioning of missing markets to solve problems in the allocation of savings, investment and risks. This is the case, for example, of the Fondo del Café in Colombia, or the compensatory fiscal policies implemented by the Chilean Government in the 1980s which were financed with the proceeds from the State-owned copper mines. It is clear, nonetheless, that there are countless failures because of the developing countries' inability to consolidate institutions. The capacity to build institutions as a determinant of growth is evident from a comparison of the system of "contests" in Asia (World Bank, 1993) with the difficulties that some transition economies have in establishing a financial structure to solve the problem of bad debt and in imposing a hard budget constraint for State-owned enterprises (Schmidt, 1996). The capacity for institution-building is determined by political and social factors, and it is not possible to generate such a capacity out of nothing. Taking institutional and political development as a constraint, the challenge is to design the optimal path to achieve a "complete" market structure.

We believe that the role of institutions in the liberalization process is under-researched. For example, more research is needed with a view to design a regulatory framework for banking supervision in a situation with a low enforcement and monitoring capacity and a high degree of macroeconomic volatility. Another important area for research is the interaction between liberalization and other reforms. For example, it could be much more important to the development of capital markets to build an efficient structure to monitor tax compliance rather than to deregulate brokers' fees. When information is credible for the tax authorities, it is also credible for investors; therefore, allocating government resources to improving tax compliance can generate important positive externalities for the development of security markets by mitigating the problems of asymmetric information.

In addition to the development of domestic financial markets and institutions, resorting to international markets is an important alternative for achieving an efficient structure of intermediation. In fact, this is the main goal of eliminating controls on capital-account transactions. Access to international markets could not only improve intertemporal allocation but also smooth macroeconomic volatility. The potential benefits resulting therefrom can be illustrated in an example. We have stressed that macroeconomic uncertainty erodes the market structure. However, macroeconomic volatility has its roots in the micro-economic structure. The lack of diversification of exports is one fundamental factor explaining the volatility of key macroeconomic variables. The low diversification of exports makes the evolution of the terms of trade more volatile and this, in turn, increases the volatility of key macrovariables, such as the real exchange rate and real national income. But it is very well known that a large variance in the cash flow in a certain sector of production does not imply that an investor in that sector will bear a higher risk. The individual investor can use the stock exchange to diversify risks. Consequently, if national investors do not use international capital markets to diversify the national risk, it could only be due to the existence of controls on the capital account. If the controls are lifted, the effects of macroeconomic volatility could be almost completely diversified away in the international markets. The argument is appealing, but we have seen that international markets show a series of imperfections that impedes the diversification of risk in that manner, the most important being segmentation, volatility and instability in the risk/return correlation function that tends to move procyclically.

From our point of view, the existence of these market failures in the international scenario largely justify actions at the international level. In the last two decades there have been important initiatives to soften the effects of volatility in real exchange rates and interest rates in developed countries. One was via policy coordination in the G-7. But there has been no comparable initiative to smooth the consequences of excessive volatility in developing economies. In a more unstable world economy, the IMF and other multilateral institutions should be prepared to assist developing countries in managing macroeconomic instability stemming from the volatility in international capital markets. Particularly important would be the development of a mechanism for "lending of last resort" to smooth the consequences of sudden reversals in capital inflows. IMF and World Bank support for the elimination of capital controls should be accompanied with a mechanism to help countries resist the temptation to restore controls to stop capital outflows.

At present, conditionality in the IMF-supported stabilization programmes primarily serves to ensure that countries adapt to the hard constraint imposed by liquidity at each point in time, rather than to permit optimal intertemporal allocation of production and expenditure. As a consequence, when there are sudden changes in the conditions for the access of developing countries to international markets, domestic absorp-tion must be adjusted swiftly. This results in sharp fluctuations in the level of domestic activity in a small economy open to capital movements.

It is clear that there could be a moral-hazard problem: if countries perceived that conditionality is being relaxed and that they would have access to soft financing, in a liquidity squeeze they would have incentives to generate excessive current-account deficits. This problem cannot be ignored. The challenge is to define the optimal design of conditionality. It would seem that the optimum is closer to IMF actions in the recent Argentine and Mexican crises than to the role the IMF played during the 1980s debt crisis.

One important issue we have tried to highlight is that in a volatile world economy free markets behave in a volatile manner, and that under such circumstances liberalization could produce unforeseen results. Under a regime of free convertibility, the volatility of capital inflows could aggravate macroeconomic instability and restrain financial deepening. The country could, to a certain extent, import the greater volatility in exchange rates and interest rates which industrial countries have been experiencing. In this world of imperfect markets, the highly pragmatic policy of the Chilean authorities in the 1990s, which combined capital controls with sterilization and managed floating within bands, proved to be much more effective in curbing volatility and smoothing the macroeconomic effects of capital movements than the orthodoxy of the Argentine currency-board arrangement.

One of the most significant points in this paper is that the ultimate result of the liberalization of the financial system and the capital account heavily depends on a series of structural and institutional features which differ across countries. Hence, there may be no such thing as correct sequencing. However, many experiences in liberalization suggest that it is very important to take into account that there will be disequilibria in the transition period and, consequently, an important goal during transition should be to assess the stability of the situation. To ensure stability, some degree of "market-friendly" financial repression might be necessary in the short run, although free financial markets are the ultimate objective. Capital controls to restrain capital inflows and to check the expansion of consumption credit during the boom which tends to follow the first stages of financial liberalization are two important examples. Tighter supervision of the financial system via strict enforcement of regulations in boom periods is another interesting alternative to which the Argentine authorities resorted after the Mexican crisis. It seems that it is worthwhile to pay the cost of controls, sterilization and/or manipulation of reserve requirements in order to maintain a stable financial system, a competitive exchange rate and a sustainable current-account deficit.

Notes

1 An important force driving the process of capital-account deregulation in developed countries was the growth of multinational corporations and international banks, as well as the market techniques to sidestep controls. The process of liberalization accelerated in the 1980s and 1990s. Iceland was the last industrial country to adopt full convertibility on 1 January 1995 (Quirk and Evans, 1995).

2 In the mid-1990s, the developing countries with an open capital account were oil exporters with strong balance-of-payment positions. Most Latin American and Caribbean countries, as well as Hong Kong, Malaysia, Singapore, Thailand, Lebanon, Gambia, Kenya and Mauritius, the Baltic countries and the Kyrgyz Republic had also liberalized their capital account. See Quirk and Evans (1995) for more details on the process of capital account liberalization in developing countries.

3 On capital flight see Goldstein et al. (1991). On financial crisis, see Sheng (1996), World Bank (1989) and Sundararajan and Baliño (1991).

4 Helleiner (1997) analyses the benefits and costs of capital-account liberalization and the purposes and efficacy of capital controls.

5 The most often cited elements of financial repression are: controlled interest rates which frequently resulted in negative real rate of return on deposits, high mandatory reserve requirements and high inflation tax because of the monetization of the fiscal deficit, the use of non-market mechanisms for credit allocation, and control of capital movements and of the exchange rate. See Fry (1995) for a survey of the liberalization approach literature.

6 According to King and Levine, financial systems affect the entrepreneurial activities that lead to productivity improvements in four ways: first, financial systems evaluate prospective entrepreneurs and choose the most promising projects; second, financial systems mobilize resources to finance promising projects; third, financial systems allow investors to diversify the risk associated with uncertain innovative activities; fourth, financial systems reveal the potential rewards to engaging in innovation, relative to continuing to make existing products with existing techniques. In contrast to traditional development work, the approach does not require that financial institutions exert influence mainly via the rate of physical capital accumulation; financial systems influence productivity growth.

7 See Akyüz and Held (1993) for a detailed analysis of the effects of liberalization on the rate of savings.

8 On sequencing, see Fanelli and Frenkel (1993) and the literature cited therein.

9 In a sense, this mirrored the history of Indonesia and Malaysia, which deregulated the capital account before the domestic financial system because of competition from Singapore (Fisher and Reisen, 1992).

10 Given that our main purpose is to discuss the linkages between the capital account and the financial system, we are not interested in discussing whether K includes human capital and other intangible and non-marketable assets. This does not make any difference to our argument.

References

AKYÜZ, Y., and G. HELD (eds.) (1993), *Finance and the Real Economy, Issues and Case Studies in Developing Countries* (Santiago de Chile: UNU/WIDER, ECLAC, UNCTAD).

BALKAN, E.M., and E.A. YELDAN (1996), "Financial Liberalization in Developing Countries: The Turkish Experience", paper presented at the Conference "Financial Liberalization in Developing Countries", Bilkent University, Ankara, June.

BERNANKE, B., and M. GERTLER (1990), "Financial Fragility and Economic Performance", *The Quarterly Journal of Economics*, Vol. 105, No. 1 (February).

BERNANKE, B., and M. GERTLER (1995), "Inside the Black Box: The Credit Channel of Monetary Policy Transmission", *The Journal of Economic Perspectives*, Vol. 9, No. 4 (Fall), pp. 27-48.

CALVO, G. (1996), "Why is the Market so Unforgiving?", paper presented at the Conference "Financial Liberalization in Developing Countries", Bilkent University, Ankara, June.

CHO, J.Y. (1986), "Inefficiencies from Financial Liberalization in the Absence of Well-Functioning Equity Markets", *Journal of Money, Credit and Banking*, Vol. 18, No. 2 (May).

DAMILL, M., J. FANELLI, and R. FRENKEL (1994), *Shock externo y desequilibrio fiscal. La Macroeconomía de América Latina en los ochenta. Los casos de Argentina, Bolivia, Brasil, Colombia, Chile y Mexico* (Santiago de Chile: CEPAL).

DANCOURT, O. (1996), "The Tequila Effect and the Peruvian Economy", paper presented at the Conference "After Neoliberalism in Latin America: What?", New School of Social Research, New York, 2-3 May.

FANELLI, J.M., R. FRENKEL, and L. TAYLOR (1992), "The World Development Report 1991: A Critical Assessment", in UNCTAD, *International Monetary and Financial Issues for the 1990s*, Vol. I (UNCTAD/GID/G24/1) (New York: United Nations).

FANELLI, J.M., and R. FRENKEL (1993), "On Gradualism, Shock Treatment and Sequencing", in UNCTAD, *International Monetary and Financial Issues for the 1990s*, Vol. II (UNCTAD/GID/G24/2) (New York: United Nations).

FANELLI, J.M., G. ROZENWURCEL, and L. SIMPSON (1996), "Financial Liberalization in Developing Countries: The Argentine Experience", paper presented at the Conference "Financial Liberalization in Developing Countries", Bilkent University, Ankara, June.

FFRENCH-DAVIS, R., and S. GRIFFITH-JONES (eds.) (1995), *Coping with Capital Surges. The Return of Finance to Latin America* (Ottawa: Lynne Rienner).

FISHER, B., and H. REISEN (1992), "Towards Capital Account Convertibility", *Policy Brief No. 4* (Paris: OECD Development Centre).

FRY, M. (1995), *Money, Interest and Banking in Economic Development* (Baltimore: Johns Hopkins University Press).

GLEN, J.D. (1993), "How Firms in Developing Countries Manage Risk", *International Finance Corporation Discussion Paper*, No. 17 (Washington, D.C.).

GOLDSTEIN, M., D.J. MATHIESON, D. FOLKERTS-LANDAU, T. LANE, S.J. LIZONDO, and L. ROJAS-SUAREZ (1991), "Determinants and Systemic Consequences of International Capital Flows", *IMF Occasional Papers*, No. 77 (Washington, D.C.).

HARRIS J.R., F. SCHIANTARELLI, and M.G. SIREGAR (1994), "The Effect of Financial Liberalization on the Capital Structure and Investment Decisions of Indonesian Manufacturing Establishments", *The World Bank Economic Review*, Vol. 8, No 1.

HELLEINER, G. K. (1997), "Capital Account Regimes and the Developing Countries", in UNCTAD, *International Monetary and Financial Issues for the 1990s*, Vol. VIII (UNCTAD/GDS/MDPB/1) (New York and Geneva: United Nations).

IDB (1995), *Economic and Social Progress in Latin America, 1995* (Washington, D.C.: Inter-American Development Bank).

IMF (1995), *Private Market Financing for Development Countries, World Economic and Financial Surveys* (Washington, D.C.).

KING, R.G., and R. LEVINE (1993a), "Finance, Entrepreneurship, and Growth: Theory and Evidence", *Journal of Monetary Economics*, Vol. 32, No. 3 (December).

KING, R.G., and R. LEVINE (1993b), "Finance and Growth: Schumpeter Might Be Right", *Quarterly Journal of Economics*, Vol. 108, No. 3 (August).

McKINNON, R. (1973), *Money and Capital in Economic Development* (Washington, D.C.: The Brookings Institution).

McKINNON, R. (1991), *The Order of Economic Liberalization. Financial Control in the Transition to a Market Economy* (Baltimore: The Johns Hopkins University Press).

NOYA, N., C. CASACUBERTA, and F. LORENZO (1996), "Financial Liberalization in Developing Countries: The Uruguayan Experience", paper presented at the Conference "Financial Liberalization in Developing Countries", Bilkent University, Ankara, June.

QUIRK, P.J., and O. EVANS (1995), "Capital Account Convertibility: Review of Experience and Implications for IMF Policies", *IMF Occasional Papers*, No. 131 (Washington, D.C.).

ROETT, R. (1996), *The Mexican Peso Crisis, International Perspectives* (London: Lynne Rienner).

ROJAS-SUAREZ, L., and S.R. WEISBROD (1995), "Financial Fragilities in Latin America: The 1980s and 1990s", *IMF Occasional Papers*, No. 132 (Washington, D.C.).

ROJAS-SUAREZ, L., and S.R. WEISBROD (1996), "Central Bank Provision of Liquidity: Its Impact on Bank Asset Quality", paper presented at a Conference on "Strengthening Latin American Banking in a Global Environment", Inter-American Development Bank, Buenos Aires, 23 March.

ROMERO, L. (1996), "Regulación y dolarización de los bancos en el Perú", paper presented for the Conference "Financial Liberalization in Peru", Instituto de Estudios Peruanos, Lima, June.

ROSS, J. (1996), "The Mexican Crisis and its Aftermath", paper presented at the Conference "After Neoliberalism in Latin America: What?", New School of Social Research, New York, 2-3 May.

SCHMIDT, R. (1996), "Banking on the Transition: Bank Credit and Enterprise Control in Central and Eastern Europe", paper presented at the Conference "Financial Liberalization in Developing Countries", Bilkent University, Ankara, June.

SHAW, I. (1973), *Financial Deepening in Economic Development* (New York: Oxford University Press).

SHENG, A. (1996), *Bank Restructuring, Lessons from the 1980's* (Washington, D.C.: The World Bank).

SUNDARARAJAN V., and T.J.T. BALIÑO (eds.) (1991), *Banking Crises: Cases and Issues* (Washington, D.C.: IMF).

SOLIMANO, A. (1996), The Chilean Economy in the 1990s: On Interpreting a "Golden Age", paper presented at the Conference "After Neoliberalism in Latin America: What?", New School of Social Research, New York, 2-3 May.

UNCTAD (1996), *Trade and Development Report, 1996* (United Nations publication, Sales No. E.96.II.D.6) (New York and Geneva: United Nations).

WILLIAMSON, J. (1990), "What Washington Means by Policy Reform", in J. Williamson (ed.), *Latin American Adjustment: How Much Has Happened?* (Washington D.C.: Institute for International Economics).

WORLD BANK (1989), *World Development Report 1989. Finance and Development* (New York: Oxford University Press).

WORLD BANK (1991), *World Development Report 1991. The Challenge of Development* (New York: Oxford University Press).

WORLD BANK (1993), *The East Asian Miracle. Economic Growth and Public Policy* (Washington, D.C.: Oxford University Press).

RESPONDING TO THE AID CRISIS

Tony Killick*

Abstract

Underlying declining official development assistance (ODA) budgets there is a crisis of confidence in the developmental value of aid. In the late 20th century aid does not command the political support of former times. There is a paucity of evidence showing ODA to have clear developmental, poverty-reducing benefits, with its impact swamped by the effects of economic policies in the recipient countries. The development model upon which the case for aid was originally based has been abandoned. A good many of the early criticisms appear to have been borne out by experience, including a tendency for large-scale aid to distort incentives for private-sector development. For these reasons, faith in, and political support for, ODA has much diminished.

This paper suggests a strategy for resolving the ODA crisis. The strategy is based on (a) reasserting an over-riding developmental purpose for aid; (b) changing to relationships with recipients based on ownership (not conditionality) and acceptance of mutual obligations; (c) increasing the selectivity with which aid is allocated across developing countries; and (d) tackling donor weaknesses which reduce the productivity of aid.

* This is an elaborated version of a paper first presented to a United Nations Expert Group Meeting in Santiago, Chile, in January 1997. I am grateful to Ranjita Rajan for valuable assistance in preparing materials for this paper and to my colleague Roger Riddell both for his helpful comments on an earlier draft and for teaching me so much about this subject. The usual disclaimers apply, however.

I.   Is there an aid crisis?

It is often asserted nowadays that there is a crisis in the international provision of development assistance, so an examination of recent trends provides a natural starting point for this paper, as a preliminary to a discussion of the factors underlying these trends.

A.   *Trends in development assistance*

First, table 1 and chart 1 set out trends in total net financial flows to developing countries, from which a number of features are immediately apparent:

- In current prices, total ODA has been roughly constant, at roughly $60 billion per annum, since the beginning of the 1990s.

- This constancy is, however, in marked contrast with strong nominal growth during the 1970s and 1980s.

- The growth trend of the 1980s was less dramatic when expressed in constant-price terms but was nonetheless still strong, whereas constant-price series show a decline since 1992 (chart 1). This change is too recent for it to be confidently described as a trend but there are, as we shall see, reasons for believing that it may well be so.

- The recent decline is far more marked when ODA is expressed relative to the GNP of donor countries, with a fall from 0.34 to 0.27 per cent in 1992-1995, i.e. by more than one fifth over only three years (see chart 1).

- Grants by non-governmental organizations (NGOs), having risen rapidly in the previous two decades, also levelled off in the 1990s (declining in real terms) and have remained at equivalent to about one tenth of official ODA (table 1). Charitable giving is not compensating for the stagnation in official aid.

- There have, nonetheless, been large increases in total net financial flows to developing countries due to a remarkable rise in the volume of private capital flows, with the share of these in total flows rising from 41 per cent in 1990 to 67 per cent five years later (table 1).

There are a few other salient facts, not included in the table and diagram, which should be added:

- Official aid[1] from non-OECD countries has dwindled to insignificance in recent years. The substantial aid programmes of the countries of Eastern Europe and the former Soviet Union are a thing of the past. Aid from countries of the Organization of the Petroleum Exporting Countries (OPEC) is also far below its peak of the early 1980s. Some former recipient countries have become net providers (e.g. Republic of Korea and Turkey), but only on a small scale. Flows from all non-OECD countries made up under 2 per cent of total ODA in 1995, and the decline of this group as providers of aid has helped to depress the global totals. OECD countries are now the only significant donors. Of these, seven countries (Canada, France, Germany, Japan, the Netherlands, the United Kingdom and the United States) contribute over three quarters of the total.[2]

- Although very large in relation to total flows to developing countries, private capital flows are heavily concentrated in a small number of (generally more industrialized) developing countries. Notable recipients of direct investment include Argentina, Malaysia, Singapore, Indonesia, Thailand and - the largest single recipient - China. Bond finance is similarly concentrated on a modest number of Asian and Latin American countries. Griffin and McKinley (1996, p. 63) show for 1993 that only 8 per cent of the total net flow of long-term private capital to developing countries went to countries classified as low-income. Sub-Saharan Africa remains almost wholly reliant on ODA and other official inflows.

- Griffin and McKinley go further and net out interest payments, profit remittances and other (non-labour) return flows attributable to private capital. The resulting net resource transfers are shown to be well under half (43 per cent) of the unadjusted figures (although the legitimacy of such adjustments is questionable). For low-income countries, the resulting net figure for 1993 (latest available) was a mere $1.6 billion, against nearly $22 billion of ODA.

- Donor-by-donor data indicate a trend towards declining aid budgets. Of 21 DAC donor countries, eight recorded a declining trend (in real terms) between 1988/89 and 1994/95, including, among the countries with the largest programmes, Canada, Germany, Italy, the Netherlands and the United States (DAC, 1997,

Table 1

NET FLOWS OF FINANCIAL RESOURCES TO DEVELOPING COUNTRIES, 1970-1994

($ billion in current prices and exchange rates)

	1970	*1975*	*1980*	*1985*	*1990*	*1991*	*1992*	*1993*	*1994*	*1995ª*
Official development finance	**8.9**	**18.3**	**34.3**	**44.1**	**69.8**	**69.7**	**69.8**	**70.1**	**71.6**	**69.4**
ODA	7.9	14.9	27.3	32.9	52.9	58.6	58.9	56.4	60.5	60.1
Other official development finance	1.0	3.4	7.0	11.2	16.9	11.1	10.9	13.7	11.1	9.3
Export credits	**2.7**	**5.6**	**16.1**	**4.0**	**4.7**	**1.8**	**1.3**	**-0.6**	**9.3**	**11.0**
Private flows	**8.3**	**22.8**	**65.5**	**30.1**	**51.8**	**50.8**	**76.8**	**86.4**	**134.1**	**158.9**
Direct investment	3.7	11.4	11.2	6.5	26.4	22.6	27.3	38.6	48.5	53.6
Bank lending	3.0	8.5	49.0	15.2	15.0	11.0	31.0	9.0	42.6	70.0
Bond issues	0.3	0.4	1.1	4.2	0.9	6.5	11.1	29.0	29.0	19.3
Other private flows	0.4	1.2	1.8	1.3	4.4	5.3	1.4	4.0	8.0	10.0
Grants by NGOs	0.9	1.3	2.4	2.9	5.1	5.4	6.0	5.8	6.0	6.0
Total flows	**19.9**	**46.7**	**115.9**	**78.2**	**126.3**	**122.3**	**147.8**	**155.9**	**215.0**	**239.3**
ODA as a percentage of total	40	32	24	42	42	48	40	36	28	25
Private flows as a percentage of total flows	42	49	57	38	41	42	52	55	62	67

Source: DAC, *Development Co-operation* (Paris: OECD), various issues.
   a Provisional.

table 6a). For the most recent 12-month period, no less than 14 of the 21 showed declines in aid volumes, including all the major donors except the Netherlands and Japan.

Beneath these global trends, significant changes have been occurring in the use of aid resources which also bear upon the availability of aid for development. Firstly, DAC statistics show that aid to the "transition economies" of Eastern Europe and the former Soviet Union increased from $0.36 billion in 1989 to $9.04 in 1995, equivalent to 15 per cent of total aid to developing countries in the latter year. There must be a high probability that some of this assistance would otherwise have been available for developing coun-

tries, so that flows to Eastern Europe and the former Soviet Union help to explain the stagnation of development assistance proper.

Secondly, there has also been an increased use of aid for debt relief. It has for some years been the Paris Club policy to encourage donor governments to forgive past aid loans, i.e., to convert them into grants. For the most part, the cost of doing so has been treated by donors as a claim on their aid budgets. However, such provisions are only a modest proportion of the aid resources devoted to debt relief. In addition, donor countries subsidized ESAF and IDA lending by the IMF and the World Bank for the purposes of refinancing these institutions' past loans and preventing

Chart 1

NET ODA DISBURSEMENTS, 1980-1995

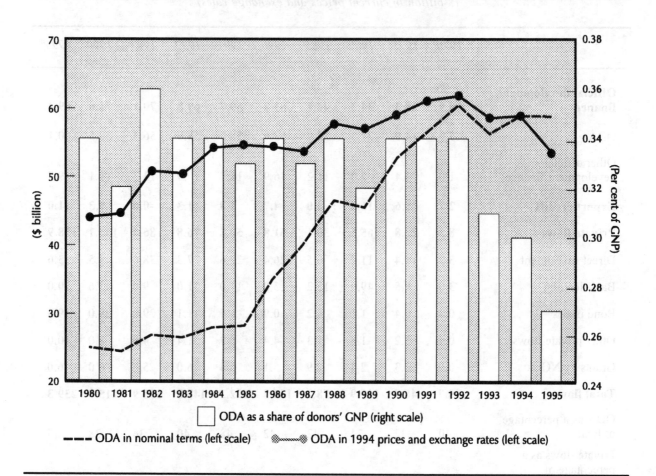

Source: IMF, 1996, Chart 2. Derived from DAC sources.

debtor countries from going into default. Such claims will increase under the recently agreed Initiative for the Heavily Indebted Poor Countries (HIPCs) for dealing with the multilateral indebtedness of low-income countries. In addition, various donor governments have participated in "Support Groups" for countries which have slipped into arrears with multilateral lenders, providing transitional finance until the debtor countries can restore their eligibility for new multilateral credits. An even larger number of donors has participated in attempts to garner additional bilateral support for debt-related adjustment programmes, e.g. through the Special Programme of Assistance for sub-Saharan Africa (the SPA). DAC figures indicate that in 1995 debt relief absorbed 11.5 per cent of total ODA, but this only covers some of the above categories. The combined amount of aid

devoted to these debt-related efforts is very large. Whether this should be regarded as a diversion from developmental applications is a moot point. Since the overhang of debt can be regarded as an obstacle to new investment and debt relief is conditional on IMF/World Bank structural adjustment programmes, the use of ODA for debt relief can be regarded as developmental, just another form of programme aid. Against this, the strength of the "overhang" argument for low-income countries is open to dispute, and the effect of using aid for debt relief is undoubtedly to divert it from investment in specific projects, and the provision of social and economic services. Allocating aid according to the severity of countries' debt problems is not at all the same as doing so by developmental or poverty criteria.

Thirdly, we should note a trend towards the use of aid for emergency relief. The sums devoted to emergency aid nearly tripled in real terms in 1990-1995, with a similar proportionate rise in the share of total aid absorbed in this way, to about 5 per cent in 1995. However, as Riddell (1996, p. 33) points out, there is no sharp distinction between emergency and development relief, particularly in the most vulnerable countries.

Although it is impossible to be precise, there seems no doubt that the three trends just described represent a substantial diversion away from more traditional developmental applications. If we assume, arbitrarily, that half of the aid going to the transition economies would otherwise have been available for developing countries, perhaps $15 billion - equal to one quarter of 1995 ODA to developing countries - could have been provided for development in the absence of these competing uses, most of which have only become significant in the 1990s.

Finally, we should note that the share of total ODA to developing countries claimed by sub-Saharan Africa has risen from 19 per cent in 1975 to 30 per cent in 1995. Southern and Central Asian countries have been the chief losers, their share declining steadily from 21 to 11 per cent over the same period. The extent of African countries' present-day reliance on aid is startling. Table 2 shows both the large size of aid inflows relative to domestic savings, investment and imports, and the severe worsening of these ratios since 1980. The contrast between Africa and the other developing regions is stark, with Southern Asia showing declining reliance on aid, and the other regions only small use of aid.[3]

This concentration on sub-Saharan Africa, while it does address the region with the greatest development problems and the most rapidly deteriorating occurrence of poverty, is also a source of difficulty, for two reasons. Firstly, the high present-day level of African dependency raises the fear that, because of

Table 2

INDICATORS OF AID DEPENDENCY FOR SELECTED REGIONS AND YEARS

	Year	Sub-Saharan Africa	South Asia	North Africa and the Middle East	Latin America and the Caribbean	All developing countries[a]
ODA in per cent of :						
GNP	1980	3.4	2.4	1.1	0.3	1.1
	1994	12.4	1.4	1.6	0.3	1.1
Gross domestic savings	1980	12.6	16.0	n.a.	1.3	3.9
	1994	77.5	7.0	n.a.	1.5	4.2
Gross domestic investment	1980	14.8	12.0	n.a.	1.2	4.2
	1994	72.9	6.4	n.a.	1.4	4.1
Imports	1994	51.5	11.5	6.3	2.2	5.2
ODA per capita ($)	1994	57	4	25	10	12
Memo item:						
GNP per capita ($)	1994	460	320	1580	3340	1090

Source: Calculated from World Bank, *World Development Report, 1996,* Development Indicator tables.

a All low- and middle-income countries.

its large relative size, aid may have become part of the problem. We shall see later that there are reasons for fearing this might be so. Secondly, Africa's limited geopolitical and trading importance weakens donor self-interest in the maintenance of large aid pro- grammes, and this may have contributed to the poor recent aid record.

Bearing all the above factors in mind, can we say that aid is in crisis? The figures certainly give reasons for grave concern. Total ODA is falling in real terms, there is a steep decline in aid relative to donor GNP and two thirds of DAC donors showed declining trends during the latest year for which data are available. There is, in addition, some tendency for aid to be diverted from traditional developmental applications, although this diversion has been in response to genuine needs, and the conflict with developmental objectives may not be large.

The view that we are facing a crisis takes on added strength when we examine the reasons for these trends. For underlying them have been important changes in the global environment conditioning rich countries' motivation for maintaining aid programmes, as well as a loss of confidence in the benefits of aid and its role in development. We therefore turn to examine these underlying influences.

B.   *Changes in the global context*

By universal agreement, the end of the cold war greatly affected the international environment for aid, for many donors had used their ODA, *inter alia,* in pursuit of foreign policy and security objectives. Various recipients lost much of their geopolitical importance and suddenly found their formerly reliable aid supplies drying up. In Africa alone, the cases of Ethiopia, Kenya, Mozambique, Somalia and the Democratic Republic of the Congo immediately suggest themselves. The ending of the East-West ideological divide may have reduced the interest of donor governments in aid programmes, even though a number of them have since integrated their aid agencies into their foreign affairs ministries. Eastern European countries and the former Soviet Union, that were previously donors themselves, became claimants on aid resources, as we have shown.

The ending of the cold war coincided with a gradual erosion of support for international co- operation in the United States. Seeing itself as having "won" the cold war against a now-defunct USSR, a Republican-dominated Congress has shown little interest in the maintenance of a major programme of development assistance (as distinct from transfers to some favoured Middle Eastern countries). Aid budgets have been cut and formal obligations, e.g. for payments to IDA, have not been honoured (with the consequence, discussed in some detail in the Appendix, that the persistence of United States arrears to IDA is endangering the future of that facility).

A more subtle and gradual change has occurred in donor-country attitudes towards developing countries, particularly among erstwhile metropolitan powers towards former colonies. There was undoubtedly an element of guilt in the relationships created in the first decades of large-scale aid. More generally, there was implicit belief both in the potency of aid to accelerate development by filling financing gaps and in the ability of recipient governments to put the finance to good developmental use.

Over time, these attitudes have changed. Guilt has faded and the plausibility of explanations of continuing underdevelopment in terms of past colonial exploitation has dimmed.[4] Frustration with the apparently limited efficacy of much past aid and increased awareness of corruption, economic mis- management and abuse of human rights has made donor governments (and their electorates) less trusting, less tolerant, more inclined to resort to conditionality, and more selective about the governments they support. Increased awareness of large-scale capital flight from poor countries, and evidence that this is correlated with inflows of capital from the rest of the world, has added further to donor-country scepticism.

This change in attitudes is illustrated by the evolution of relationships between the European Union and the ACP group of developing countries, as embodied in successive Lomé Treaties. By its original ideals, the relationship (which went beyond ODA to the provision of trade privileges) was to be based on Treaty obligations by co-equal partners (although inevitably the reality never matched up to this). In the aid area, unconditional medium-term country allocations were agreed. Such rights have gradually been eroded, however. The European Commission increasingly has recourse to policy conditionality, or provides programme aid in support of IMF/World Bank adjustment programmes, as well as concerning itself with the extent of democracy and rule of law within recipient countries. The future renewal of a Lomé-style relationship is now in question, and the Commission looks increasingly like other donor agencies in its somewhat more wary and selective approach to the allocation of aid.

The increasing globalization of product and financial markets has also had an impact on the aid environment. As we shall see shortly, it is becoming more difficult to explain why large-scale public development aid (as distinct from emergency relief or humanitarian assistance) is needed in the face of burgeoning and increasingly efficient international capital markets. Finally, for reasons that will also be discussed later, the total budgets of virtually all donor governments are coming under increasing strain. It has become more difficult for them to reconcile their electorates' resistance to taxation with their demands for public services and transfers. With public services under stress, it is harder to sustain aid budgets.

C. Evidence on the effectiveness of aid

The difficulties created by the global developments described above have been compounded by the results of academic attempts to measure the impact of aid inflows on economic growth in recipient countries. Most of these studies fail to find a significant association.[5] Mosley's (1987) conclusion is fairly representative of this literature: "... there appears to be no statistically significant correlation in *any* post-war period, either positive or negative, between inflows of development aid and the growth rate of GNP in developing countries when other causal influences on growth are taken into account" (p. 139). He is, however, careful to point out that there may be good reasons for this and that care has to be taken in deriving any judgements from it about aid effectiveness. The multitude of other factors bearing upon growth, and the complex interactions between them, make it difficult to isolate the impact of any one input into the system. An even more fundamental difficulty is that countries experiencing severe economic problems, resulting in substandard growth, are regarded by donors as therefore requiring more assistance. This is precisely what has happened in Africa. Donors, in other words, are not in the business of picking winners, nor do they design aid interventions simply in order to maximize growth. Nonetheless, the scarcity of evidence that aid has growth- (or investment-) enhancing effects is nonetheless a source of disquiet.

Academic investigators have gone further, trying to isolate the main determinants, at the macroeconomic level, of the growth and investment effectiveness of

aid. The survey of the Overseas Development Institute (ODI, 1993, p. 27) concluded that the main correlates were: (a) the rate of return on public and private capital; (b) the allocation of aid between the recipient government's development and recurrent budgets; and (c) the impact of aid on the structure of prices facing the private sector, particularly private investment. Other investigators, too, have found the fungibility factor to be an important determinant. There is (now seriously out-of-date) evidence of a tendency for aid to be used to reduce taxation (Heller, 1975), and also far stronger and more recent evidence that much aid leaks into public-sector consumption.[6] A recent World Bank study (Feyzioglu et al., 1996) found that of every $1 of net ODA roughly three quarters went to increase governments' current expenditures and only one quarter to capital spending.

Several studies have focused on the quality of domestic economic policies as a determinant of the ability of aid to make a difference to growth and investment. The connections between this and the factors mentioned in the previous paragraph are clear. The allocation of revenues as between recurrent and capital expenditures is largely a matter of policy priorities. Similarly, there is much evidence of the impact of the policy environment on the rates of return to public and private investment. Burnside and Dollar (1996) confirm other findings that, taking all countries together, aid receipts have little impact on economic growth. However, both studies take the analysis further by developing (largely macroeconomic) indicators of the quality of country policies and investigating the influence of this factor, obtaining "a robust finding that aid has a positive impact on growth in a good policy environment" (Burnside and Dollar, 1996, p. 33). Hadjimichael et al. (1995, pp. 51-55) arrive at virtually identical conclusions, and the results of these studies are in line with others showing the importance of the policy environment as a possible explanation of contrasting country economic performances.[7] Their result is consistent with the overall absence of an aid-growth correlation because of the limited extent to which donors discriminate among recipients on the basis of the quality of policies; they found that, on balance, "good" policies were rewarded by more aid but that "other variables, which we regard as reflecting donor interests, have even greater explanatory power" (*ibid.*).

Moreover, they found that aid does not appear to induce improvements in policy. This finding is strongly confirmed by the present writer's own ongoing work on donor conditionality, which finds much evidence of donor reluctance, or inability, to punish poor policy performance by withholding aid (Killick, forthcoming, chap. 6). Absence of effective enforcement of conditionality helps explain the weakness of evidence on the effectiveness of that large segment of aid devoted to the support of structural adjustment programmes.

Assessment of the effects of these is fraught with controversy, but enough evidence has accumulated to show that programmes have had limited ability to achieve their own objectives.[8] While both IMF and World Bank programmes have been associated with improvements in export performance and other balance-of-payments indicators, they are not systematically correlated with increased economic growth. One reason for this is that they are associated with reduced investment levels. Programmes seek to achieve improved economic performance by raising the quality of domestic policies and strengthening institutions but the evidence suggests, in common with Burnside and Dollar's (1996) findings, that programmes have only modest impact on key policy variables (except the exchange rate), even less on institutions. Even such limited claims as can be made probably overstate the degree of programme influence because some of the policy changes would have been introduced in any case. Moreover, a good many of the reforms are not sustained, with some governments regressing, reverting to old practices or introducing equivalent interventions through the back door.

Leaving donor foreign policy, security and commercial interests to one side, the basic justification for aid transfers from high- to low-income countries is that it reduces poverty. Here too, however, the evidence is not encouraging. Looking at the broad trends in the distribution of ODA described earlier, while the rise in the share of sub-Saharan Africa may be regarded as a positive response to the large and growing poverty of that region, we should also remember that much of this reallocation has been at the expense of Southern and Central Asian countries, a region also beset with much absolute poverty. At a less aggregated level, a wealth of studies show that country allocations of aid are poorly correlated with the average income levels of the recipient countries, although some donors have been better at this than others.[9]

However, even though it is a cliché of the aid industry, it is necessary to remind ourselves here that aid transfers to *governments of poor countries* does not necessarily mean that much of it benefits *poor people*. Although this does not appear to be an aspect which has been studied much, casual observation suggests that donors have not systematically favoured

governments with effective poverty-reducing policies. Not the least of the problems of aid to Africa is that only a minority of the governments of that continent can demonstrate that they give priority to poverty reduction and have initiated substantial anti-poverty programmes. From this point of view, the net poverty effect of the reallocation from Southern Asia to Africa is ambiguous at best, probably regressive.

How effective have donors been in getting their aid directly to those living in absolute poverty? Mosley (1987, p. 181) concludes his examination by suggesting that while donors continue to say that they wish to help the poor, "that desire does not penetrate very far into administrative procedures, so that such help as the poor and destitute get from aid is largely adventitious ...". While not going as far as this, Riddell (1987, p. 226) also stresses the difficulties that donors have encountered in reaching the poor. Perhaps alone among independent observers, Cassen (1994, pp. 54-55) reaches a more positive conclusion, stressing the importance to the poor of aided projects which raise agricultural productivity and improve social services. However, he also stresses the way that donors' non-developmental objectives constrain the targeting of aid for poverty-reduction, as well as the limitations on what can be done in the face of recipient-government indifference. One of the points of difficulty is that most of the poor live in rural areas. While the World Bank (1990, p. 130) has drawn attention to a range of rural projects which have aided the poor, virtually all evaluations are agreed that agricultural and other rural projects have among the lowest success rates.[10]

Further insight is obtained from the preliminary results of ongoing ODI research into the use of aid for poverty reduction by the countries of the European Union. These appear to validate today Mosley's 1987 assessment, just quoted. Preliminary results indicate that European donor agencies have varied records with respect to the weight attached to poverty-reduction objectives, country allocation priorities and procedures for tracing poverty effects in project monitoring and evaluation procedures, and that in few of them does poverty reduction permeate as an overriding operational objective. Some still argue that their aid, by promoting economic growth, reduces poverty indirectly, but without articulating any clear connection between their aid interventions and the welfare of those living in poverty. The error of conflating aid to the governments of poor countries with aid to poor people remains remarkably common. Only exceptionally are specific poverty groups identified. The collection of data to permit evaluation of the poverty effects of specific projects is even rarer. There appears to be a large gap between present practices and what would be possible on a best-practice basis, confirming that this major group of donors (with honourable exceptions) has yet to give direct poverty-reduction high priority.

Finally in this catalogue of woe, we should add that in concentrating increasing proportions of their ODA on sub-Saharan Africa, donors have selected the region which, by common consent, presents the greatest difficulties. As much is suggested by comparing Africa's very high levels of aid dependency, illustrated in table 2, with the poor economic performance of that continent, both absolutely and by comparison with other developing regions. Less impressionistically, studies indicate lower rates of return - and higher failure rates - from aid projects in Africa, particularly weak relationships between aid inflows and economic growth, and especially large difficulties with adjustment programmes.[11]

The above admittedly presents an unbalanced picture. For one thing, it ignores the more positive outcome of assessments of aided *projects*, which generally find well over half of these to have produced satisfactory outcomes (although these assessments have often been criticized for exhibiting "evaluation optimism"). It also ignores the multiplicity of donor objectives in supplying aid. The main point, however, is that it is difficult for advocates and practitioners to point to convincing evidence that ODA produces clear developmental benefits. This puts them on the defensive and undermines faith in the value of the activity, making it harder to defend aid budgets in conditions of general budgetary stringency.

D. Models of aid and development

The condition just described is worsened by growing doubts about how aid fits into a present-day understanding of the dynamics of economic development. In the early years of explicit concern with the problems of "underdeveloped countries", when development economics emerged as an important sub-branch of the wider discipline, the notion of financial transfers from rich to poor nations fitted comfortably within the predominant model of development of that period. This tended to conflate development with growth and largely saw the latter in terms of investment. Thus, with the incremental capital-output ratio (ICOR, approximately, the inverse of the marginal productivity of capital) taken as a

given, the well-known Harrod-Domar model showed that the rate of growth was determined by the ratio of investment to gross domestic product (GDP). It was therefore possible to state the investment rate necessary to produce a given target growth rate (always assuming a constant ICOR).

Given further assumptions (or information) about domestic savings capabilities, it was then simple to estimate required levels of capital inflows from the rest of the world and, by subtracting likely inflows of private and other sources of capital, to derive residually estimates of needed aid inflows. Since "underdeveloped countries" were by definition poor and saving propensities were regarded as rising with income, it was reasonable to postulate that domestic savings in those countries were likely to fall well below the level required to sustain investment at levels that would generate a satisfactory pace of economic progress. And since private capital inflows were at that time generally modest (and there was, in any case, much debate about the benefits of foreign direct investment), ODA needs were shown to be large, both in aggregate and in a high proportion of individual underdeveloped countries.

This rather simple approach subsequently gave way to a rather more sophisticated "two-gap" model. This added to the savings-investment gap of the Harrod-Domar model the idea of a second gap, between the supply and demand for foreign exchange, which might be even more difficult to fill. Two-gap analysis introduced the important idea of structural rigidities preventing the ready conversion of domestic savings into an equivalent release of foreign exchange. In relatively inflexible underdeveloped economies, it was argued, resources and demand could not readily be switched between tradables and non-tradables, a condition which may be worsened by protectionism in industrial countries and by shortages of imported inputs. In such situations, foreign exchange gaps may exceed savings-investment gaps, in which case the former would be the dominant constraint on growth and would define the volume of ODA needed to achieve a given growth rate.

More recently, three-gap models have been introduced, with the government's revenue-expenditure balance identified as another potentially binding constraint. This was developed particularly in the context of the debt crisis of the 1980s, when the servicing of large external debts necessitated the generation not merely of large savings-investment and balance-of-payment surpluses but large budgetary surpluses too.

In the meantime, however, almost all the thinking which underlies such estimates of need has been discredited. We no longer equate development with growth (although that dies as hard as most bad habits). We no longer think that the marginal productivity of capital is unaffected by the volume of investment (and many countries have combined periods of high investment and unsatisfactory growth because resources were poorly invested). Indeed, we no longer think that physical capital formation, *per se*, is the prime mover of economic development. Moreover, experience has shown that quite poor countries can sustain high savings rates if the right policies and incentives are in place. The relevance of two-gap models has been reduced by the movement towards more flexible exchange rates and by the diversification of many (non-African) developing countries away from reliance on primary product exports.

These changes of view, together with the rise in private capital flows to developing countries, inevitably raise questions about the place of ODA in development. The arguments of writers of the political Right, who have long been critical of aid, appear in a number of respects to have been validated by experience, which has further undermined intellectual support for ODA.[12] These critics see development as essentially driven by domestic forces, often of a deep-seated cultural-historical nature. Aid is therefore not indispensable for development and may get in the way by distorting incentives. Particularly pernicious, in their view, is the tendency for ODA - being channelled almost exclusively to governments - to reinforce a bias towards extensive State interventionism, to the disadvantage of private enterprise.

Looking back from the vantage point of 1996, Lal (1996) sees large-scale official ODA as a historically unique response to the breakdown of international capital markets in the inter-war period, reinforced by a welfare-based humanitarian ethic in favour of transfers to reduce poverty. Appreciation that aiding the governments of poor countries is not the same as aiding poor people, plus ODA's limited success in actually reducing poverty, has sapped the humanitarian motive, just as the growth in size and efficiency of private capital markets has undermined the efficiency case. While Lal acknowledges that private capital still shuns some low-income countries, chiefly in Africa, he attributes this not to their poverty but to the "predatory" nature of their governments. Unless this is addressed, not only will private capital stay away but aid is unlikely to bring developmental benefits either. "The foreign aid programmes of the last half-century are a historical

anomaly ... an idea whose time has gone!" (Lal, 1996, pp. 12-13).

It is not surprising, therefore, that those who agree with this type of critique question the rationale for the continued existence of multilateral lending agencies, such as the World Bank and the various regional development banks. These institutions, in particular, are confronted with the question of what they can do which international markets cannot now do. It is probably fair to say that no very clear answer has so far been forthcoming, as it relates to their "hard window" lending, which is on near-commercial terms. As will be argued later, a strong market failures case can still be made out for concessionary "soft window" lending, but that constitutes only a small part of the operations of the multilateral development banks (MDBs).

It is in this context that the threat to IDA resulting from the continuing problem of arrears by the United States (see Appendix) should be seen. If indeed inability to solve this problem should cause non-renewal of IDA resources and a consequential tailing-off of new IDA lending - a real, if ultimately unlikely, possibility - this would raise particularly serious issues concerning the future nature and size of the World Bank (spilling over inevitably to the position of the other MDBs), for IDA is overwhelmingly the Bank's most important vehicle for concessionary lending.

In fact, much of the thinking upon which the Rightist critique is based now finds acceptance across a wider spectrum of opinion. As much has already been indicated earlier in this paper. In particular, the lessons of experience - in developed and developing countries alike - have forced a re-evaluation of the role of the State in development, and this foment has inevitably raised questions about the value of ODA in its traditional forms. The emphasis now is on raising the *quality* of State interventions (see also World Bank, 1997) but, while it is not difficult to see how aid might obstruct institutional reform and development, it is less clear that external donor agencies can do much to promote the needed institutional changes.

The danger that large-scale aid inflows may distort incentive signals finds a similarly wide acceptance today. There are both specific and general aspects of this. Food aid, for example, was long criticized along these lines (although most food aid donors are nowadays more careful than they used to be to avoid weakening incentives for production by local farmers). Another specific distortion relates to the possible "Dutch disease" effects of ODA receipts. The danger here is that, by providing a major additional supply of foreign exchange, aid affects exchange rates, such that the local-currency price of foreign exchange is lower than would otherwise be the case, causing overvaluation and discouraging exports.[13] A different line of explanation that leads to the same policy outcome points out that, since aid finances imports, this leads to an underpricing of imported goods (including capital goods) relative to exports and non-tradables (including local labour). The underpricing of tradables vis-à-vis non-tradables is, of course, synonymous with currency overvaluation.

Moreover, this is not merely a theoretical possibility. Van Wijnbergen (1986) explored this and found empirical evidence that aid has a Dutch-disease effect. Younger (1992) investigated this for Ghana and also found evidence of a currency-appreciating effect. At a more casual level, the length of time the Western and Central Africa countries of the Communauté Financière Africaine (CFA) were able to cling on to an increasingly inappropriate exchange rate until the pressures for devaluation of the CFA franc eventually became irresistible in 1994 was surely only possible because of the large volume of aid and monetary support they received from France and other sources. Similarly, logic alone suggests that, in the absence of policy correctives, aid at the levels for Africa reported in table 2 is most likely to have an upward effect on exchange rates, where these reflect supply and demand. The implication, of course, is that large-scale ODA tends to discourage exports - a serious charge in relation to the small, trade-dependent economies of Africa and elsewhere.

Official ODA also affects the incentive system facing governments in their conduct of fiscal policy. As noted earlier, it may weaken the tax effort, with aid substituting for local revenues. This is a type of moral-hazard problem, a member of a larger class of situations in which the "soft budget constraint" offered by relatively stable and large inflows of assistance may dissuade governments from unpopular but economically desirable actions (e.g. reducing the size of inflated public services) that they might otherwise be unable to avoid. My own research on the effects of programme aid has yielded many examples of this (Killick, forthcoming, chap. 6).

Quite apart from moral hazard, ODA which is large relative to total government revenues may distort the composition of government spending in favour of the type of activity, or project, which can most easily attract aid. This may have a number of undesirable

characteristics: skewing expenditure in favour of large new projects with high import contents, and giving rise to under-budgeting for the maintenance and utilization of past capital projects, as with roads whose maintenance is neglected until their condition is bad enough for them to be justified as (aid-funded) "rehabilitation" projects. At its worst, this type of bias may so undermine the utilization of past aided projects that the process threatens to become nugatory.

Furthermore, donor practices have sometimes undermined budgetary control and discipline in recipient countries, often because of agency desires to spend their budgets. Sometimes donors have pursued the tactics of the Pied Piper, deliberately selecting for assistance activities in sectors they believe to be neglected, in the expectation that this will force a government to spend more because of the recurrent costs of aid projects (Howell, 1985, p. 13). More generally, past neglect of the recurrent cost implications of aid projects has added to the difficulties of budgetary planning. Even more seriously, donors sometimes evade normal budget procedures altogether, setting up quasi-autonomous project administrations, or augmenting the salaries of local civil servants, or paying suppliers direct, all undermining the fiscal authority of the Treasury. See, for example, Adams (1989, pp. 187-188) for a description of the situation in Sudan in the 1980s:

> Sudan's total dependence on foreign assistance constrains its ability to control the free-wheeling activities of donors. The hold of the Ministry of Finance and Economic Planning over the donor agencies is tenuous. Even some of the long-established bilateral donors ... are disbursing outside the government budget, in some instances without any formal agreement with the central authorities. For most intents and purposes, the government system of annual budgeting of development and recurrent expenditure has collapsed. In the circumstances, bilateral agencies tend to become a law unto themselves, preferring to retain their freedom to disburse funds in the most opportune manner and to provide the authorities with just sufficient information to justify their continued presence. Projects are often funded through informal, ad hoc channels. For example, to ensure the loyalty and commitment of government staff attached to projects, donors find it necessary to make incentive payments and to pay retainers to senior government personnel to act as "consultants".

There is also the danger, identified in the earlier description of the Rightist critique of aid, that, being channelled to governments, it hampers private-sector development. Quite apart from allegedly buttressing a *dirigiste* approach to economic management, aid may discourage private investment (in the tradable goods sector, at least) through its Dutch-disease effects, just discussed. It may do this directly or, as found by Younger for Ghana, as an unintended by-product of policies designed to counter the macro-economic effects of large aid receipts:

> ... the aid flowing towards Ghana has worked at crosspurposes with some of the reforms in recent years by driving up aggregate demand and by making foreign exchange relatively abundant. The Ghanaian authorities' attempts to counter the increased aggregate demand by tight monetary policy have made credit extremely scarce, thus crowding out private investment (Younger, 1992, p. 1595).

Yet another channel through which ODA might act as a disincentive for private investment is through the so-called "debt overhang" effect. It is well known that among many aid-reliant, low-income, developing countries indebtedness to the IMF, the World Bank and other multilateral agencies has been growing rapidly, to which the recent HIPC Initiative is a response. The argument here is that the overhang of this debt and the increasing claims that its servicing makes upon debtor-country resources act as a kind of tax on increments to private-sector output and increase uncertainties about future profitability.

Against these potential disincentive effects, there is the countervailing influence - for the existence of which there is a large volume of accumulated evidence - that certain public-sector investments stimulate private investments by raising the expected rate of return (or lowering the perceived risks) of private projects, e.g. when public-sector investments in transport and communications reduce private-sector production or distribution costs (the so-called "crowding-in" effect).

In the face of these contrary impulses, the net effect of ODA on private investment is an under-researched issue, but one study of 36 developing countries in 1977-1991 (Snyder, 1996) has found a negative association between ODA and private investment, particularly in low-income countries: "The results clearly show that countries which receive larger aid allocations experience lower subsequent levels of private investment" (p. 735) (note the word "subsequent", implying that causality runs from aid to reduced private investment). Another study by Hadjimichael et al. (1996) also examines the con-

nection between these two variables, obtaining rather mixed results, but concluding that ODA appears to have a negative influence on private investment once account is taken of the influence of other explanatory variables.

There is a further aspect of the Rightist critique which now receives wider acceptance, namely, a view of national economic development as essentially driven by domestic forces. This has entered the conventional wisdom on aid via the concept of "ownership". In the context of policy reform, I have described this in the following terms:

> Government ownership is at its strongest when the political leadership and its advisers, with broad support among agencies of state and civil society, decide of their own volition that policy changes are desirable, choose what these changes should be and when they should be introduced, and where these changes become built into parameters of policy and administration which are generally accepted as desirable (Killick, forthcoming, chap. 4).

The opposite case is given when reforms are donor-initiated and designed, with little domestic support and few local roots. The danger, of course, is that aid that is large relative to total resource availabilities will undermine local ownership. One obvious way it might do this is through donors' use of policy conditionality. Conditionality stands in opposition to ownership, not least because it is apt to generate nationalist resentment of outside "interference". Where it exists, such hostility can add powerfully to perceptions of differences of interest as between donors and recipients. It can sometimes undermine the prospects of policy reform by creating a generalized suspicion of changes advocated outside which has little to do with the merits of the case. Donors contradict themselves when paying lip service to ownership while insisting on conditionality, for conditionality implies involuntary action, policies that would not otherwise be undertaken and which are agreed simply in order to gain access to money.

Technical "cooperation" (TC) is another component which, as it is practised, often swims against the tide of ownership. Thus, the ODI study of aid effectiveness (1993, p. 55) concludes that TC has been largely donor-driven in sub-Saharan Africa, with little recipient involvement, limited local commitment and weak local ownership. Not coincidentally, a growing number of evaluation studies of TC are quite negative about its achievements. Berg (1993), for example, chronicles the change from an earlier presumption of the beneficial effects of TC to a rising chorus of doubts and criticisms in the 1980s, on the grounds that it does not appear to be fostering greater self-reliance in recipient countries: "Despite thirty years of a heavy technical assistance presence and much training, local institutions remain weak and this type of assistance persists" (p. 244). More recently, the World Bank evaluation department (1996a) has assessed that only 19 per cent of the Bank's technical assistance projects have been successful.

A large-scale donor presence can weaken local impulses for self-improvement and development initiatives in more insidious ways too, as the present writer found in a 1995 mission to the United Republic of Tanzania (DANIDA, 1995). There, the over-whelming donor presence, their large financial and other resources relative to local resources, the multi-plicity of their projects and of their reporting and other stipulations appeared to have swamped local capabilities. Local officials felt overwhelmed, power-less to insist on local priorities. If they tried to stand up to a donor, more often than not it would use its higher political contacts in favour of its project, or would find another agency willing to implement it. For this reason, among others, the United Republic of Tanzania in 1995 displayed most of the undesirable characteristics of aid dependency (see also Sobhan, 1996).

E. Conclusion: there is a genuine aid crisis

We started by asking whether it is justified to view aid as being in crisis. Data on total aid flows indeed suggest serious reasons for concern. Total ODA is falling in real terms and two thirds of DAC donor countries reduced their aid volumes during 1995. In addition, some ODA is being diverted from traditional applications, although this is in response to genuine needs, and the conflict with developmental objectives may not be large. Moreover, aid remains at historically high levels, when account is taken of the diminishing number of aid-reliant countries.

However, if we look below the statistics of ODA at the underlying condition of the aid industry, we can see that it is indeed in poor condition. A turning away from post-war ideals of international cooperation in some major donor countries has coincided with a period when political support for aid as an extension of security policy has faded. Attitudes towards recipient governments have

changed, with past waste and frustrations creating a less trusting, less tolerant view. The resulting desire to be more selective is powerfully reinforced by increasing budgetary stringency within most donor governments.

This situation has been aggravated by a paucity of evidence showing ODA to have clear developmental and poverty-reducing benefits. It appears that aid has little ability to improve the performance of recipient economies. Its effects tend to be swamped, *inter alia*, by the effects of recipient governments' economic policies, but donors have not discriminated efficiently in favour of those with good policy performance, nor does aid itself appear to bring much leverage over policy. Evidence that aid has a direct poverty-reducing impact is even weaker. Moreover, most of these negative judgements apply with particular force to African countries, the region on which donors have concentrated their greatest efforts over the last two decades and where there are special concerns about the negative effects of aid dependency. Indeed, one of the features to emerge above is that many of the weaknesses identified are associated with *large-scale* aid.[14] Aid, it seems, is like red wine: beneficial in modest amounts but toxic when taken in large quantities over a long time.

When we turned to examine the place of aid within the dominant present-day view of the nature of development, we concluded that the intellectual underpinnings of aid have been seriously undermined. The development model upon which the case for aid was originally based has been abandoned in the light of experience and changing intellectual perceptions. A good many of the early criticisms of the Right appear to have been borne out by experience, not least the tendency for large-scale aid to distort incentives for private-sector development. Aid appears less obviously suited for approaches to development which see development as essentially an internally driven process, propelled largely by private initiatives and market mechanisms. Furthermore, given the now widespread criticism of much past TC aid as in-effectual, ODA similarly fits less readily into models of development which view human skill creation, institutional development, technological capabilities and the quality of policy interventions as among the key determinants.

Even accepting that the above view is one-sided and that, at more micro-economic levels, many aid projects appear to have been quite successful, the cumulative effect of the influences just summarized in eroding belief in ODA has been powerful. Much past aid is now perceived to have been wasted, not so much as a result of the corruption that is receiving so much media attention but by being placed within unfavourable policy and administrative environments (that are also likely to result in capital flight). Burnside and Dollar (1996) have found that aid is associated with improved economic performance when it goes to countries maintaining good macroeconomic policies, but that donors' use of ODA to promote non-developmental objectives has prevented an efficient concentration of resources on such countries. Instead, donors have placed ill-founded faith in a conditionality which has not in practice brought much assurance of favourable policies within recipient countries.

In brief, faith in, and political support for, ODA has been gnawed away. That is the true crisis. Let us therefore turn now to consider the future and to the changes in aid policy which might avert this crisis.

II. The future

A. *Prospects for the future volume of ODA*

It is likely that the adverse trends in the aid budgets of some donors, reported earlier, are a reflection of the eroding political support for the type of expenditure just described. If the sources of weakness are not adequately addressed, it is possible to predict that more donors will follow suit and that a declining trend could well accelerate.

One reason for this pessimism is that virtually all donors are confronted by similar sources of budgetary pressure and these will inevitably intensify competition for scarce revenues. On the one hand, there is a rather general perception that, despite attempts to reduce it, the burden of taxation (along with the distortions which taxes bring) has become as high as electorates are willing to pay. If so, and if governments continue to give priority (reinforced in Europe by the movement towards monetary union) to the anti-inflationary strategy of reducing budget deficits and reversing the climb in public-debt-to-GDP ratios, then the burden of fiscal adjustment will necessarily fall on the control of expenditures. At the same time, most donor countries are, in varying degrees, confronted with powerful long-term pressures for larger expenditures: on State pensions (related to ageing populations), unemployment benefits (related in many cases to a long-term rise in structural unemployment), the rising cost of health care and the

increased claims of interest payments on the public debt.

Even though aid budgets are everywhere small relative to total government spending, they are unlikely to flourish in the fiscal environment just described. The United Nations' aid target of 0.7 per cent of GNP is supposed to act as a safeguard against large budgetary cuts (at least in the majority of donor countries which have not exceeded that target) but, even though it was reaffirmed at the Rio Summit, experience gives no grounds for thinking that it actually offers protection. As Riddell (1996, pp. 27-28) puts it:

> ... there is little evidence in the past, and less today, to suggest that the 0.7 per cent target contributed in a major way to quantitative aid expansion. Some donors passed the target and continued increasing their aid; some donors never reached it and never looked as though they would; some donors whose aid volume always fell below the target increased their ODA/GNP ratio but then let it fall away; and, most recently, a number of those which exceeded an ODA/GNP ratio of 1 per cent are seeing that (self-imposed) target slipping back.

To appeal to a 27-year-old target adopted by a General Assembly in which donors were in a minority in economic circumstances radically different from today's is simply not a weighty bargaining chip for a Minister of Development to use in arguments with the Ministry of Finance about budgetary allocations.

Faced with the likelihood of a continuing squeeze on aid budgets, there has been considerable recent interest in possible "new" sources of aid finance.[15] The idea which has perhaps attracted the greatest attention is that of a tax on international financial transactions, the "Tobin Tax". However, conflicting purposes are ascribed to such a tax, which is seen as both a potential deterrent to speculative capital movements and a possible new source of revenue for ODA (or other internationally agreed purposes). The dilemma here is that if the tax is successful in deterring speculation it will bring in little revenue. On the other hand, if it is set low enough to maximize revenue, it will necessarily provide little deterrent to speculation: the deterrence and revenue objectives are in conflict. There would also be large problems with enforcement: near-universal adoption would be necessary if evasion were to be kept to acceptable levels. There would probably be technological problems of monitoring and collection, too, and a danger that the ingenuity of international financiers would always keep them one step ahead of the tax collectors.

The United Nations Law of the Sea Convention arguably demonstrates both the difficulties of achieving international agreement, even on a relatively uncontroversial measure, that took 18 years to negotiate, and the potential that exists for the international taxation of common resources. There are other ideas along similar lines, and also for various environment-related international taxes. The sale of all or some of IMF gold reserves is another frequently nominated candidate. Indeed, it appears likely that a small part of these will be sold during the next few years, with the proceeds reinvested to place the IMF Enhanced Structural Adjustment Facility (ESAF) on a permanent footing. However, even this modest proposal has met fierce resistance from some donor countries and, in any case, the finite resources represented by IMF gold could not provide the basis for a significant long-term increase in global ODA.

The basic difficulty which all these ideas confront is that the major industrial countries show very little interest in them:

> The states which would find themselves contributing most ... are precisely those whose conventional aid programmes are under greatest political pressure. They are also the countries where vested interests would be most adversely affected. In many of them, such as the United States, distrust of public-sector and multilateral intervention is widespread. The potential beneficiaries, for various reasons, have not progressed far beyond rhetoric. As a result, despite much activity by international secretariats and outside experts, no nation or group of nations has made concrete proposals for action, in an appropriate forum with power to carry the action forward (ODI, 1996, p. 4).

Given this situation, it would be unwise to look to new international taxes as offering more than a very long-term escape from the constraints on bilateral aid budgets. However, given the past waste of much aid and doubts about its effectiveness, excessive concern about aid volume may be mistaken, and it would be a tactical mistake to concentrate on quantitative aspects, such as the 0.7 per cent/GNP target. Political support for ODA has to be won back through demonstrations of aid effectiveness. Therefore, it matters more to improve the results obtained from the considerable volume of aid that remains.

B. Tackling the crisis - A strategy to raise the effectiveness of ODA

The most urgent task, then, is to raise the demonstrable effectiveness of ODA. This would bring the twin benefits of (a) bolstering the defence of aid budgets, and (b) raising the productivity of such aid as is available. But how might this be achieved? The strategy set out below has four elements:[16]

- Reasserting an overriding developmental purpose for aid;

- Changing to donor-recipient relationships based on local ownership and acceptance of mutual obligations;

- Increasing the selectivity with which aid is allocated across developing countries;

- Tackling donor weaknesses which reduce the quality or productivity of aid.

1. Reasserting the development goal

It is well recognized that aid effectiveness has been undermined by a multiplicity of donor goals of a developmental, humanitarian, commercial, financial, foreign-policy and military nature. This has led to such maligned practices as procurement tying and obstructed a more developmental pattern of aid allocations. Complaints about this have long been commonplace but little improvement is observable, except that the ending of the cold war has downgraded foreign-policy and security considerations to some extent.

This latter development, and also the move towards freer systems of trade and payments, does provide a political opportunity to strip out, or seriously downgrade, the increasingly redundant commercial and foreign-policy-cum-security goals, which remain attached to aid programmes like long-dead crustaceans. Ministers of Development faced with a threat of budget reductions should offer a deal: acceptance of cuts in return for freedom to concentrate on the promotion of long-term development, with its implications of greater freedom to shift aid between countries (and to cut some off altogether) and to reduce procurement-tying.

However, in urging this we have to be careful about how we interpret "development". We should emphatically *not* equate it with economic growth. It deserves to be repeated that the moral case for ODA rests ultimately on aid's ability to reduce poverty, in this and future generations. Growth is necessary for poverty reduction but will not achieve that result unless it occurs in an environmentally sustainable manner and within a policy framework which ensures that the benefits of growth are widely shared.[17] We have suggested earlier that a good many donors still do not give poverty reduction much priority and that there is typically a large gap between best practice and what mostly happens on the ground. Taking poverty reduction more seriously would involve selecting more projects with explicit poverty-reduction objectives; favouring projects and programmes whose outputs are particularly likely to benefit identified groups of poor people (which agricultural projects directed to the production of staple foodstuffs and the provision of primary education and basic training are obvious examples); working in close partnership with potential beneficiaries; and building distributional objectives into the design of all projects, e.g. by skewing technology choices in favour of employment creation.

There is probably also value in continuing the tendency of the last decade in channelling more poverty-directed ODA through NGOs on the ground that, being closer to the grass roots, NGOs are more likely than official agencies to reach the poor. The danger, of course, is that using NGOs as a conduit in this manner will change the nature of these organizations in ways that impair precisely the advantages that were the reason for channelling aid through them in the first place. It should not just be taken for granted that NGOs have a comparative advantage in poverty-reduction interventions, nor should official donor agencies cease attempting to directly reach the poor themselves.[18] Most importantly of all, donors should withhold aid from governments pursuing seriously inegalitarian policies and should increase allocations to governments with a demonstrated commitment to improve the welfare of the poor. The same principles apply with respect to the quality of governments' environmental policies.

Interpretation of the development objective also needs to take due cognizance of the importance for human advancement of more qualitative factors, e.g. as they relate to personal security and the rule of law, the observance of human rights (including the right to freely determine their own political status enshrined in the Charter of the United Nations), and reasonable access to health and education.

2.   Changing relationships

As pointed out above, traditional relationships between aid donors and recipients placed few obligations upon the latter, apart from formal requirements for financial accountability, procurement and the like. In the case of the Lomé Treaties, ACP governments received ODA as a right. In most other cases there was a presumption of a shared development objective and that governments would pursue policies consistent with a productive use of aid received. It has also been pointed out that trust has been eroded, exemplified by the growth of conditionality, not merely by multilateral agencies but by bilateral donors too (see Hewitt and Killick, 1996). This has established the important principle of aid being based on *mutual* obligations, as stressed in the 1996 DAC restatement of the principles of aid (DAC, 1996a). The problem is, as already argued, that using financial leverage does not appear to be a generally effective way of securing better policies, even less of promoting human rights and parliamentary democracy.

There has thus been a search for a more workable model, still based on the acceptance of mutual obligations. Within the World Bank, a major report on long-term development in Africa advocated placing aid on "parallel tracks", with programme and project aid being based on past performance in the implementation of governments' own programmes (World Bank, 1989b, p. 14). Within the Bank's Africa Department there has been discussion of the desirability of shifting in favour of greater use of "*ex post* conditionality", implementing the parallel-tracks approach.

A related, but more radical, idea is for the expression of aid relationships in *development contracts*.[19] The idea is that these would be based on mutual interests and embody reciprocal, long-term donor and recipient obligations. It would be for recipient governments to design the policy content of these contracts. They would formally commit themselves to these actions in return for donor commitments to agreed levels of assistance over a number of years, preferably including compensatory and contingency mechanisms to ensure that policy reforms are not blown off course by external shocks. The assistance in question would not necessarily be confined to ODA; it could also extend to debt relief and trading relationships. Whether development contracts would be workable must be doubted, however. They rely on the right of either party to cancel the contract if the other party does not fulfil its obligations The threat of withdrawal would have to be credible. There would be a tendency for recipient governments to press donors for guidance on what they would need to do in order to qualify for assistance, with the danger of restoring conditionality by the back door.

However, the most significant thing about the ideas just described is that they all embody the idea of "ownership", i.e. of aid in support of policies devised by recipient governments. The evidence confirms the superiority of results obtained from government-initiated measures, with donors chiefly influencing the course of events through their intellectual contributions and practical help. This points strongly to the conclusion that the effectiveness of aid could be greatly enhanced by concentrating it more selectively in favour of governments which have decided for themselves to pursue, and persist with, a pro-development, anti-poverty policy strategy, a conclusion strongly reinforced by the evidence of the economic benefits of aid in countries pursuing "good" macroeconomic policies. The recipient government's obligation in this case would be restricted to persevering with a policy strategy it had already adopted of its own volition.

3. Increasing selectivity

However, if donors are to become more selective they need to develop objective indicators of ownership (and expertise in that area).[20] These indicators are liable to be highly specific to the policy area with which they are concerned, which means that there is a potentially large number of specific indicators that might be deployed. Consistent with the approach advocated here, the World Bank now makes a systematic attempt to relate its IDA lending to country policy and poverty-reduction indicators, although insufficient information is available to permit its methods to be assessed. For the period of IDA-10 (1994-1996) a positive correlation is reported (World Bank 1996b, table 4.1) between assessment of country performance and IDA commitment levels: the 20 per cent of the countries that performed best received commitments of SDR 13.4 per capita, against only SDR 1.1 per capita for the bottom fifth (although there was less evidence of correlation within the "middle" 60 per cent). The Bank points out that commitments cannot be wholly determined by performance indicators, however: it is important to retain the flexibility to be able to respond to exceptional financing needs, e.g. for postwar reconstruction or debt workouts.

A broad-brush approach to the prediction of government ownership, would be to use past performance as a predictor of the future. This is what was meant by the earlier reference to *ex post* conditionality. There are problems with this, however, mainly arising from the impermanence of political life. Governments come and go. They may also change course in mid term, for good or ill. The concept of government ownership is difficult to apply when there is serious political instability. What, then, to do in countries plagued by chronic political instability? In the worst cases, it is probably an illusion to think there is anything at all to be done with development aid. In the absence of a tolerably settled government, or when the very institutions of the State are under threat, the prerequisites for effective ODA are not met and the most that donors can do is to respond to humanitarian needs until stability is restored.

It is in less extreme situations that the value of having indicators of government commitment would be of value. At the political level, these should be sensitive enough to differentiate between situations where a government is making a tactical retreat from a reform to better manage opposition to it, as against cases where the government loses heart and abandons the endeavour altogether. Indicators of ownership should also provide evidence on the extent to which affected interest groups have been consulted about the reforms in question, and the degree to which reforms command broad-based support.

Another test suggests itself: the government's willingness to prepare its own policy document formally requesting finance in support of reforms. This appears a basic requirement, but it is one whose observance is startlingly sporadic. The IMF usually insists on drafting letters of intent in Washington, and this is surprisingly common practice within the Bank as well. Here, however, a distinction between willingness and ability is crucial. Governments that lack the technical capability should be provided with expertise, if they ask for it. Donors should steer clear of governments having that capability but with such weak commitment to a developmental policy framework that they cannot put a persuasive request together, while taking a more eclectic view than has sometimes been taken in the past of what constitutes a "persuasive" programme.

A further aspect of greater selectivity is that aid should be concentrated on those countries without adequate access to private capital markets. As noted earlier, Lal (1996) attributes lack of creditworthiness among poor countries to the predatory nature of their governments, but that is a very partial view. It overlooks the large structural weaknesses of these economies, the poor functioning of their markets (particularly financial markets), the skill shortages and weak technological capabilities, and the tiny size of their internal markets. All these characteristics depress the prospective profitability of investment. They also make it less worthwhile for potential international investors to incur the costs necessary for a knowledgeable view of local investment opportunities, leading to informational inefficiencies. Moreover, creditworthiness on private capital markets does not necessarily ensure sufficient resources for investments where social returns exceed private returns (e.g. primary education and health care), even less for environmental protection and poverty-reduction measures. There is, in other words, a market-failures case for continuing with aid to low-income countries, filling a major gap which private capital is unlikely to occupy for some time.

In practice, as Riddell (1996, pp. 29-30) points out, much aid still goes to countries with good credit ratings, so that the share of ODA going to upper-middle- and high-income countries has actually been rising. Argentina, Brazil, Egypt, Indonesia, Mexico and Thailand are among creditworthy countries still receiving substantial amounts of aid. Donors have resisted the idea of a cut-off point of eligibility, with the United States and Japan particularly reluctant to have their freedom limited by any commitment to restrict assistance to poor countries - another example where mixing developmental, foreign policy and commercial objectives undermines aid effectiveness.

It should be frankly admitted that there is difficulty with a strategy based on a more selective concentration of aid on the countries most in need of it and best able to put it to good use. A consequence of this would be to reduce the number of recipient countries (very probably to the disadvantage of Africa and to the advantage of some Asian countries), with the prospect that the "chosen ones" would receive substantially larger inflows than at present. Yet one of the lessons emerging from our earlier discussion is that there are diminishing returns to aid to a given country: too much of it is liable to generate progressively the ill effects associated with aid dependency. A partial solution would be to provide a larger proportion of ODA in the form of programme support. But this would not entirely get rid of the problems because, as Younger (1992) found for Ghana, large amounts of programme aid are apt to have Dutch-disease effects and may discourage private-sector

investment. Better use of a smaller global volume of aid is consistent with an enhanced developmental impact.

4.   *Addressing donor weaknesses*

The fourth leg of a strategy to raise the effectiveness of ODA is to address various specific donor weaknesses in the implementation of aid. These can be dealt with summarily because they are thoroughly familiar and the direction of desirable action is already clear.

The desirability of contributing more to local-currency recurrent costs has been urged and mechanisms for this have been proposed.[21] Various proposals have been made to strengthen donor agencies and reform the incentive systems that create pressures to spend, regardless of developmental value. More and better *ex post* evaluation has been advocated, as well as an improvement in learning from the results. Everybody is in favour of better coordination and a consequential amelioration of the problems of the proliferation of donors, projects and conditions, but actual progress in this respect is limited. There is a similarly long-standing struggle to reduce procurement tying, but here too the trend is unclear.

In principle, one attractive route for avoiding bilateral donor weaknesses is to switch more aid to multilateral agencies. These are less beset by multiple objectives, better able to concentrate on maximizing developmental effects. They are relatively immune from tying and some of the other practices which reduce aid quality, are likely to have greater freedom in decisions on country allocation, and are better placed to engage in constructive policy dialogues with recipient governments.

However: (a) some multilateral agencies are more professional, efficient and non-political than others; this is not a blanket recommendation for more resources to any agency that happens to be international; (b) there would be obvious dangers of spawning yet larger international bureaucracies, with even greater concentrations of power vis-à-vis recipient governments; (c) there is little sign of a shift to multilaterals actually happening. Their share in total aid has actually declined in recent years (DAC, 1996b, table A3), and a reversal of this trend would be resisted by many donor governments. Once again, we come up against donors' multiple objectives, for it is the resulting loss of freedom to use aid for foreign policy and commercial advantages that have been among the prime reasons for donor governments to resist larger proportionate allocations to multilateral agencies.

One specific issue confronting donor governments in their financial relations with the MDBs - specifically the World Bank - concerns the future of IDA, referred to earlier. This is dealt with in more detail in the Appendix. It is possible, although unlikely, that present difficulties over the financing of IDA, arising from continuing large-scale United States arrears, will prove intractable, because of the strength of other donors' attachment to the burden-sharing principle. As suggested in the Appendix, it would be possible, should an impasse arise, to continue much the same level of IDA lending at a smaller budgetary cost to donor governments by converting the financing of IDA to an interest-subsidy basis, as in the case of ESAF, although this would be at a cost to IDA's longer-term level of activity and would raise some practical problems.

The IDA situation illustrates a far wider point: the politics of the situation is the key, among both donors and recipients. If there is to be a fresh start, it is at the political level that it will have to be initiated. The approach of the new millennium may be a good time to attempt a fresh start. There have been important policy improvements and political stirrings within recipient countries; and there has been a radical re-evaluation of security and foreign policies among donor countries. Both developments may permit some of the old obstacles to aid effectiveness to be overcome.

Appendix

The position and future of IDA

Introduction

The International Development Association (IDA) is the World Bank's principal source of highly concessional capital aid. Its credits are repayable over 40 years following a 10-year grace period and are interest-free, although they bear an 0.75 per cent service charge. The grant element in such credits is thus large. These credits are available to two classes of borrower countries, depending on levels of per capita income[22] and commercial creditworthiness: "IDA only" countries, who received 62 per cent of all IDA-10 commitments in 1994-1996, and "blend" countries receiving a mix of IDA and IBRD credits (38 per cent).[23] A quarter of IDA-10 credits were in

support of adjustment programmes; the remainder were investments in projects and sectoral programmes. IDA credits are the principal form of lending by the World Bank Group to the countries of sub-Saharan Africa, making up two thirds of total lending to that region in 1995/96.

The capital for IDA is provided in the form of grants from aid donor governments, overwhelmingly OECD countries. Contributions are made on the basis of a burden-sharing formula, although some donor governments also augment their regular IDA contributions by "co-financing" specific projects or programmes. Return flows ("reflows") on past credits are also assuming importance as a source of funding. Financing is replenished in a three-year cycle, with agreement on the 11th replenishment (IDA-11) having been reached in March 1996, to cover the period July 1996 to June 1999. The size of recent replenishments and level of annual IDA commitments is shown in table A1.

The IDA-11 settlement, down by one third on IDA-10, was only the second time that replenishment occurred at a lower level than that of the preceding replenishment.[24] It was possible to avoid an equally sharp reduction in projected annual lending levels only through what the President of the World Bank described as a "one-time drawdown of accumulated non-donor resources".[25] The President regards the size of the IDA-11 replenishment as inadequate, "because it does not provide IDA with the capacity to respond to policy improvements in large IDA-eligible countries ...", and argues the need for higher levels of replenishment in the future.

IDA-11 and the American problem

Many of the present difficulties associated with IDA derive from the refusal of the United States Congress to approve budgetary provisions for American dues to IDA under the burden-sharing formula. As a result, at the time of the IDA-11 negotiations the United States in arrears on payments due for IDA-10 amounted to $935 million. This created difficulties for other donors, which saw themselves making larger proportionate contributions than had been agreed, to the prejudice of the burden-sharing principle.

The March 1996 settlement sought to overcome the difficulty by exempting the United States from IDA-11 contributions for FY 1996/97 (to be covered by a special "interim fund"), during which period it

Table A1

IDA: RECENT REPLENISHMENTS AND ANNUAL COMMITMENTS

($ billion)

Period		Size of replenishment	Annual commitment level
IDA-8	1987/88-1989/90	12.2	3.8
IDA-9	1990/91-1992/93	14.7	4.7
IDA-10	1993/94-1995/96	18.3	5.7
IDA-11	1996/97-1998/99	11.8ᵃ	4.8 (proj.)

a This amount is made up of an "interim fund" of $4.38 billion and two annual contributions totalling $3.7 billion per annum.

was expected to clear its IDA-10 arrears. For the other two years of IDA-11, the burden-sharing formula would be restored, with the United States pledging to contribute $800 million per annum.

However, although the United States Administration made provision in its 1996/97 budget to honour the commitments entered into, Congress declined to approve that level of provision. United States payments in 1996/97 were expected to be about only half the intended level, insufficient to clear IDA-10 arrears. This carries the problem forward into the second year of IDA-11, and undoes the March 1996 agreement. If the United States were to clear its IDA-10 arrears in FY 1997/98 and make its agreed contribution to IDA-11, it would need to contribute over $1 billion in that year, well in excess of the maximum likely to be acceptable to Congress. The prospects were probably dimmed further by the announcement by the United States Administration that, following the election of a new Secretary-General of the United Nations, it would give priority to reducing its arrears to the United Nations. It would take a major lobbying effort to persuade Congress to approve the budget provision for that, and it is unlikely (and might be counterproductive) for the White House to choose simultaneously to fight for IDA.

If these expectations are correct, the key question becomes how the other donors will react to continuing United States arrears, either in 1997 or - more likely - in 1998. Some adhere very strongly to the burden-

sharing principle because it has ramifications which go well beyond IDA (e.g. financing of the United Nations), and two donors - Canada and Germany - have reduced their own contributions to IDA in the same proportion as the United States shortfall. Some sense of their frustrations is given by the following reported remarks of the then World Bank Executive Director from the Netherlands:[26]

> How can we explain to the Netherlands taxpayers that they are bailing out the United States? I find it very irritating that the Americans are always asking us to understand their special situation. Can't they think for once about someone else? Unemployment in Europe is much worse than in the United States and our budgetary situations are just as bad. The American Congress should understand that the elected representatives of the Netherlands, Britain and other countries don't understand why they should foot the bill for America, which is a far richer country.
>
> The poorest countries in the world would receive not a penny less in aid if there was no IDA. Maybe it is time to say "Bye, Bye IDA". We can use bilateral aid, European Development Fund, through the United Nations system and the NGOs ...

Were such sentiments to prevail when the donors meet to consider the situation, the IDA-11 agreement would collapse and fundamental doubts would be raised about the future existence of IDA. With aid budgets under pressure in many donor countries (see main text), a number of them might welcome an opportunity to make savings through a collapse of IDA. For some donors, that motive might be reinforced by a concern to reverse a long-term tendency for multilateral commitments to absorb ever-increasing shares of their total aid budgets, in order to be able to boost - or protect - bilateral programmes.

However, IDA is by no means defenceless. A good number of donor agencies have a rather strong commitment to it, as an efficient means of channelling assistance to poor countries, and they would presumably try hard to find ways round the American problem. By no means all would agree with the Dutch Executive Director that the poorest countries would receive not a penny less if IDA were to be wound up. Another factor which will carry weight is that the recently negotiated HIPC Initiative for providing greater debt relief to heavily indebted low-income countries is predicated on a continuing substantial level of IDA lending. That this initiative would unravel if IDA were to be discontinued would provide a further reason for retaining it at substantial levels of activity. Further, it would be a mistake to underrate the force of inertia. All countries, as well as the international scene, are littered with institutions that have outlived their original blueprints, but which continue in existence because they have been able to present themselves as doing useful things, or simply because no one wants to incur the odium of closing them down. This factor alone creates some presumption that IDA is more likely than not to survive its present difficulties.

This presumption is further strengthened by the fact that a more cost-effective method of financing IDA is available which would make smaller short-term (and perhaps long-term) claims on donor aid budgets, and for which a highly pertinent international precedent already exists.

Alternative methods of financing IDA

In a 1997 article Jonathan Sanford of the United States Library of Congress explores various alternative ways of financing IDA (showing, incidentally, that they are *all* superior to the existing method in terms of the net present value (NPV) of costs to contributing governments (Sanford, 1997). We shall focus here on one alternative which appears most pertinent to dealing with the situation described above, where various donors are confronted with intensifying budgetary constraints and where burden-sharing

considerations also point to smaller levels of contribution.

Under the present method, most contributing countries make their funding available in the form of non-revocable letters of credit which are encashed by IDA as they are needed, i.e. as funds are disbursed in the borrowing countries. This contrasts with the position of the IMF ESAF, whose concessional terms (0.5 per cent interest, normally repayable over 10 years) are made possible by donor contributions to a subsidy account to lower the cost to borrowers of funds available from a loan account.

Sanford explores the possibility of introducing a donor-financed interest-subsidy account for IDA, subsidizing the cost of borrowing from international capital markets. This idea has been raised before, when it was opposed by the Bank on the grounds that it could raise the cost of borrowing funds for the IBRD by adversely affecting market sentiment (but then, as Sanford points out, the Bank originally resisted the creation of IDA itself for the same reason). On the basis of certain necessary but reasonable simplifying assumptions, Sanford compares the financial cost to contributing donors of the present system and of an interest-subsidy system, per $1,000 of loan committed in year 1 and disbursed over six years. The resulting claims on contributing governments for the first seven years are given in table A2.

Table A2

CLAIMS ON CONTRIBUTING GOVERNMENTS UNDER THE PRESENT IDA SYSTEM AND AN INTEREST-SUBSIDY SYSTEM

(Dollars per $1,000 of loan commitment in a single year)

	Present system	Subsidy account
Year 1	50	3
Year 2	150	13
Year 3	300	31
Year 4	300	50
Year 5	100	63
Year 6	100	62
Year 7	0	63

It shows that there are large short-term savings for donors, as the capital resources are now coming from the financial markets, with donors only making such contributions as are necessary to lower the cost to borrowers to their present concessional levels. It is only in year 7 that subsidy payments become larger. Moreover, Sanford shows that in NPV terms the subsidy system results in significantly lower costs to contributors than the present one (648 against 789 - an 18 per cent saving).

The above figures relate only to a single year 1 commitment of $1,000. We can extend Sanford's analysis to a case where commitments of $1,000 are made annually in years 1 to 7 (table A3). Retaining all other assumptions (and ignoring the possibilities of financing new loans by reflows) the financial outcome is again strongly in favour of the subsidy option. In fact, with continuous annual new commitments of $1,000, it is not until year 17 that the balance moves in favour of the present system. In the meantime, donors are liable to be particularly attracted by the large short-term net savings revealed above.

Table A3

CLAIMS ON CONTRIBUTING GOVERNMENTS UNDER THE PRESENT IDA SYSTEM AND AN INTEREST-SUBSIDY SYSTEM

(Dollars per $1,000 of annual loan commitment over 7 years)

	Present system	Subsidy account
Year 1	50	3
Year 2	200	16
Year 3	500	47
Year 4	800	97
Year 5	900	153
Year 6	1,000	216
Year 7	1,000	278

It would be easy to devise modified versions of the subsidy account illustrated above. One, explored by Sanford, is an interest subsidy account financed by future reflows. Another would be a hybrid scheme, with donors making a mixture of contributions to new

capital and to a subsidy account. All would reduce the short-run budgetary costs to donors of sustaining the existing level of IDA lending, as well as the total cost in NPV terms.

Of course this short-term attractiveness can also be a danger. An interest subsidy account of the type illustrated above would risk a medium- to long-term reduction in new IDA lending because capital repayments would not return to IDA (the money having been borrowed on commercial terms by IBRD), leaving smaller reflows for re-lending. To put it another way, in order to maintain a given time-profile and volume of IDA lending, donors would need to stand ready to provide additional capital in later years (a factor which, however, is taken into account in Sanford's NPV calculations). Judgements about the weight that should be given to this make it necessary to look at the longer-term demand for loans on the highly concessional terms offered by IDA. If the need is expected to continue on a large scale well into the 21st century, changes in IDA's financing structure which might prejudice its long-term ability to sustain lending levels would need to be approached with great care. Against this, it would be possible to take the more optimistic view that needs should diminish appreciably over the next 20 to 30 years - or that, if needs are undiminished after so long a time, IDA (and aid in general) would have been shown not to offer a solution to the problem of poverty.

A potentially serious practical problem (although it is one which the IMF has apparently solved in the case of ESAF) would be the difficulty for the Bank of entering into *contractual* commitments on the basis of donor *promises* to make interest-subsidy payments in the future. The present United States arrears are a sufficient signal of such danger. The problem might, perhaps, be dealt with by establishing a reserve account against the danger of future donor slippages, but (a) this reduces the financial attractions of the move, and (b) it might introduce moral hazard considerations. This is a matter that would need careful consideration.

There may also be a Bank concern that introducing an interest subsidy might be misread by the markets as increasing the risks of lending to the Bank because of the inherently higher risks of default on loans to IDA-eligible countries, raising the spreads which the Bank would have to pay on its bonds. This would be a good reason for structuring the arrangements carefully so as to minimize the risks of such an interpretation, keeping a sharp distinction between IBRD and IDA operations, and retaining the Bank's present "preferred creditor" status and the financial sanctions that go with it.

The question of geographical coverage

There is a final matter to be mentioned: the very low levels of lending, at United States insistence, to India and China. In the latter case, the IDA-11 agreement envisages that China will be lent only about 4 per cent of total commitments (against 11 per cent in IDA-10), after which it will altogether cease to be regarded as eligible (Sanford, 1997). India's share is also due to fall further during IDA-11, from its 15 per cent share of IDA-10.

The grounds on which these two countries have been squeezed is that they are "blend" countries, enjoying creditworthiness on private capital markets. It can be argued, however, that they are countries where a vast number of people is still living in absolute poverty, and whose international creditworthiness provides no assurance that adequate public resources will be available for the provision of educational, health and other services accessible by the poor. Moreover, both countries can reasonably be represented as following economic policies favourable to the productive utilization of aid, a claim that may be made much less plausibly for a good many other countries which receive far larger amounts of IDA lending in per capita terms.

There would be a good case for revisiting this issue in the context of the problem arising from the United States arrears, particularly given the concerns expressed by the President of the World Bank, quoted earlier, that at present IDA is unduly limited in its ability to respond to the potential needs of eligible countries.

Notes

1 "Aid" and "ODA" are used synonymously in this paper.
2 Based on statistics of the Development Assistance Committee of the OECD (DAC) for 1995, net disbursements by these countries to developing countries and multilateral organizations amounted to $46.3 billion, or 77 per cent of the DAC total for that year. Of course, total flows do not provide a good indicator of aid performance because they take no account of donor country size or economic circumstances. The aid programme of the United States, for example, was the fourth largest in absolute terms in 1995 but, relative to GNP, was by far the smallest of all the DAC donor countries: at 0.10 per cent, against an average for all of them of 0.27 per cent. By this criterion, the top performers

were Denmark, Norway, the Netherlands, Sweden and France (in that order). Source: DAC (1997, table 6a).
3 However, it is likely that the steep deterioration shown for Africa in table 2 is somewhat overstated by exchange-rate movements. It is likely that the average degree of currency overvaluation in Africa in 1980 was substantially larger than in 1994, which would have the effect of overstating the rate of deterioration. I owe this point to Nguyuru Lipumba.
4 But see Killick (1994), among others, for an account of the continuing retarding influence of conditions at the time of independence on the development of African economies.
5 These studies are usefully surveyed in an (unfortunately unpublished) ODI survey of the aid-effectiveness literature (ODI, 1993), on which I shall draw quite heavily below. See also the recent contribution by Boone (1994), Burnside and Dollar (1996), and ongoing work by Mosley and associates.
6 We should remember, however, that some of what is counted as "consumption" could more appropriately be regarded as investment (or at least developmental) spending, most notably the ongoing costs of public educational and preventative health services.
7 See Killick (1991, pp. 20-26), for a survey of some of this literature.
8 Here I am paraphrasing the results of a detailed survey of the evidence on the effects of adjustment programmes in Killick (forthcoming, chap. 2).
9 See ODI (1993, pp. 5-7) for a survey of this evidence.
10 Four fifths of all World Bank (1989a) projects surveyed in the Operations Evaluation Department's 15-year overview which yielded negative *ex post* economic rates of return were agricultural.
11 See Killick (1991, pp. 14-17) for documentation of the statements made here.
12 See Bauer (1971) for a trenchant statement of the following line of criticism and Lal (1996) for a recent restatement of the Rightist critique. Riddell (1987) provides a balanced assessment of the arguments of this school.
13 It can be argued that, so long as the aid inflows in question can be depended on over time, there is no Dutch-disease effect, for the current account adjusts to the net capital inflows that can finance a current-account deficit. Against this two points can be made: (a) if the effect of large-scale aid inflows is to result in an exchange rate that discourages exports (especially non-traditional exports) that will tend to perpetuate reliance on aid, which recipient and donor governments alike say they do not wish; and (b) in the light of the aid trends discussed earlier, it is, in any case, questionable whether future aid will be sustained at past levels, with currency over-valuation leaving recipient economies poorly equipped to respond to any substantial aid declines.
14 Consistent with this, Hadjimichael et al. (1995, p. 51) found that the growth effects of aid varied according to its volume: "... foreign aid stimulates growth initially; beyond a certain threshold, however, the impact on growth appears to be negative". However, the threshold level indicated by their regressions suggested that aid only began to exert a negative influence when it exceeded 25 per cent of GDP, which can be compared with the 1994 ratio reported in table 2 for sub-Saharan Africa (12 per cent of GNP).
15 For a succinct survey of the advantages and disadvantages of the leading contenders, see ODI (1996). This lists no less than 20 recent suggestions.

16   For an important attempt by the OECD donors to respond to the challenges described above, see DAC (1996a).

17   Modern approaches to the macroeconomics of poverty reduction are based on decomposing the growth and distributional components of the performance of an economy. Research suggests that most poverty reduction is a result of growth, rather than redistribution. This has been the case in much of Asia. However, where initially very inegalitarian income distributions are reinforced by policies which perpetuate the inequalities, as in much of Latin America, growth can occur in the midst of worsening absolute poverty.

18   For an account of the evidence on the advantages and disadvantages of NGOs, and a sceptical evaluation of the use of NGOs in Norwegian aid programmes, see Marcussen (1996).

19   For treatments of this topic see Ofstad et al. (1991), Jayawardena (1993), and Stokke (1996, pp. 101-04). See also Hyden (1995) for a related proposal to create politically autonomous "Development Funds".

20   A recent World Bank study illustrates this approach very well. *Bureaucrats in Business* (World Bank, 1995) is concerned with the performance and reform of State-owned enterprises. Its conclusions are close to the position taken here: that there is little that conditionality by itself can do, that ownership and domestic politics are all-important, and that certain pre-conditions must be satisfied for effective enterprise reform. This raises the question of how to identify situations in which the conditions for successful reform are satisfied. Its authors therefore undertook research to identify predictive indicators. These included whether reform had come to be regarded as *politically desirable* by the government; that the proposed enterprise reforms should be *politically feasible*, seen as having two elements, the extent of control which reformers have over the policy-making process, and their ability to overcome resistance; and the *credibility* of the process, disaggregated into the reputation of the government for keeping its promises, the existence of legal and/or political constraints on policy reversals in this area, and the extent of any international constraints, e.g. as constituted by treaty obligations or by membership of regional or other groupings.

21   Back in 1979 the DAC published *Guidelines on Local and Recurrent Cost Financing* which made provision for a transition of financial responsibility from donor to government, with a gradual tapering-off of support. In its report on sub-Saharan Africa, the World Bank advocates donor acceptance of "time slicing", involving agreement by a donor to finance a specified proportion of total financing in a chosen area (World Bank, 1989b, p. 181).

22   The current cut-off point for IDA-only eligibility is a 1995 per capita income of $905, using the methodology employed in the World Bank's *Atlas* (World Bank, *Annual Report, 1996*, p. 234)

23   This and subsequent information about IDA-10 is taken from World Bank (1996b).

24   At $9.0 billion, IDA-7 (1985-1987) set the precedent, down from the IDA-6 level of $12.0 billion.

25   From a September 1996 note by the President of the World Bank to members of the Development Committee.

26   As reported in the Bread for the World Institute's *News and Notices for World Bank Watchers*, No. 15, November 1996, p. 17.

References

ADAMS, M.E. (1989), "Aid Co-ordination in Africa: A Review", *Development Policy Review*, Vol. 7, No. 2 (June).

BAUER, P.T. (1971), *Dissent on Development* (London: Weidenfeld and Nicolson).

BERG, E.J. (1993), *Rethinking Technical Cooperation* (Bethesda, MD: Development Alternatives Inc).

BOONE, P. (1994), "The Impact of Foreign Aid on Savings and Growth", mimeo (London School of Economics).

BURNSIDE, C., and D. DOLLAR (1996), "Aid, Policies and Growth", mimeo (Washington, D.C.: Policy Research Department, The World Bank).

CASSEN, R. et al. (1994), *Does Aid Work?*, 2nd edition (Oxford: Oxford University Press).

DAC (Development Assistance Committee of the OECD) (1996a), *Shaping the 21st Century: The Contribution of Development Co-operation* (Paris: OECD), May.

DAC (1996b), *Development Co-operation, 1995* (Paris: OECD).

DAC (1997), *Development Co-operation, 1996* (Paris: OECD).

DANIDA (1995), "Report of the Group of Independent Advisers on Development Co-operation Issues Between Tanzania and Its Donors" (Copenhagen), October.

FEYZIOGLU, T., V. SWAROOP, and M. ZHU (1996), "Foreign Aid's Impact on Public Spending", *World Bank Policy Research Working Paper*, No. 1610 (Washington, D.C.), May.

GRIFFIN, K., and T. McKINLEY (1996), *New Approaches to Development Cooperation*, UNDP Discussion Paper, No. 7 (New York: UNDP).

HADJIMICHAEL, M.T., D. GHURA, M. MÜHLEISEN, R. NORD, and E.M. UÇER (1995), "Sub-Saharan Africa: Growth, Savings, and Investment, 1986-93", *IMF Occasional Paper*, No. 118 (Washington, D.C.: IMF), January.

HADJIMICHAEL, M.T., M. NOWAK, R. SHARER, and A. TAHARI (1996), "Adjustment for Growth: The African experience", *IMF Occasional Paper*, No. 143 (Washington, D.C.: IMF), October.

HELLER, P.S. (1975), "A Model of Public Fiscal Behaviour in Developing Countries: Aid, investment and taxation", *American Economic Review*, Vol. 65.

HEWITT, A., and T. KILLICK (1996), "Bilateral Aid Conditionality: A first view", in O. Stokke (ed.), *Foreign Aid Towards the Year 2000: Experiences and Challenges* (London: Frank Cass).

HOWELL, J. (ed.) (1985), *Recurrent Costs and Agricultural Development* (London: Overseas Development Institute).

HYDEN, G. (1995), "Reforming Foreign Aid to African Development", *Development Dialogue*, No. 2, pp. 34-52.

IMF (1996), "Official Financing for Developing Countries, Their Debt Situation, and Recent Developments in Commercial Bank Debt Restructuring" (SM/96/230) (Washington, D.C.).

JAYAWARDENA, L. (1993), *The Potential of Development Contracts* (Helsinki: UNU-WIDER).

KILLICK, T. (1991), "The Developmental Effectiveness of Aid to Africa", in I. Husain and J. Underwood (eds.), *African External Finance in the 1990s*, World Bank Working Paper, WPS 646 (Washington, D.C.: The World Bank).

KILLICK, T. (1994), "Africa's Post-Independence Development Experiences", in E. Grilli and D. Salvatore (eds.), *Economic Development* (Westport, CT: Greenwood Press).

KILLICK, T. (forthcoming), *Conditionality: Donors and the Political-Economy of Policy Reform in Developing Countries*.

LAL, D. (1996), "Foreign Aid: An idea whose time has gone", *Economic Affairs*, Vol. 10, No. 4 (autumn), pp. 9-13.

MARCUSSEN, H.S. (1996), "Comparative Advantages of NGOs: Myths and realities", in O. Stokke (ed.), *Foreign Aid Towards the Year 2000: Experiences and Challenges* (London: Frank Cass).

MOSLEY, P. (1987), *Overseas Aid: Its Defence and Reform* (Brighton: Wheatsheaf Books).

ODI (Overseas Development Institute) (1993), *Aid Effectiveness. A Report for The World Bank* (London), October.

ODI (1996), "New Sources of Finance for Development", *ODI Briefing Paper* (London), February.

OFSTAD, A., A. TOSTENSEN, and T. VRAALSEN (1991), *Towards a "Development Contract". A New Model for International Agreements with African Countries* (Bergen: Chr. Michelsen Institute; DERAP - Development Research and Action Programme), December.

RIDDELL, R.C. (1987), *Foreign Aid Reconsidered* (London: Overseas Development Institute and James Currey).

RIDDELL, R.C. (1996), *Aid in the 21st Century*, UNDP *Discussion Paper*, No. 6 (New York: UNDP).

SANFORD, J. (1997), "Alternative Ways to Fund the International Development Association (IDA)", *World Development*, Vol. 25, No. 3 (March).

SNYDER, D.W. (1996), "Foreign Aid and Private Investment in Developing Countries", *Journal of International Development*, Vol. 8, No. 6 (November-December), pp. 735-746.

SOBHAN, R. (1996), "Aid Dependence and Donor Policy", in SIDA, *Aid Dependency: Causes, Symptoms and Remedies* (Stockholm: SIDA).

STOKKE, O. (ed.) (1996), *Foreign Aid Towards the Year 2000: Experiences and Challenges* (London: Frank Cass).

van WIJNBERGEN, S. (1986), "Aid, Export Promotion and the Real Exchange Rate: An African dilemma" (Washington, D.C.: Development Research Department, The World Bank), October.

WORLD BANK (1989a), Annual Review of Evaluation Results, *Operations Evaluation Department Report*, No. 8164 (Washington, D.C.), October.

WORLD BANK (1989b), *Sub-Saharan Africa: From Crisis to Sustainable Growth* (Washington, D.C).

WORLD BANK (1990), *World Development Report 1990* (New York: Oxford University Press).

WORLD BANK (1995), *Bureaucrats in Business* (Oxford and New York: Oxford University Press).

WORLD BANK (1996a), *Annual Review of Evaluation Results, 1995* (Washington, D.C., Operations Evaluation Department, The World Bank).

WORLD BANK (1996b), *The Pursuit of Sustained Poverty Reduction: Review of the IDA-10 Program (FY94-96)* (Washington, D.C.: Resource Mobilization Department, The World Bank), December.

WORLD BANK (1997), *World Development Report 1997* (New York: Oxford University Press).

YOUNGER, S.D. (1992), "Aid and the Dutch Disease: Macroeconomic management when everyone loves you", *World Development*, Vol. 20, No. 11 (November), pp.1587-1597.

EXTERNAL DEBT, STRUCTURAL ADJUSTMENT AND ECONOMIC GROWTH

Jeffrey D. Sachs

Abstract

There is widespread recognition in the international community that the excessive foreign indebtedness of many developing countries remains a major impediment to their economic growth and stability. The G-7 and the multilateral institutions have voiced their support for new initiatives to promote the reduction of the multilateral debt of the heavily indebted poor countries (HIPCs), although the extent of multilateral debt reduction and the mechanisms for such reduction remain unresolved. This paper asks how an improved debt management process can best support rapid and sustained economic growth in the developing countries.

The main conclusions are as follows:

- *The foreign debt crisis should be understood mainly as a crisis of State insolvency;*

- *The fiscal burden of debt servicing is extremely inimical to economic growth in HIPCs, and is an important reason for the repeated failure of structural adjustment programmes to restore economic growth in many of them;*

- *Debt "sustainability" should be judged mainly according to the fiscal burden of debt servicing, rather than export-related indicators or the "external financing gap";*

- *The current approach to debt reduction in the HIPCs falls far short of what is required to re-establish the conditions for sustained economic growth;*

- *Bankruptcy law provides a useful analogy to the issues of international, sovereign debt reduction.*

- *The recent IMF/World Bank initiative on multilateral debt reduction for the HIPCs is a step in the right direction but falls short of what is needed;*

- *The IMF/World Bank proposals can be modified within the current international framework to provide a much improved basis for economic recovery and growth in the HIPCs.*

Introduction

There is widespread recognition in the international community that the excessive foreign indebtedness of many developing countries remains a major impediment to their economic growth and stability. The G-7 and the multilateral institutions have voiced their support for new initiatives to promote the reduction of the multilateral debt of the heavily indebted poor countries (HIPCs), although the extent of multilateral debt reduction and the mechanisms for such reduction remain unresolved (see, in particular, Sachs, 1996). This paper will not address many of the details of the current debate on multilateral debt reduction - such as the use of IMF gold, the specific nature of the proposed trust fund for financing the reduction of World Bank debt, and so forth - but will instead return to first principles, to ask what should be accomplished by a new and comprehensive approach to debt reduction. It is of utmost importance to insure that an improved debt management process will support rapid and sustained economic growth in the developing countries.

I.   External debt and economic growth

Despite a decade of IMF/World Bank structural adjustment programmes, the HIPCs have failed to achieve high and sustained rates of economic growth. In fact, per capita growth in sub-Saharan Africa (where of 33 of the 41 countries classified as HIPCs are located) was negative every year between 1989 and 1994, and only became slightly positive in 1995. Not surprisingly, economic growth in countries classified by the World Bank as suffering from "recent debt service difficulties" has fallen far short of growth in countries without debt service difficulties. In general, countries engaged in IMF/World Bank structural adjustment programmes, almost all of which continue to suffer from a heavy external debt burden, have continued to grow very slowly despite years of structural adjustment lending.

There are two interpretations of the continuing poor growth performance of countries undertaking structural adjustment programmes. One is that the countries in question have failed to abide by the requirements of the programmes, i.e. implementation has fallen short of promise. An alternative interpretation is that the programmes themselves are poorly designed for producing a sustained recovery in economic growth. The evidence suggests that both

interpretations have merit. Countries that comply with IMF/World Bank programmes seem to outperform countries that do not. At the same time, however, even countries in compliance with the programmes have poor to mediocre growth performance. The typical "success stories" in Africa, as cited by the World Bank, have hovered at zero rates of per capita GDP growth during the past five years, with very few exceptions (e.g. Uganda, which has experienced very rapid increases in per capita income in the past five years). There are evidently serious problems in programme design, not just in programme implementation.

While the reasons for failure are difficult to prove rigorously (especially since IMF and World Bank programme documents are confidential and therefore not systematically available for independent analysis), experience suggests two fundamental shortcomings in typical IMF/World Bank programmes with the HIPCs. First, many programmes are simply poorly designed, in the sense that they do not emphasize the policy measures most likely to promote economic growth. Second, and relatedly, the IMF/World Bank programmes typically fail to resolve the overhang of extreme external indebtedness. The heavy debt burdens of the adjusting countries depress economic growth through a variety of channels mentioned below. Even the best designed IMF/World Bank programmes would be unlikely to restore economic growth without a bolder approach to debt reduction.

To understand the limitations of current IMF/World Bank adjustment programmes, it is useful to look at the considerable body of recent evidence on economic growth in developing countries. A veritable explosion of academic work in recent years on cross-country growth experiences has identified the following basic lessons (see, in particular, Barro and Sala-i-Martin, 1995; Sachs and Warner, 1995; and Sachs and Warner, 1996):

(1)   Poor countries, all other things being equal, have the opportunity to grow more rapidly than richer countries through various mechanisms of "catching up", including the importation of capital and advanced technologies from the wealthier nations;

(2)   Open international trade (convertible currencies, low tariffs, low quotas and the absence of licensing restrictions on imports and exports) is the virtual *sine qua non* for catching up. Developing countries that are open to international trade and foreign investment vastly

outperform countries that are closed to international trade and foreign investment;

(3) Low rates of taxation and low rates of government expenditure on current (non-investment) items tend to increase economic growth, mainly by promoting higher rates of investment and saving in the economy. High rates of taxation and government expenditure, on the other hand, promote extensive black-market activity, capital flight and low rates of investment expenditure, all of which translate into slower growth;

(4) Rapidly growing countries focus government expenditures on a few priority areas - basic health, education and infrastructure - while expenditures on consumer and producer subsidies and other income transfers to households and firms are generally kept to a minimum;

(5) A heavy foreign debt burden of a developing country government impedes economic growth through several channels. Higher debt tends to undermine macroeconomic stability by increasing budget deficits. If debt service is covered by higher taxes rather than by an increased budget deficit, the high rates of taxation tend to undermine growth by introducing serious distortions in the economy, including heightened barriers to trade (via trade taxes), capital flight, tax evasion and reduced work effort.

IMF/World Bank adjustment programmes should incorporate these basic lessons in order to ensure the swiftest possible recovery of developing countries to high and sustained rates of growth. Unfortunately, typical programmes are not sufficiently growth-oriented. First, despite much rhetoric to the contrary, insufficient priority is given to the basic policies of openness, low taxation and export-led growth. IMF/World Bank programmes often tolerate gradual trade liberalization stretched out over five to ten years, even though the continuing trade barriers during that period virtually preclude export-led growth. The IMF/World Bank programmes in Zimbabwe during the first half of the 1990s, to cite just one example, took no less than five years to establish partial convertibility of the currency. The continued overvaluation of the Zimbabwean currency during the five-year adjustment period virtually guaranteed that the IMF/World Bank programme would imply painful austerity measures not offset by gains from new export growth. Similarly, the IMF/World Bank adjustment programmes in the CFA franc

zone imposed ten years of austerity before the necessary CFA franc devaluation was finally incorporated in the adjustment process in January 1994. Once again, the result was ten years of pain, without the compensating gains of export-led growth.

Part of the problem in IMF/World Bank programme design is an overflow of conditionality. The IMF and the Bank impose conditionalities on virtually every aspect of economic policy: monetary policy, exchange arrangements, trade measures, government spending, tax reform, tax administration, public sector reorganization, civil service reform, social programmes, privatization, regulatory reform, infrastructure investment, labour market operations, public health, education, and so on. No doubt there are many worthy goals and projects in such extensive lists, but the overall practical result is a ludicrous excess of conditionality, sometimes totalling more than 100 separate items. Not only does an excessively long list breed cynicism - since all parties to the agreement know that many items on the list cannot possibly be fulfilled on time - but also it subverts the urgent need to set policy priorities, especially priorities focused on the restoration of economic growth. In this regard, it is ironic that some NGOs are pressing for still more conditionalities within IMF/World Bank programmes, e.g. on social policies, as part of the debt reduction process. The developing countries, together with the IMF and World Bank, should strongly resist the further proliferation of conditionalities in these programmes. Indeed, both the debtor governments and the IMF and World Bank should aim to streamline conditionalities back to the essentials needed for renewed economic growth.

The second main problem with IMF/World Bank programmes has been the failure to address the continuing external debt overhang with any overall logic or consistency. Of course, there has been progress in this area. Following the outbreak of the debt crisis in the first half of the 1980s, the official community rejected the notion of debt reduction, insisting that the crisis was merely a problem of liquidity. This began to change in the second half of the 1980s, with the introduction of debt reduction by the Paris Club, and then by the commercial banks under the Brady Plan introduced in 1989. Terms of bilateral debt reduction have been extended (from the so-called Toronto Terms to the Enhanced Toronto Terms to the Naples Terms, and now to the proposed Lyon Terms), and the current discussions aim to introduce multilateral debt reduction. Of course, the darker implication of this progressive extent of debt reduction is that the terms of debt relief have been inadequate at each point in the past decade. It is crucial to come to a quick solution of this problem, rather than dragging it out further in still more incremental steps.

In heavily indebted countries, the fiscal burdens of debt servicing are often many times greater than the budgetary expenditures on health and education. Rather than emphasizing adequate debt reduction, IMF programmes typically call for a combination of tax increases and spending cuts on non-debt-service items (including health and education) in order to accommodate the contractual debt servicing obligations. Since there is no overall growth framework, or adequate growth targets, to set the parameters of IMF/ World Bank programmes, expenditure cuts in vitally needed infrastructure projects or basic health and education are often demanded in those programmes in order to make room for debt service.

As is now appreciated in theory as well as in practice, the results of excessive demands for debt servicing can be damaging not only to the debtor countries, but ultimately to the creditors as well. As the result of creditor demands for full repayment of unpayable debts, the adverse consequences for growth in the debtor country can actually reduce the present value of debt servicing in the future. Excessive demands for debt servicing can cause social and political instability, a fall in investment spending and a decline in growth, which all undermine the long-term capacity to pay a portion of the debt. Thus, the reduction of a debt overhang through a negotiated reduction of the contractual debt burden is often mutually beneficial for both debtor and creditors. Even when this is not strictly the case, small reductions in the ultimate payments to creditors may still result in very large gains for the debtors. Thus, deep debt relief for HIPCs may easily dominate new inflows of funds in terms of their relative stimulus to future growth. The HIPCs should continue to insist on deep debt relief at this juncture, as the key to renewed growth in the context of growth-oriented policy reforms.

A typical pattern of IMF programmes is to pressure debtor governments to raise tax revenues beyond the rates consistent with rapid economic growth, with the pressure for tax increases often arising from the demands of debt servicing. Ironically, the IMF has frequently been an opponent of rapid trade liberalization measures, especially sharp reductions in tariff rates, because it puts much more operational emphasis on increasing government revenues than on increasing growth. If the IMF were to propose debt service reductions balanced by deep

cuts in tariff rates, it would find widespread acceptance among the HIPCs. In other words, debt reduction operations would help to leverage extensive trade liberalization. Instead, the IMF tends to ignore debt service reductions, while rejecting tariff cuts! The result is slow growth, with much of the debt service bill going unpaid in any event as a consequence of the slow growth.

In many cases, IMF/World Bank programmes target overall government spending of 30 per cent or more of GDP (including debt servicing of 5-10 per cent of GDP) in countries with per capita incomes as low as $1,000 (Egypt, Kenya and Ukraine are three recent examples). These rates of government spending virtually guarantee slow economic growth via excessive rates of taxation, excessive tariff barriers, widespread tax evasion and capital flight. Of course, debt servicing burdens are only a part of the overall excessive government expenditure. Overambitious social policies, loss-making state enterprises and misconceived development spending also take their toll. For whatever reason, these rates of government expenditure vastly exceed the rates of government spending relative to GDP observed in those developing countries that have been growing rapidly. In eight very fast growing economies (Chile, Hong Kong, Malaysia, Mauritius, Republic of Korea, Singapore, Taiwan Province of China, and Thailand) government expenditure in 1995 averaged around 20 per cent of GDP, with Hong Kong at just 16 per cent.

In order to reach rates of government expenditure in the HIPCs consistent with rapid growth, there is no doubt that deep debt reduction will be necessary. Consider a country with a ratio of debt to GDP of more than 80 per cent (with debt measured in present value terms). If the average interest rate on the debt is 7 per cent, the interest service burden on the debt will be in the order of 5.6 per cent of GDP. Overall contractual debt servicing, including amortization, could easily reach 8-10 per cent of GDP. Even after adjustments for refinancing, and for the reductions of the real debt burden through US-dollar inflation, the fiscal burdens of debt servicing will be enormous, and are likely to match or exceed the budgetary outlays for health, education or infrastructure. There is very little fiscal room for debt servicing if overall spending is to be kept at modest levels consistent with rapid growth (e.g. below 20 per cent of GDP), with the necessary outlays on basic public goods still being maintained.

To get some sense of the numbers involved, consider the following very rough illustration.

Suppose, on the basis of the international evidence, that a poor country can target tax revenues in the order of 10-15 per cent of GDP without damaging long-term growth prospects, but that attempts to raise more than that in government revenues would result in severe distortions that would undermine economic growth. Suppose also that the government can rely on sustained flows of foreign assistance in support of budgetary outlays of around 3-5 per cent of GDP.[1] Typically, the government will have very little additional recourse to private capital markets, either domestic or foreign. Thus, in the absence of inflationary financing from the central bank, overall expenditures should be limited to a range of some 13-20 per cent of GDP, depending on the precise flows of foreign assistance, and on the specific sources of domestic revenues available to the government. (Of course, many developing and developed country governments regularly spend more than 20 per cent of GDP without collapsing; they simply do not have rapid economic growth, however.)

A government can live within such constraints if spending is very carefully targeted. For example, a well-designed budget might include current expenditures on education (mostly at the primary and secondary level) of some 5 per cent of GDP; public health outlays of some 3 per cent of GDP; costs of public administration of 2 per cent of GDP; and expenses on police and defence of some 3 per cent of GDP. Infrastructure spending is sure to require at least 5 per cent of GDP, even if the government leaves much of the infrastructure finance to the private sector (e.g. for power, telecommunications and ports) and focuses attention on items (e.g. rural roads) that are much harder to finance through the market. The total outlays in this illustration total 18 per cent of GDP. Evidently, there is virtually no room for debt servicing, nor for subsidies to households and firms or income transfer programmes other than in health and education. As experience has shown, attempts to collect more than a minimum in external debt servicing results in (a) serious budget deficits; (b) unacceptable cuts in education, public health, or basic infra-structure; or (c) tax rates at levels that jeopardize economic growth.

One of the significant costs of a continuing debt overhang is the difficulty, or impossibility, that the debtor country faces in tapping the private financial markets for new loans. As long as the debt overhang continues, the debtor government is unable to return to private capital markets. This tends to make many countries continuing "wards" of the international institutions. Economic policy is increasingly politicized

in this way, since it is not tested by the international capital markets. In cases where deep debt reduction is granted (e.g. in Poland in the early 1990s), on the other hand, debtor governments can return to the international capital markets. Economic policy tends to become much more focused on market signals, and much less politicized, as a result.

II. Mechanisms for providing debt reduction

The current IMF/World Bank arrangements need fundamental reform if the external debt burden is to be reduced to levels consistent with high and sustained growth in the poorest countries. They need modi-fication as regards (a) the standards for judging the sustainability or unsustainability of the debt burden, and (b) the mechanisms for arriving at the necessary debt reduction. We shall consider each of these in turn.

A. *Standards for judging the sustainability of debt*

One of the oddest aspects of the current debt-management practices of the IMF, the World Bank and the Paris Club is that the fiscal burden of the debt is actually given very little systematic analysis. The focus is almost entirely on external indicators such as the "balance-of-payments financing gap" and the "ratio of debt service to exports" that have little economic meaning or merit. The IMF judges whether the debt service burden is too high relative to exports, but rarely relative to the exigencies of fiscal policy in the debtor country. This is especially odd since, as we have stressed, the overwhelming proportion of the debt is owed by the public sector, and thus the burden of the debt should naturally be measured relative to government revenues rather than to exports, which have little to do with the government's capacity to service the debt. (The creditor governments should understand the situation very well indeed, since the main reason they are resistant to offering greater debt reduction to the poorest nations is their own budgetary concerns![2])

In a standard IMF/World Bank programme, the viability of a given level of indebtedness is judged by the calculation of the balance-of-payments gap. The IMF makes an estimate of the "import needs" of the country, and then estimates the likely exports and the anticipated inflows of foreign capital. The financing gap is calculated, roughly, as "import needs" plus debt-servicing obligations, minus the sum of exports plus anticipated inflows of foreign capital. If import needs plus debt service obligations cannot be matched by exports plus capital inflows, a financing gap is said to exist. The gap may be "closed" by cutting the estimate of import needs, reducing the debt service burden (either through rescheduling or partial forgiveness) or increasing capital inflows, typically through increased official flows.

This standard procedure essentially neglects the fiscal issues raised by the debt service burden. The IMF may estimate that private capital inflows to industry will be large - so that there is no balance-of-payments gap, even though the government itself lacks the revenues to service its own foreign debt obligations. Or the IMF may cut the estimate of import needs, since the calculation of "needs" is rather arbitrary, and thus the assessment of import needs may easily be cut when it is necessary to "close" the financing gap. The weight of the debt on fiscal policy is only addressed indirectly when the IMF pressures the debtor government to close the budget deficit. The extreme pressures implied by debt servicing may lead the IMF to recognize informally the need for debt service reduction, but there is no formal test of debt sustainability linked to the fiscal burden. All too often, the IMF/World Bank response to a heavy debt service burden is to press for increased tax collections, or drastic cuts in education, health and infrastructure.

This analysis suggests that the IMF, the World Bank, the Paris Club and the heavily indebted developing countries should immediately begin to search for new standards for assessing the sustainability of external debt, based on the fiscal consequences of the debt burden. At a minimum, a fiscal test should accompany the balance-of-payments test. The debtor government and the international institutions would agree on a multi-year fiscal scenario based on a number of principles: (a) macroeconomic stability, i.e. government expenditures (including debt servicing) consistent with non-inflationary financing; (b) domestic rates of taxation consistent with rapid growth, i.e. at levels which promote open trade and preserve strong incentives for investment, labour market activity and compliance with tax laws; (c) adequate financing for core public goods, including education, public health and basic infrastructure; and (d) debt reduction as necessary to achieve these goals, taking into account the realistic time path for budgetary and tax adjustments, as well as the magnitude of budgetary assistance that the debtor governments can expect from donor countries. This

exercise would differ from current IMF/World Bank structural adjustment negotiations by putting debt reduction as an explicit balancing item of the budget, by stressing the growth orientation of public spending and taxation, and by focusing negotiations on the adequacy of budgetary funding for core public goods. The debt reduction programme would be presented to the Paris Club on the basis of the fiscal analysis, instead of (or at least in addition to) the traditional balance-of-payments gap calculations.

The procedures recommended here would have two consequences. On the one hand, the case for debt reduction would be much more realistically framed. On the other hand, the focus would be brightly on the excessive rates of government spending that characterize most developing countries. Negotiations between the IMF and the debtor governments would still be tough, with the IMF pressing for deeper spending cuts than many governments would like to make. At the same time, however, debt reduction would be the sweetener, assuring the debtor governments that deep spending cuts would translate at least into higher economic growth, rather than into increased debt-servicing.

B. *Efficient debt reduction: a digression on bankruptcy law*[3]

We have learned repeatedly over the past 15 years that it is one thing to calculate the need for debt relief, and quite another to achieve it in practice. Even when it is clear that deep debt relief is called for in a particular debtor country, there are several enormous barriers to achieving a timely, negotiated reduction of the debt in line with financial needs. In practice, debt reduction negotiations may drag on for years; individual creditors, or particular classes of creditors, may block tentative agreements that are widely supported by most other creditors; the final extent of relief may be clouded in uncertainty, thereby undermining the confidence of the public and potential investors in economic recovery; and the system may "tax" good policy measures by reducing the amount of debt relief precisely for those governments that make the largest policy adjustments. Perhaps most unfortunately, during the prolonged period of negotiation on debt relief, the debtor government is usually strapped for funds, and is unable to obtain working capital that is vitally needed for the effective functioning of the State. In short, even if the analytical phase of debt relief is properly worked out, it will still be necessary to reform the negotiating phase.

An efficient system for debt reduction would have the following features. First, it would reduce moral hazards by rewarding countries for maintaining their debt servicing and by punishing countries adequately for managing their affairs in a manner which leads to default on debt obligations. Second, it would ensure the effective functioning of the debtor government at all stages of the debt restructuring, from the onset of the crisis to its final resolution. Third, it would create mechanisms for coordinating the actions of creditors, so as to achieve an efficient arrangement for renegotiating the financial terms of the problem debts.

Fifteen years' experience with the international debt crisis has demonstrated that current institutional arrangements do not meet the needs in question, even though the international system has evolved over time in a more efficient direction. As a recent IMF report (1995, p. 11) states, "Because there exists no well-defined and accepted legal process that is applicable in such cases, the process of debt resolution by involuntary restructuring is necessarily ad hoc with an uncertain outcome". The implications of the lack of a legal framework may be appreciated by comparing the ad hoc international arrangements with the legal structure that governs financial workouts under the bankruptcy laws of the advanced economies. The United States Bankruptcy Code - Chapter 9 (municipalities) and Chapter 11 (corporations) - provides a particularly relevant contrast with international arrangements, since these chapters are explicitly designed to handle cases of financial restructuring rather than liquidation.

The United States Bankruptcy Code recognizes that efficient workouts of financial insolvency require a regulatory environment at three stages in the workout. At the outset of insolvency (or at least the outset of creditor recognition of insolvency), the Code provides for an automatic standstill on debt servicing. Creditors are not allowed to pursue legal remedies to seize assets or to force the payment of debts. The law recognizes that each creditor, acting individually, has the incentive to enter a "grab race" for assets, to their mutual detriment. The automatic standstill prevents the premature liquidation or impairment of the insolvent entity, which would lower the overall value of the entity to the collective detriment of the creditors.

The second stage occurs between the beginning of the stay and the exit from bankruptcy through reorganization. During this interim period, the insolvent entity (whether a municipality under Chapter 9 or a corporation under Chapter 11) will generally need access to new working capital. The overhang of pre-bankruptcy debt precludes a routine return to the capital markets, and high transaction costs among the current creditors normally preclude new lending by the existing creditors (since each creditor would like the others to make the emergency loans). The Bankruptcy Code solution is "debtor-in-possession (DIP) financing", through the assignment of priority to the repayment of the new, emergency loans ahead of the pre-bankruptcy claims. The bankruptcy court must approve the DIP financing, so as to ensure that the new loans actually enhance the value of the entity (thereby increasing the value of the pre-bankruptcy debts). Note importantly that, unlike the IMF, the bankruptcy court does not dispose of any money itself; its ability to deliver working capital lies in its power to assign priority to new market borrowing by the insolvent entity.

The third stage of the workout is the final balance-sheet reorganization (debt reduction, debt service reduction, new loans, debt-to-equity swaps, etc.), usually combined with an operational re-organization (closure of loss-making units, divestiture, change in management, etc.). The key role of the bankruptcy law is to provide a negotiating framework which (a) brings together all the parties; (b) establishes mechanisms for across-the-board settlements involving all classes of creditors; and (c) discourages free-riding or holdouts by individual creditors, and pushes the process towards an expeditious resolution. The main tricks to avoid free-riding and holdouts are non-unanimity among creditors in the confirmation of the reorganization plan, and the possibility of a court-led "cramdown" of a plan that is resisted by a particular group of creditors. A plan is confirmed if it is accepted by two thirds or more of each creditor class by amount of claims, and by more than one half of each creditor class by number of claimants.

By these standards, the shortcomings in the international system are clear. There is no automatic standstill. An insolvent government typically faces legal harassment, or at least the threat of legal harassment, by individual creditors for months or years after the onset of the crisis. There are continued threats to seize aeroplanes, ships and bank accounts, and to otherwise disrupt trade credit lines. The legal basis of these threats usually does not subside until the final confirmation of a Paris Club and London Club deal, and by that time individual creditors may have done great damage to the debtor government's effectiveness. Moreover, many types of private creditors, such as providers of suppliers' credit, may not be parties to the London Club agreement (which is limited to bank creditors). Thus, legal harassment may well continue even after a London Club agreement has been reached.

There is essentially no debtor-in-possession financing other than the IMF lending. Early in the debt crisis, the IMF orchestrated a few "involuntary lending" programmes of the existing creditors, but the loans were very hard to arrange, and the IMF gave up by the mid-1980s. In the case of Mexico in 1995, for example, there was no active attempt to round up "involuntary" or voluntary private financing. Unfortunately, there are typically very long delays between the onset of insolvency and the start of IMF lending. During this period, the debtor government is starved of working capital, and often loses much of its capacity to govern.

Russia during 1992 and 1993 offers a vivid illustration of how the absence of debtor-in-possession type financing in the international setting undermines economic reforms in debtor countries (see Sachs, 1995b, for details). By coincidence, both Russia and Macy's Department Store in the United States went bankrupt in the same month (January 1992). Macy's filed for Chapter 11 protection, while in the same month the Russian Government informed the G-7 creditors that it would be unable to continue to service its debt. Under the United States Bankruptcy Code, Macy's received an immediate standstill on debt servicing, and within three weeks of filing for bankruptcy it was able to arrange a new loan of $600 million from several New York commercial banks as part of court-supervised debtor-in-possession financing. Russia had no such luck! It received no standstill on debt servicing, and the Russian Government had to wait over a year to receive from the IMF and World Bank as much money as Macy's was able to borrow in three weeks. As a result of the long delay in getting working capital, the Russian Government was politically weakened. By the time the financing was arranged, many of the leading reformers had already been ousted from government and Russia's stabilization programme had been thrown far off track.

In addition to lacking mechanisms for a debt-service standstill and for timely debtor-in-possession financing, the international system lacks effective rules to ensure an expeditious overall settlement that overcomes free-riding and holdouts. The Paris Club and London Club have evolved norms of behaviour to keep the major creditors fairly united. Nonetheless, there are still sharp divisions among various creditor classes (bilaterals versus multilaterals versus com-

mercial banks versus suppliers; large banks versus small banks) which incite strategic moves among the creditors, and which in extreme cases lead to individual holdouts that significantly delay a debt rescheduling or debt reduction operation. The process requires a large input of time and energy from the United States Treasury and other leading finance ministries. Large, high-profile countries (e.g. Poland, Mexico and Argentina) get vastly more attention and more adequate remedies than smaller countries off of the world's political radar screen. The HIPCs, not surprisingly, have come in last in the queue in terms of official attention, so that in many cases of poor, out-of-the-way countries, the debt overhang has continued for a decade or more without resolution.

On the basis of earlier writings (for example Sachs, 1995b) I have been interpreted as recommending an "International Chapter 11", i.e. an international bankruptcy court. This is too literal an interpretation of my critique of current arrangements. What I am recommending is that we recognize and attempt to establish the functional equivalents of the key bankruptcy-code mechanisms: automatic standstills, priority lending and comprehensive reorganization plans supported by non-unanimity rules. We do not need a literal bankruptcy court in order to move in the direction of such mechanisms. We could begin with a clear statement of IMF operating principles regarding each stage of the workout. We could search for ways to establish emergency priority lending from private capital markets, under IMF supervision. The IMF and governments could recommend model covenants for inclusion in future sovereign lending instruments that would allow for emergency priority lending and for efficient renegotiation of debt claims, should future circumstances so require.

In ideal circumstances, the basic standards of debt reduction would include the following:

(1) Standstill: upon determination by the Executive Board of the IMF, the debtor government would be protected from legal challenges by its creditors for immediate debt collection;

(2) Debtor-in-possession financing: the IMF would establish clear procedures for emergency lending on an expedited basis, as in the Mexico crisis of 1994-1995. Debtor governments would be able to pursue emergency relief via direct appeal to the Executive Board;

(3) Comprehensive and timely workout: the IMF would provide the forum for bringing all creditor

classes into negotiation with the debtor government, on principles of parity (comparability) within and across creditor classes. It would provide moral suasion, if not legal backing, to prevent creditor holdouts, and to ensure comparability of settlements across banks (London Club), bilateral creditors (Paris Club), multilateral creditors (see below), and other creditor groups that are often outside negotiations (e.g. suppliers);

(4) Conditionality: debt reduction would be accompanied by strong conditionality, in the form of a growth-oriented structural adjustment programme agreed with the IMF and World Bank, along the lines discussed earlier.

One more point can be made about the bankruptcy analogy. It is sometimes claimed that the analogy does not apply to sovereign debtors, because bankruptcy deals with private-sector debtors rather than government debtors. The bankruptcy judge, for example, is said to have the power to change the management of a bankrupt firm, while the IMF cannot change the management of a bankrupt, poorly run country. In fact, this criticism is simply wrong. First, the United States Bankruptcy Code applies to governments as well as to the private sector. Chapter 9 of the Code deals with bankrupt municipalities. The same principles - standstill, debtor-in-possession financing and comprehensive debt settlement - apply as much to government debtors as to private-sector debtors. The recent successful workout of the Orange County Government was under Chapter 9 of the Code. Second, in most cases, the bankruptcy judge does not remove the management of the bankrupt firm, nor does he or she dictate business policy. Under Chapter 11, the debtor management remains in place during the period of the workout. The creditors or the court generally cannot force a change in management, contrary to what is often believed.

C. Debt-reduction mechanisms for multilateral creditors

Recent proposals for the reduction of HIPC debts to multilateral creditors (especially the World Bank and the regional development banks) represent a potentially important advance in the management of the debt crisis of the poorest countries. Following the initial onset of the developing-country debt crisis in the early 1980s, many developing countries borrowed heavily from multilateral sources in order

to finance debt servicing to private creditors, thereby shifting the balance of debt from private to public creditors. In addition, many countries borrowed heavily in the context of IMF/World Bank structural adjustment programmes. The poor performance of countries under these programmes, described earlier in this paper, has left much of the borrowing simply unrepayable. For both reasons, a large number of HIPC governments now require a large reduction of obligations to multilateral creditors in order to restore long-term financial viability.

The multilateral debt initiative should be coordinated with Paris Club and London Club arrangements, in order to ensure a comprehensive and efficient reduction of debt in the context of principles enunciated earlier. Without dwelling on the arcana of the current debate (e.g. the terms under which the IMF might sell gold to finance its contribution to the debt reduction operations), a few general principles are worth stressing:

(1) Even if the multilateral debt-reduction operation is stretched out over several years, as is now being proposed, the extent of reduction should be committed at the start of the operation so that the government and the markets can have confidence that the debt overhang will be eliminated. For example, the IMF/World Bank programme may call for a 90 per cent reduction in multilateral debt, to be carried out in the third year of a structural adjustment programme. Even though the debt reduction will not take place until the third year, and will be conditional on the successful completion of the adjustment programme, the eventual amount of debt reduction will be known at the outset. This will ensure maximum clarity for the process and will provide a strong incentive for the successful completion of the adjustment programme. If, instead, the amount of reduction is to be determined at the conclusion of the programme, the debtor government will face the unhappy reality that strong adjustment measures would be likely to result in less, rather than more, relief at the end of the process.

(2) There is a case for differentiating the treatment of claims owed to the IMF and to the World Bank. In particular, there is a much stronger case for writing down debts owed to the World Bank while insisting on repayments of debts owed to the IMF. The reason is that the IMF is, or at least should be, the emergency lender of last resort to the international community, while

the World Bank is a financier of long-term development projects. In order to preserve the unique role of the Fund as lender of last resort - and, indeed, to encourage the Fund to make emergency loans in a timely way when they are needed - the lender of last resort needs the security of high priority for debt repayments. The World Bank, on the other hand, should face the reality that long-term lending is risky and, as in the case of other creditors, may subject the Bank to losses. This possibility of losses on long-term loans would provide an important incentive within the Bank to scrutinize loans carefully, and to link lending to growth-oriented programmes ensuring the greatest possibility of debt repayments. If the Bank has no fear of losses on its own loans, it is subject to well-known bureaucratic pressures to "push" loans onto uncreditworthy clients.

(3) After ten years of incremental debt reduction operations (e.g. from Toronto Terms to Naples Terms, to Lyon Terms, etc.), in which each step of debt reduction has been inadequate to restore the viability of the debtor governments, it is now especially crucial that debt reduction finally be deep enough and bold enough to resolve the crisis. On the one hand, many countries are suffering from extreme reform fatigue, after ten years of structural adjustment with little or no economic growth. These countries need the financial, political and psychological boost of deep debt relief in order to keep the reforms on track. On the other hand, after ten years of structural adjustment efforts, many of these countries are now capable of renewed growth. They have undertaken enough reforms in trade liberalization, fiscal consolidation and privatization to make rapid economic growth a real possibility. It is crucial, therefore, to seize the historic opportunity at hand.

Conclusions

The main conclusions of this paper are the following:

(1) The foreign debt crisis should be understood mainly as a crisis of State insolvency, i.e. financial distress of the public sectors of HIPCs. The main goal of debt reduction operations should be to restore the financial viability of the public sector as an underpinning to macro-economic stability and renewed economic growth.

(2) The fiscal burden of debt servicing is extremely inimical to economic growth in HIPCs, and is in fact an important reason for the repeated failure of structural adjustment programmes to restore economic growth in many of them.

(3) Debt "sustainability" should be judged mainly according to the fiscal burden of debt servicing, rather than the ratio of debt to exports, the ratio of debt service to exports or the "external financing gap".

(4) The current approach to debt reduction in the HIPCs falls far short of what is required to re-establish the conditions for sustained economic growth. This is true with regard not only to the amount of debt reduction, but also to the timing, standards and procedures that are applied.

(5) Bankruptcy law provides a useful analogy to the issues of international, sovereign debt reduction. The international community would benefit from recognizing the underlying principles of debt workouts under bankruptcy law, in order to create new mechanisms for sovereign debt reduction for the poor developing countries.

(6) The recent IMF/World Bank initiative on multilateral debt reduction for the HIPCs, supported by the G-7 at the Lyon Summit, is a step in the right direction but falls short of what is needed. The recent proposals do not focus adequately on the fiscal burden of external debt, nor do they propose mechanisms for comprehensive and timely restructuring of that debt.

(7) The IMF/World Bank proposals can be modified within the current international framework to provide a much improved basis for economic recovery and growth in the HIPCs.

Notes

1   Overall foreign assistance may exceed 5 per cent of GDP, but much of it will go directly to enterprises and households, and thus will not be available as a source of revenue support for budgetary outlays.

2   When the United States Government considers the policy implications of debt relief, it is not concerned about the loss of debt service flows relative to total United States

exports. It cares about the loss of debt service revenues relative to United States government revenues, since the Government must obtain Congressional approval, as part of the overall budget, for debt reduction operations.

3   This section draws upon my paper on "Alternative Approaches to Financial Crises in Emerging Markets" (Sachs, 1995b), and forthcoming in a volume on international capital markets edited by Miles Kahler (Council of Foreign Relations, 1997).

References

BARRO, Robert, and Xavier SALA-I-MARTIN (1995), *Economic Growth* (New York: McGraw-Hill).

IMF (1995), *International Capital Markets: Developments, Prospects, and Policy Issues* (Washington, D.C.), August.

SACHS, Jeffrey D. (1995a), "Do We Need an International Lender of Last Resort", Frank D. Graham Lecture, Princeton University, April 1995.

SACHS, Jeffrey D. (1995b), "Alternative Approaches to Financial Crises in Emerging Markets", paper presented at the Bank for International Settlements, December 1995.

SACHS, Jeffrey D. (1996), "A Framework for Action to Resolve Debt Problems of the Heavily Indebted Poor Countries", Development Committee of the World Bank and International Monetary Fund, Washington, D.C., 12 April 1996.

SACHS, Jeffrey D., and Andrew WARNER (1995), "Economic Reform and the Process of Global Integration", *Brookings Papers on Economic Activity*, No. 1, pp. 1-118.

SACHS, Jeffrey D., and Andrew WARNER (1996), "Sources of Slow Growth in Africa", *Development Discussion Paper* (Cambridge, MA: Harvard Institute for International Development).

THE SIGNIFICANCE OF THE EURO FOR DEVELOPING COUNTRIES

Jacques J. Polak

Abstract

The creation of a European Economic and Monetary Union (EMU), together with the introduction of a new currency, the "euro", will bring about a radical change in the international monetary system, with important consequences for the developing countries.

The question whether the euro will be a strong currency cannot be answered for along period ahead, and the emphasis that the Maastricht Treaty lays on "stability" holds out no promise for a stable value of the euro in the exchange markets. The focus in the EMU is on domestic or price stability rather than on external or exchange-rate stability. While the IMF should exercise leadership with respect to stability among the major currencies, it is also necessary for the developing countries to acknowledge, in the management of their exchange rates and their reserves, the risk that the system may continue to show considerable currency instability.

In the last 25 years the main issue in the choice of an exchange-rate regime for a developing country has switched from that of choosing the best peg to the relative merits of pegging to provide an "anchor" for domestic stability, and floating to deal with uncontrolled inflation or with persistent one-way capital flows. Nevertheless, if the wide swings among the major currencies of the last few years continue, some countries might benefit from pegging on a simple basket or the SDR. If the introduction of the euro leads to still more instability among the major currencies, the problems of reserve management can only increase.

EMU members are likely to remain individual members of the IMF, at least during a transition period, but this does not necessarily mean continuation of their representation in the Executive Board by directors from nine different countries. Representation of the EMU by a single director could reduce the size of the Board from 24 to 19 or 20 members.

The creation of the euro is not expected to have important systemic implications for the SDR and is unlikely to foster its increased use.

I.   Introduction

Since concluding the Treaty of Maastricht in 1991, the members of the European Union (EU) - at the time 12 and now 15 in number[1] - have been preoccupied with the measures necessary to start an Economic and Monetary Union (EMU), based on a single currency, the "euro". Important lacunae in the Treaty needed to be filled and formidable technical problems to be solved, but these will not occupy us here. The central issue for all EU members soon became whether they would want to join the EMU and, if so, whether they qualified by the criteria laid down in the Treaty. Three countries (Denmark, Sweden and the United Kingdom) made it clear that they would not become members of the EMU from the start, which the Treaty specified as 1 January 1999 at the latest. Of the 12 others, only Greece can at this stage be considered certain not to meet the entrance criteria, of which a reduction of the budget deficit in 1997 to no more than 3 per cent of GDP has proved the most difficult to meet at a time when unemployment rates in many continental countries have reached painfully high levels. Many of the remaining 11, including both Germany and France, will not quite meet this criterion but it appears at this time (and in contrast to what was considered the most likely outcome only a few months ago) that, if the EMU is to start on time at all, the only politically viable decision for the membership will be to vote all of them in, using a rather liberal interpretation of the Treaty. These votes will be taken at a meeting of the Heads of State or Governments of the Union to be held in the spring of 1998.

The creation of the EMU, together with the introduction of the euro, will bring about a radical change in the international monetary system. A number of European currencies, among them the most important ones in the system after the United States dollar and the Japanese yen, will abruptly cease to exist and their place will be taken by something that has no precedent: a major currency that belongs to no single individual country but to a community of countries. As they give up their respective currencies, the members of the EMU cease to have control over their monetary policies and the exchange rates at which they trade with non-Union countries: these matters will be determined by the group collectively. At the same time, their trade among each other, conducted in the Union's single currency, the euro, will become freed from the effects of exchange-rate fluctuations, and so will capital transactions among EMU countries. These changes will, of course, be

of the greatest importance to the members of the EMU, and after that to the other members of the European Union, but there will also be important consequences for the rest of the world.

This paper focuses on the impact of the new arrangements on the developing countries. Part I analyses the impact on developing countries of the changes in the international monetary system in general. Part II then discusses the effects that will occur through changes in the International Monetary Fund. A brief list of conclusions is provided at the end of the paper.

At the time of writing there are still many uncertainties about the EMU, with rapid changes in public perceptions as political winds change in member countries. Apart from the uncertainties already mentioned about the starting date and initial participation, certain questions may remain unanswered for some time after the EMU has begun to operate, such as how the balance of power will work out between the common central bank, which is generally expected to take a conservative view on monetary policy, and the Council of Ministers where, perhaps, more expansionary, employment-motivated views may dominate.

This paper will not indulge in guesswork on these matters but concentrate on those aspects of the EMU/euro mechanism that are likely in any event to be relevant to developing countries. Certain obvious uncertainties, e.g. regarding the future strength of the euro, will be pointed out and conclusions drawn for the exchange rate and reserve policies of non-EU countries.

II.   The impact of the euro on the international monetary system

A.   What is the euro?

To understand the functioning of the euro it is necessary to familiarize oneself with the wholly novel characteristics of this monetary asset, and in particular its radical difference from the ECU. The ECU, both a monetary unit and a unit of account, was created in 1979 to implement the exchange-rate provisions and the settlement mechanism of the European Exchange Rate System. Following the practice established for the SDR in the mid-1970s, the ECU was designed as a basket of currencies. Hence its value, in terms of any currency at any moment of time is calculated by multiplying the market values of the currencies in the "basket" by their respective weights in the ECU. Like the SDR, the ECU is no more nor less than a package of currencies. It has no value of its own; its value is the value of the package.

Although it was widely expected until two years ago that the new monetary unit would also be called "ECU", the euro is in fact wholly different from the ECU. It is not a basket of currencies, but as the Maastricht Treaty puts it, "a currency in its own right". Its value is not based on that of the currencies of the countries participating in the EMU, because when the euro is born, these currencies will cease to exist. The notes denominated in these currencies that will continue to circulate for a few years will become in economic reality euro notes of odd, non-decimal, denominations. The value of deutsche mark notes, French franc notes, etc., will be based on, and rigidly linked to, the value of the euro, and it is expected that, in order to head off last-minute speculative disturbances, these links (the "conversion rates") will be announced well before the end of 1998, perhaps at the time of the decision on the list of participating countries. The value of the euro in terms of, for example, the United States dollar will be determined by the market, in just the same way as the value of the Swiss franc against the dollar is.

This does not mean that the value of the euro at the beginning of 1999 will come as a total surprise. The Council of Ministers has declared that 1 euro = 1 ECU, and while this identity cannot refer to two currencies, for the two will never coexist, it does create a market link between ECU assets held before the end of 1998 and euro assets held after that time. Anyone holding a 1000 ECU bond in 1998 will be considered to be holding a 1000 euro bond after the turn of the year, and will receive interest and ultimate repayment on that basis. Nobody guarantees the holder that the dollar value of the euro bond will be the same after the turn of the year as the value of the ECU bond before. But a forward exchange market in euros will permit arbitrage between the ECU and the euro.

The euro, then, has to be seen as a full-fledged currency, like the United States dollar or the Swiss franc, but with one very important difference: it will be the first major currency not backed by a single national state. If the dollar comes to face pressure and corrective action is needed, one would expect not only the Federal Reserve System but also the United States Government to swing into action, as both did in November 1978. In the case of the euro, the European Central Bank can take action, for example by raising interest rates, but if any supporting governmental measures in the fiscal field were deemed necessary, they would have to be the result of an agreement among the governments of the EMU. The likelihood that such agreement might prove difficult or time-consuming to reach could work towards instability of the euro in the exchange markets.

The original blueprint for the euro, the Delors Report, recognized the need for the coordination of the fiscal policies of members to complement their common monetary policy. A need for collective expansionary fiscal policies might arise to meet an EMU-wide lack of aggregate demand, or a need for collective contractionary fiscal policies to contain an excessively expansionary trend in the European economies. Beyond that, individual countries might need to take fiscal action (which could differ from one country to another) to offset the asymmetrical shocks to which they had been exposed. These attempts to anticipate the need for discretionary fiscal action to mitigate any possible untoward effects of the common currency were not translated into the Maastricht Treaty (Kenen, 1995, p. 91). Instead, the fiscal dimension of the adoption of a common currency was addressed only to the extent of the incorporation of measures against "excessive fiscal deficits". Yet, the success of the euro and hence the cohesion of the EMU in the event of its being subjected to severe external strains will depend on the ability of the Union both to adopt a non-dogmatic application of these measures and to be ready to agree on collective action when the fate of their economies and that of the euro makes this necessary.

B. *The euro and the international monetary system*

The introduction of the euro will bring about a radical change in the structure of the international monetary system. At present, that system is dominated by the United States dollar. More than 60 per cent of official currency reserves are held in dollars and, although the United States continues to run a current account deficit, around 80 per cent of external bank loans and about 40 per cent of external bond issues are denominated in dollars (table 1). By any of these standards of importance, there is a wide gap from other "major currencies". But three or four of the G-7 currencies (the deutsche mark, the French franc, the Italian lira and perhaps the pound sterling) will disappear to make place for the euro. At one stroke

Table 1

CURRENCY DISTRIBUTION OF FOREIGN EXCHANGE RESERVES, EXTERNAL BANK LOANS, AND EXTERNAL BOND ISSUES, 1995

(Per cent of total)

Currency	Reserves	Bank loans	Bond issues
United States dollar [a]	61.5	76.8	39.5
Deutsche mark	14.2	4.1	15.5
Japanese yen	7.4	0.2	12.6
Pound sterling	3.5	11.7	5.9
Swiss franc	0.9	0.1	5.6
European currency unit	...	3.8	1.7
Other [b]	12.5	3.3	19.2

Source: Henning, 1997, pp. 10 and 11.
    a ECU issued against dollars treated as dollars.
    b Includes unspecified.

(on present plans, the stroke of midnight between 1998 and 1999), the dollar-dominated system will be replaced by a tripolar one (or perhaps more accurately a "two-and-a-half-polar" one) in which the euro will become, if not at once fully the equal of the dollar, at least a plausible contender for that place - with the yen at a considerable distance as the world's third currency.

There have been a number of serious attempts to guess how closely and over what time span the share of the euro in, for example, other countries' reserves would approach that of the dollar. The details of these estimates need not concern us. It suffices to establish the likelihood that, within a horizon of perhaps a decade, the countries then constituting the EMU will account for a large proportion (somewhere between one-half and equality) of the United States in terms of international financial aggregates. The world in which the developing countries will have to select their international financial policies will be a world consisting of two colossi, with Japan as a pretty distant third in financial terms and, of course the substantial economic presence, but probably not a commensurate financial presence, of China and Russia looming in the background.

The preponderant role of the euro next to the dollar will be a central factor that developing countries

will have to take into account in designing (a) their exchange-rate policies and (b) their reserve policies. Two characteristics of the euro will be of particular relevance in this connection:

(1) Can they expect the euro to be a strong currency or a weak currency compared to the main alternative, the dollar?

(2) Should they expect the euro to be essentially stable in its relation to the dollar, or should they reckon with the possibility, or perhaps even the likelihood, of considerable volatility between these two currencies?

The two questions are of course interrelated, but they deserve separate consideration in the next two sections.

C. The euro: a strong or a weak currency?

At its meeting in Dublin on 13 and 14 December 1996, the European Council stressed that it was essential that the four criteria of sustainable convergence be "strictly applied" if "the euro [was] to be assured of its status as a strong currency".[2] Since that time, voices (especially in the new French government) have suggested that the rigours implied in the call for a strong euro could be overdone, and the Managing Director of the IMF recently called for a "euro that should seek to be neither strong nor weak, but well managed" (*Reuters*, 10 June 1997). But while differences may from time to time appear in the zeal with which different European countries view the benefits of a strong euro, it is fair to say that they all have learned from their experience with the Exchange Rate Mechanism since 1979 (in so far as they had not learned this before) that the pursuit of a weak currency in the hope of stimulating the economy through enhanced exports and reduced imports will not yield lasting benefits, because of both the inflation it will cause and the high interest rate level that must accompany it. However, the same sentiments guide the policies of other industrial countries, in particular the United States and Japan. The question, therefore, whether the euro will be a strong currency in the exchange markets has to be approached not in absolute but in relative terms: will the relevant authorities of the EMU want to see or promote a relatively high or a relatively low value of the euro against the dollar (and, secondarily, against the yen)?

Much has been written in the last year or so on both sides of this issue. At one stage there seemed to be almost consensus that the dominance of the Bundesbank in the design of the euro would guarantee that it would emerge as a very strong currency (Kenen, 1995, p. 116), with the expectation that its natural strength could be further enhanced by bandwagon movement as foreigners rearranged their portfolios towards the strongest currency. It is perhaps somewhat ironic that these musings on the innate strength of the euro coincided with a definite weakening in the money markets of the major European currencies, other than sterling. From the middle of 1995 to August 1997, both the deutsche mark and the French franc depreciated by more than 20 per cent against the dollar - a movement that did not seem to evoke strong expressions of regret on the part of the authorities in either country. But even this experience has been interpreted by Bergsten (1997) as heralding a strong euro: he sees the European authorities taking advantage of the current environment in exchange markets to engineer a depreciation of their currencies to allow the euro, once it has made its entry, to move in the opposite direction.

The more reasonable interpretation of the available evidence is that, while it may be possible to judge the strength or weakness of the euro or any other currency in the near future, there is no basis for a judgment on the long-run strength of the major

currencies against each other. In each country or currency bloc, there will always be some balancing between the benefits (even if modest) of a relatively high value of the currency in containing inflation, and those (again modest) of a relatively low value of the currency in promoting employment. Depending on the relative severity of inflation and unemployment at any point in time, the financial authorities may be seen to lean one way or the other in promoting a stronger or tolerating a weaker outcome for the national currency. In the past two years, with unemployment in the United States at record lows since the oil shocks of the 1970s and inflation stubbornly staying at close to 3 per cent per annum, the US authorities have stressed the benefits of a strong dollar. At the same time, the difficulties encountered by Japan in bringing about a solid recovery have made the gradual depreciation of the yen, from an over-valued 85 yen to the dollar in mid-1995 to more than 120 yen to the dollar in the spring of 1997, appear on balance as beneficial to the authorities in that country.

Such national views, however, are likely to change with the cycle, and there would seem to be no reason to assume that the European authorities would on average be either more or less attached to the strength of their currency than their colleagues in the United States or Japan. For the non-industrial countries, the safest expectation with respect to the strength of the euro, as with respect to that of the dollar or the yen, will be to avoid dogmatic views and to hedge currency risks as far as possible.

D. Will the euro be a stable currency?

"Stability" is touted as a major objective of the Maastricht Treaty. The "primary objective" laid down for the European System of Central Banks (ESCB) is "to maintain price stability". If the Council of Finance Ministers wants to express any "general orientations for exchange-rate policy", it must watch that any such orientations be "without prejudice to the primary objective of the ESCB to maintain price stability". To reinforce the fiscal threshold for entry into the EMU (a deficit not in excess of 3 per cent of GNP) by a permanent bar against fiscal profligacy, the Treaty was complemented by a "Stability Pact" (subsequently, no doubt for public relations purposes, renamed a "Stability and Growth Pact") laying down permanent rules with respect to the permissible magnitude of fiscal deficits, defining some exceptions and containing the possibility of stiff fines for countries that flout these rules.

It is important to be aware of the fact that all this emphasis on "stability" holds out no promise at all for a stable value of the euro against other currencies in the exchange markets. To begin with, the focus in the EMU is on *domestic* or *price* stability, not on *external* or *exchange-rate* stability. For a small, or even a medium-sized, country the distinction between internal and external stability would usually not be important: if the external value of the currency of such a country declines, domestic inflation is almost always either the cause or the effect, or indeed both. But for very large countries, or for a large grouping of countries such as the EMU, the distinction is crucial. Such countries have the option of using upward changes in the value of their currencies to stabilize the domestic price level and may be in a position to use downward changes for employment purposes with minimal inflationary implications. Japan's experience in the last two years provides the most striking example of the room for manoeuvre available to large countries with a good anti-inflationary reputation. Faced in mid-1995 with a weak economic situation and an overvalued currency, Japan adopted a set of policies, including an extremely low rate of interest and at times massive intervention in the exchange markets, which reduced the value of the yen by about one third in 18 months. Nevertheless, inflation in Japan remained as subdued as before, at a rate of less than one per cent per annum. The depreciation of the deutsche mark and other European currencies over the past year appears, similarly, not to have had any untoward inflationary consequences.

Observations such as these are in agreement with a widely held view that the relative insensitivity of the economies of large currency blocs to factors coming from abroad enhances the possibility of wide swings in the exchange rates of such blocs (Kenen, 1995, pp. 122 and 123; Bergsten, 1997).

There is little in the Maastricht Treaty that would suggest concern about such swings. Indeed, as pointed out by Henning (1997, p. 44), "the provisions of the Maastricht Treaty contain a strong bias against exchange-rate stabilization and in favour of flexible exchange rates". It is true that the relevant Article 109 begins by defining a set of rules that could govern a central-rate system between the euro and non-Community currencies. That clause, however, reminds one of the Fund's Article IV, Section 4 on "Par Values", complete with a detailed *modus operandi* of a par value system in Schedule C, all of which was inserted in the second amendment on the very occasion when the par value system was officially abandoned. Compared to the 85 per cent majority required for the introduction of par values in the Fund, Article 109 specifies unanimity among EMU members - and it would of course also require the consent of any non-Community partners, such as the United States, before a central-rate system could be introduced. In brief, therefore, the message from the Treaty is that the euro will float - and may well float with wide swings - until there is a complete change of heart in the world on the desired exchange-rate system among the main currencies. This conclusion suggests, as observed by the G-24 in their Communiqué of 27 April 1997, that "major implications of EMU for IMF surveillance", including "an urgent need for the IMF to exercise leadership to ensure that the transition to a tripolar currency system proceeds with much closer international coordination to minimize instability in the exchange and capital markets and to enhance the prospects for global prosperity".

E.   *Towards greater stability among the principal currencies?*

It is obvious that the bilateral surveillance of the IMF over the exchange-rate policies of the United States and Japan, and of the EMU countries as a group - with surveillance over the latter, a task that will raise serious procedural difficulties of its own (for details see Polak, 1997) - cannot deal with this multilateral question. This will leave a clear need for an international mechanism that can address the potential conflicts of interest arising from the movements of the exchange rates among the three reserve currencies. Experience over the last 10 years or so has shown that the G-7 does not provide such a mechanism (Bergsten and Henning, 1996, p. 34), and this will become increasingly obvious as, with the arrival of the euro, only two or three of the seven members of the Group will remain as issuers of world currencies. The G-7 has found a different niche in the global system than to be (as Bergsten would have it) the "steering committee for the world economic system", or the coordinator of the economic and financial policies of their respective countries. Instead, as stressed recently by the Managing Director of the Fund, the G-7 performs a useful task by once a year putting on the table the most important economic issues, drawing the world's attention to them and committing the members of the group to work towards the resolution of these issues (Camdessus, 1997, p. 1). One can expect that even with the creation of the EMU, the four European countries that now belong to the G-7 will remain there as individual centres of economic influence. Indeed, as shown in Denver, there is a strong case for some enlargement of this group over time.

In a world financial system where only three currencies matter - the dollar, the euro and the yen - the Managing Director of the IMF should take the initiative to organize a process of regular consultations between both the political and the central bank authorities of these three centres of influence (Polak, 1997). The aim of these consultations would not be to arrive at a set of fixed rates or target zones among these currencies but the achievement at any time of a triangle of acceptable exchange rates among them.

In weighing the chances of success of such an initiative, one should bear in mind that a high degree of exchange-rate volatility is a likely, but not un-avoidable, result of the existence of three large currency areas. The relatively small impact of foreign to domestic factors on the economies of such areas makes "benign neglect" of the exchange rate (within rather wide limits) a tolerable option - an option with which they, unlike smaller economic units, can live. It is also a least-effort option that avoids many difficult choices. But it follows in no way from this that it is also the best one even for these countries - or for the world at large - or that a strong push directed towards a common search for a better, more stable, outcome would be doomed to fail.

While it is therefore right for the developing countries collectively to urge the IMF to move in the direction indicated, it is also necessary for them individually to acknowledge the risk that the system may continue to show considerable currency in-stability. In the two sections that follow, we discuss what such an outcome would imply for exchange-rate policies and policies on the reserve composition of developing countries.

F. Implications for the exchange-rate policies of developing countries

The collapse of the par value system at the beginning of the 1970s has, gradually over time, brought about major changes in the views held on the exchange-rate policies appropriate to developing countries. Fifteen years ago it was still widely agreed that independent floating was either not feasible or was undesirable for most developing countries (Williamson, 1982, p. 39). On the assumption, then, that the great majority of developing countries would want to continue to peg the value of their currencies

in one way or another while the currencies of the dominant trading countries floated, much thought was given to the question of the optimum basket of partner currencies to which individual countries should peg.[3]

In recent years this subject appears to have almost vanished from the discussion, and for a number of good reasons. To begin with, many developing countries have found floating to be both feasible and the least objectionable answer (even if sometimes only a second- or third-best answer) to their balance-of-payments problems, whether as a way to liberalize an overly restrictive system, to remain competitive in the face of persistent domestic inflation, or to help ward off excessive inflows of capital. Accordingly, the number of developing countries with independently floating currencies has increased dramatically, from three in 1983 to 43 in 1996, while over the same period the number of countries pegging on baskets (SDR or other baskets) has declined sharply (table 2). Accordingly, the debate has switched from that on the choice of the best basket to the relative merits of pegging (including the possibility of a crawling peg) to provide an "anchor" for domestic stability, and floating to deal with uncontrolled inflation or with persistent one-way capital flows (Polak, 1995, pp. 754-757). In these new circumstances, the view has gained ground that "on the whole, the choice of pegging to a single currency or a basket of currencies is likely to be of secondary importance, as long as the underlying financial policies are consistent with maintaining the announced peg" (Aghevli et al., 1991, p. 17).

Certainly, when the peg is intended to signal the country's determination to solidly "anchor" its currency, the transparency of a single-currency peg will be more helpful than the opacity that is inevitably associated with a basket. And when a country goes one step beyond "anchoring" its currency by the introduction of a currency board, the link with a single currency becomes an essential part of that option. Nevertheless, if experience shows a continuation of the wide swings among the major currencies of the last few years, some countries might see a stability benefit outweighing the inconvenience of moving from a single-currency peg to a simple currency basket. Any refinement beyond a two- or three-currency basket (the latter including the dollar, the euro and the yen), with very rough weights, such as 50/50 or 50/25/25, would almost certainly not be worth the effort. And among small baskets without the pretence of fine-tuned weighting, the SDR, slimmed down to three or four currencies (see below) might be found as suitable as any other one.

Table 2

EXCHANGE RATE ARRANGEMENTS OF DEVELOPING COUNTRIES, 1975-1997

	Mid-1975	End-1983	Mid-1987	Mid-1990	March 1997
National currencies pegged to a single currency	77	60	57	48	44
United States dollar [a]	52	42	38	29	21
French franc	13	13	14	14	15
Other currencies [b]	12	5	5	5	8
National currencies pegged to a currency basket	15	35	33	37	21
SDR	6	12	10	7	2
Other basket [c]	9	23	23	30	19
Flexible arrangements	14	30	40	40	88
Based on indicators [d]	4	5	5	3	0
Managed floating [e]	9	22	22	20	45
Independent floating [f]	1	3	13	17	43
Total	**106**	**125**	**130**	**125**	**153**

Source: IMF, *International Financial Statistics*, various issues.

[a] Including currencies maintained with relatively narrow margins to the dollar and one transition economy.

[b] Including eight countries pegging to the pound sterling in 1975, one in 1983 and none in 1987 and 1997. In 1997, three countries pegged their currencies to the South African rand and the other six countries pegged to the deutsche mark, Italian lira, Indian rupee, and the Singapore and Australian dollar, of which two are transition economies.

[c] Including two transition economies that became IMF members after 1990.

[d] In 1997, the IMF reclassified three countries to reflect their exchange rate arrangements more accurately and this category was eliminated.

[e] Including 13 transition economies that became IMF members after 1990.

[f] Including eight transition economies that became IMF members after 1990.

Not much is likely to change in this panorama as a result of the introduction of the euro. Naturally, countries now pegging on the deutsche mark or the French franc will switch to the euro as their anchor, in the process gaining currency stability for an EMU-wide trading area. But the finance ministers of the 15 countries of the franc zone and of France have formally stated that the transition of the French franc to the euro "will have no effect on the parity of the CFA franc or on the monetary cooperation between France and the African member countries of the franc area" (press communiqué, meeting of the Finance Ministers of the Franc Area, Cotonou, Benin, 17 April 1997).

The argument has sometimes been made that in choosing a single currency as an anchor, countries that had some doubt about their ability to match the inflation performance of the most stable of the major currencies might select a somewhat weaker reserve currency as their anchor. The recent experience of the sharp appreciation of the dollar against both the yen and the deutsche mark and the unpredictability of exchange rates for the major currencies over any extended period raise serious doubts about the practicability of such an exchange-rate policy.

G. *Implications for foreign reserve management*

Almost 20 years ago, the IMF noted the problems that the increase in exchange-rate fluctuations posed for the reserve policies of developing countries. Countries pegging to a single currency whose future value in terms of other major currencies was uncertain faced the dilemma of needing to hold larger working balances in that currency while at the same time wishing to diversify their reserves (IMF, 1978, p. 40). A few years later, field investigations confirmed these problems faced by the managers of foreign exchange reserves (Helleiner, 1981, para. 136). If the introduction of the euro leads to still more instability among the major currencies, these problems can only increase. Yet there does not seem to be an agreed view on the rules of thumb that could guide the managers of foreign exchange portfolios in their task. A model based on both the expected return on the foreign assets portfolio and the avoidance of portfolio risk is developed in Dooley et al. (1989). Williamson (1988, p. 172) points out that monetary authorities should make hedging, rather than the expected rate of return, "the dominant determinant in the choice of reserves", on the ground that the market probably equates expected rates of return on different currencies better than monetary authorities can speculate. And he also observes that option markets may in future, as their maturities lengthen, offer better opportunities to hedge currency risks than changes in the composition of the reserve portfolio. Helleiner's (1981, para. 138) conclusion that more work on this subject is needed remains unfortunately all too true.

III. The impact of the euro on the IMF

The first and by far the most important issue emerging from the EMU for the functioning of the IMF relates to the consequences that at least a partial merger of the policies of major group of members could have on the structure and the governance of the Fund. Secondly, the interest that the developing countries have always shown for the SDR requires a discussion of the changes, if any, that the EMU will bring to the future of the SDR.

A third set of issues is raised by the fact that, as a result of the EMU, the Fund's financial assets will include large amounts of euros (rather than these countries' own currencies) in the accounts of EMU members. For example, how does the Fund decide whether to sell in its transactions euros from the account of Germany or Italy? Does it focus on the balance-of-payments strength of individual EMU members or on that of the EMU as a whole? While some of these issues may involve difficult technical aspects, none of them seems to be fundamental to the successful operation of the institution, and they are therefore not treated in this paper.

A. *Structure and governance*

The formation of the EMU will, if not at once at least in the somewhat longer run, have a profound impact on the structure and hence on the governance of the IMF. One can imagine, as an ultimate construction, a situation in which political and policy integration among the members of the European Union (or a somewhat more restricted EMU) would have gone so far as to make joint membership of the Fund, with a common quota, of the countries concerned a natural outcome. Presumably, if this were to materialize even though the countries concerned had not merged into a single country, an amendment of the Articles of Agreement would be necessary to accommodate such a joint membership; however, this legal aspect need not detain us here. I share the view of the chairman of the Fund's Interim Committee (the Belgian Minister of Finance, Philippe Maystadt) that "it is most likely that EMU members will remain individual members of the Fund, at least during a transition period and perhaps forever" (Maystadt, 1997). The principal reason for the continuation of separate membership is that cited by Maystadt, namely that the EMU Treaty leaves countries' economic policies mainly within their national competence. But there is also an obvious financial inducement for countries to retain their individual membership in the Fund: the right of members to have access to its credit facilities. It is true that none of the 15 current members of the European Union has made use of that right in the last 15 years. But one of the reasons that they did not was that the European Community provided an alternative mechanism of medium-term balance-of-payments assistance. Between 1974 and 1993, four members of the European Union (France, Greece, Ireland and Italy) drew approximately $1.5 billion under this mechanism (Polak, 1997). Yet, in its zeal to ensure that a member of the EMU will not be "bailed out" from the effects of its own improvident financial policies, the Treaty stops access to these arrangements the moment a country joins the EMU, while continuing access for countries that do not join.[4] In the event of a particularly unfavourable constellation of foreign and domestic economic circumstances, the potential access of EMU members to the credit of the Fund may not only assist these countries but may also contribute to the cohesion of the EMU itself. And the fact that Fund credit is available on conditional terms only ensures that such credit is not a soft option (not a "bail-out") for the country that has recourse to it.

Beyond these basic economic reasons for the continuation of the present membership structure of the Fund, there are no doubt legal difficulties in having a group of countries as "a member" of the Fund, as well as political difficulties of agreement on a consolidated quota for the group, and even on the location of the Fund's principal office, which, according to Article XIII, Section 1, of the Fund, "shall be in the territory of the member having the largest quota".[5] But this does not necessarily entail continuation of the present representation by members of the European Union in the Executive Board and its replica, the Interim Committee. At present, the 15 member countries of the European Union are represented on the Board by nationals of nine different countries. Germany, France and the United Kingdom each appoint a director because their quotas are among the five largest. Belgium, the Netherlands, Italy and Sweden head constituencies that also include six other EU countries and 25 non-EU countries. Ireland and Spain belong to two Western hemisphere constituencies.

Whatever its historical explanation, the present structure of the representation of the EU countries on the Board of the IMF would prove hard to reconcile with the degree of policy integration envisaged of the EMU. Article 109 of the Maastricht Treaty stipulates that "the Council shall, acting by a qualified majority, decide on the position of the Community at the international level as regards issues of particular relevance to economic and monetary union" and, in a slightly different context, that "the Community expresses a single position". The European Union might well find that the most efficient way of carrying a single opinion in the councils of the Fund would be to have a single Executive Director and a single member of the Interim Committee. Also, the position of directors representing both one or more members of the European Union and a large number of non-EU members might become increasingly incongruous, as the weight of the European Central Bank and EU organs in Brussels in the positions taken by EU directors increased.

The concept of a single Executive Director representing the interests of a regional group of members is, of course, a well-established feature of the Fund's structure. But an EU constituency would be unusually large in terms of the number of countries (only the two African constituencies have more than 15 members), and particularly in terms of voting strength: on the basis of present quotas, an Executive Director casting the votes of the 15 members of the European Union would have 26.6 per cent of the vote, as compared to the 17.8 per cent of the vote cast by the Executive Director for the United States, even though a consolidated quota for the 15 countries combined would be only marginally (by about 10 per cent) larger than that of the United States (based on 1995 data for GNP and trade in Bergsten, 1997, table 1). But the continuation of the present voting strength of the seven separate EU directors, 30.7 per cent, including the votes of 25 non-EU countries in their constituencies, would appear even more anomalous.

Representation of the EMU, or the larger European Union, by a single director - which would of course happen automatically once the European Union became a single member of the Fund - might not be a practical possibility until all major members of the European Union had joined in the EMU, and even then it might it might need to overcome many reservations in individual capitals. In any event, whatever its appeal to the members of European Union, it would be a rearrangement in the Fund that could have attractive aspects for the non-industrial countries. For these countries, which are the main users of the Fund's financial resources, the efficient governance of the Fund is a matter of prime concern (see Woods in this volume). A single EU director could contribute to better governance in two respects. First, it would make it possible to reduce the size of the Board from 24 to 19 or 20 members: one European Union director, instead of the present seven, and one or at most two new directors to represent the countries in Eastern Europe and the former Soviet Union that now give their votes to Belgium, the Netherlands, the Nordic group and Italy, the precise number depending on how many of these countries would join the European Union or other existing constituencies, such as those of Switzerland or Russia. The end result would be a board consisting of the directors from the United States and the European Union, four from other industrial countries (Australia, Canada, Japan and Switzerland), China, Russia, Saudi Arabia, and 10 or 11 groupings of developing and "transition" countries (three in Latin America, three in Asia, two in Africa, one or two in Eastern Europe, and one in the Middle East).

Second, the presence on the Board of what would no doubt be a very senior person, as the Board member from the European Union could be expected to facilitate decision-making, as compared with a Board of seven directors whose instructions from capitals would need to be coordinated in Brussels and Frankfurt to ensure that they voiced the common opinion of the European Union.

Further consideration would need to be given to the precise technique whereby a single person selected by the appropriate organ of the European Union would become the Executive Director for the EU countries. The three largest members (Germany, France and the United Kingdom) would presumably be free to exercise their right to appoint a director by appointing the same person. The other Fund members from the European Union could then either all cast their vote for that same person, or they could abstain from voting in the biannual election of executive directors (as for example South Africa has done for many years) and then ask the appointed "EU director" to look after their interests. There would be only one practical difference in the outcome between these two approaches:[6] under the first approach, the "EU director" would cast the votes of all members of the European Union (at present, 26.6 per cent of the total), while under the second approach he would only have the voting strength of the three largest EU members. On present quotas, this would be 15.5 per cent - still a blocking vote for decisions requiring an 85 per cent majority and at the same time close to the voting strength of the United States (17.8 per cent), and thus perhaps attractive as a forerunner of an ultimate structure in which the United States and the European Union would have equal or close to equal voting power.

The ideas put forward in this section are, of course, speculative in nature and they would obviously require extensive, and no doubt time-consuming, international discussion before a decision could be taken whether to proceed to putting them into effect. An interesting aspect of this discussion might be whether the choice in favour of a single EMU director in the Fund would need to be matched by a similar choice in the World Bank.

B. The euro and the future of the SDR

The creation of the euro does not, it would appear, have important systemic implications for the SDR. It poses one immediate, essentially technical, problem, namely the currency composition of the SDR basket, but it is unlikely to enhance the role of the SDR in the system.

1. The SDR basket

The current SDR basket consists of specified amounts of the United States dollar, the yen, deutsche mark, French franc and pound sterling. As two or perhaps three of these currencies vanish from the scene, it will be necessary to replace them at once by the corresponding amounts of euro, turning the SDR into a basket of three or four currencies, rather than five as at present. In the somewhat longer run, more fundamental questions about the composition of the SDR basket will need to be addressed, such as the number of currencies to be included and the manner of determining the weight of each of them. In the light of the experience with SDRs over the past 15 years or so, it does not seem likely that any plausible decisions taken on these issues would greatly affect the status of the SDR.

2. Future allocations of SDRs

Ever since the second decision to allocate SDRs in 1978, the outlook for further general allocations has become increasingly bleak as it has become evident that all industrial and many developing countries could satisfy their needs for increasing reserves in the world's capital markets at a cost only marginally in excess of the SDR interest rate. The often acrimonious discussions in the past three years on an "equity" allocation of SDRs that would be directed mostly to new members of the Fund have done nothing to brighten the outlook for a general across-the-board allocation to meet "a global need to supplement reserves". The introduction of the euro is unlikely to improve the climate for such an allocation since it will reveal an excess of reserves held by EMU members as their "foreign transactions", to be defined as those with non-EU countries only, decline sharply. That excess may even increase if there is a general tendency on the part of non-EU countries to convert a portion of their reserves from dollars into euro and the European Central Bank decides to intervene in the exchange markets to avoid an excessive appreciation of the euro.

3. An SDR substitution account?

In 1978/79, concern about an "overhang" of excessive dollars in country reserves led to an active discussion in the Fund aimed at absorbing these excess dollars in a substitution account in the Fund. The creation of such an account was agreed in principle at the meeting of the Interim Committee in October 1979 in Belgrade,[7] but support for the idea evaporated soon thereafter as the dollar strengthened in the exchange markets.

Although there has been extensive discussion on the extent to which EMU countries might find themselves collectively with excess holdings of dollars, this does not, for understandable reasons, appear to have revived the idea of an SDR substitution account, although Bergsten (1997) in passing mentions the possibility of this. First, these holdings are in excess not because they are in the form of dollars, but because they are not needed as reserves; accordingly there would be little point in converting them from direct claims on the United States into indirect claims via a substitution account in the IMF. Second, excess dollars in the reserves of EMU countries, if they materialize, will be under the control of the European Central Bank, which could prevent them being dumped on the market and might negotiate a deal with the United States on their use.

As far as the developing countries are concerned, the partial diversification of their dollar reserves occurred some 15 years ago (Kenen, 1995, p. 113) and the share of European currencies in their reserves (most of which will automatically become holdings of euros) has been stable at a little over 20 per cent for many years (see IMF, 1978 and 1980, table 1.2), with the share of yen holdings at around 7-8 per cent. Moreover, almost 80 per cent of the reserves of developing countries are held in Asia and the Western hemisphere, regions that trade more with the United States than with Europe. Kenen's conclusion seems reasonable, therefore, that "unless the advent of the [euro] leads to shifts in the pricing of major commodities such as oil, it is unlikely to induce another round of diversification by the developing countries" (p. 113).

It would appear therefore that if there is an exchange market problem as a result of rather massive portfolio shifts, the origin of these shifts would lie with private rather than official holders, and an SDR substitution account does not offer an answer to that problem.

Conclusions

(1) Within a horizon of perhaps a decade, the countries then constituting the EMU and using the euro as their currency will account for some-

where between 50 and 100 per cent of the United States in terms of international financial aggregates.

(2) Whether the euro will be a strong or a weak currency in the exchange markets cannot be predicted for any long period ahead. For the developing countries, the safest expectation with respect to the strength of the euro, as with respect to that of the dollar or the yen, will be to avoid dogmatic views and to hedge currency risks as far as possible.

(3) The emphasis that the Maastricht Treaty lays on "stability" holds out no promise for a stable value of the euro against other currencies in the exchange markets, and the evidence that the relative insensitivity of the economies of large currency blocs to factors coming from abroad enhances the volatility in their exchange rates supports the call by the G-24 for the IMF to exercise leadership with respect to this issue.

(4) In the management of their exchange rates and their reserves, it is necessary for the developing countries to acknowledge the risk that the system may continue to show considerable currency instability. In the last 25 years, the main issue in the choice of an exchange-rate regime for a developing country has switched from that of choosing the best peg to the relative merits of pegging (preferably on a single currency for reasons of transparency) to provide an "anchor" for domestic stability, and floating to deal with uncontrolled inflation or with persistent one-way capital flows. But if the wide swings among the major currencies of the last few years continue, a simple basket of a few currencies, or the SDR, might appear attractive to some countries. If the introduction of the euro leads to still more instability among the major currencies, the difficulties of managing foreign exchange portfolios can only increase.

(5) EMU members are likely to remain individual members of the Fund, at least during a transition period, but this need not mean a continuation of their representation on the Executive Board by directors from nine different countries: Having a single Executive Director for the European Union could reduce the size of the Board from 24 to 19 or 20 members.

(6) The creation of the euro does not have important systemic implications for the SDR and is unlikely to foster its increased use.

Notes

1   The members of the European Union in 1997 were: Austria, Belgium, Denmark, Finland, France, Germany, Greece, Ireland, Italy, Luxembourg, Netherlands, Portugal, Spain, Sweden and the United Kingdom.

2   The warning of the Council was no doubt addressed primarily against a weakening of the fiscal criteria, but in that event the logic of the statement is questionable. On the assumption that the independent European Central Bank would offset any weakening of the fiscal criteria by tightening its monetary policy, the effect would be to harden, not to weaken, the euro.

3   A number of papers on this overworked subject are cited in Polak (1988).

4   A new, much more restrictive provision of the Treaty opens the possibility for the Council, by unanimous action, to extend credit to an EMU member suffering from "severe difficulties caused by exceptional occurrences beyond its control".

5   Henning (1997, pp. 56 and 57) suggests that these could ultimately be resolved by agreement on equal quotas for the European Union and the United States (with an increase in the quota shares of other Fund members) and on the maintenance of the Fund's main office in Washington.

6   The other EU members would in any event have the right (under Article XII, Section [3][j]), to "send a representative to attend any meeting of the Executive Board when a request made by, or a matter particularly affecting, that member [was] under consideration".

7   In paragraph 7 of its communiqué, the Committee "concluded that [a substitution] account, if properly designed, could contribute to an improvement of the international monetary system and could constitute a step towards making the SDR the principal reserve asset in the system ... The Committee ... asked the Executive Board to continue to direct priority attention to designing a substitution account plan ..." (IMF, 1980, p. 154).

References

AGHEVLI, B.B., M.S. KHAN, and P.J. MONTIEL (1991), "Exchange Rate Policy in Developing Countries: Some Analytical Issues", *Occasional Paper*, No. 78 (Washington, D.C.: IMF).

BERGSTEN, C.F. (1997), "The Impact of the Euro on Exchange Rates and International Policy Cooperation", in P. Masson, T. Krueger and B.G. Turtleboom (eds.), *EMU and the International Monetary System* (Washington, D.C.: IMF).

BERGSTEN, C.F., and C.R. HENNING (1996), *Global Economic Leadership and the Group of Seven* (Washington, D.C.: Institute for International Economics).

CAMDESSUS, M. (1997), "Les grands enjeux du G-7 - La perspective du FMI", mimeo (Washington, D.C.: IMF).

DOOLEY, M.P., J.S. LIZONDO, and D.J. MATHIESON (1989), "The Currency Composition of Foreign Exchange Reserves", *IMF Staff Papers*, Vol. 36, No. 2, pp. 385-434.

GROUP OF 24 (1997), Communiqué of 27 April 1997, *IMF Survey*, Vol. 26, No. 9, p. 142.

HELLEINER, G.K. (1981), *The impact of the exchange rate system on the developing countries*, UNCTAD/MFD/TA/13 (Geneva: UNCTAD).

HENNING, C.R. (1997), *Cooperating with Europe's Monetary Union* (Washington, D.C.: Institute for International Economics).

IMF (1978), *Annual Report 1978* (Washington, D.C.).

IMF (1980), *Annual Report 1980* (Washington, D.C.).

IMF (various issues), *International Financial Statistics* (Washington, D.C.).

KENEN, P.B. (1995), *Economic and Monetary Union in Europe* (Cambridge: Cambridge University Press).

MAYSTADT, P. (1997), "The Implications of EMU for the IMF", in P. Masson, T. Krueger and B.G. Turtleboom (eds.), *EMU and the International Monetary System* (Washington, D.C.: IMF).

POLAK, J.J. (1988), "The Choice of an Exchange Rate Regime", in D.M. Sutalaksana (ed.), *Development Issues in the Current International Monetary System* (Singapore: Addison-Wesley), pp. 132-148.

POLAK, J.J. (1995), "Fifty Years of Exchange Rate Research and Policy at the International Monetary Fund", *IMF Staff Papers*, Vol. 42, No. 4, pp. 734-761.

POLAK, J.J. (1997), "The IMF and its EMU Members", in P. Masson, T. Krueger and B.G. Turtleboom (eds.), *EMU and the International Monetary System* (Washington, D.C.: IMF).

WILLIAMSON, J. (1982), "A survey of literature on the optimal peg", *Journal of Development Economics* (August), pp. 39-61.

WILLIAMSON, J. (1988), "Exchange Reserves as Shock Absorbers", in R. Dornbusch and F.L. Helmers (eds.), *The Open Economy*, EDI Series in Economic Development (New York and Oxford: Oxford University Press).

WOODS, N. (1998), "Governance in International Organizations: The Case for Reform in the Bretton Woods Institutions", in UNCTAD, *International Monetary and Financial Issues for the 1990s*, Vol. IX (New York and Geneva: United Nations).

THE ROLE OF SPECIAL DRAWING RIGHTS IN THE INTERNATIONAL MONETARY SYSTEM

Hannan Ezekiel*

Abstract

Since the last allocation of Special Drawing Rights (SDRs) over the period 1980-1982, the proportion of cumulative total SDR allocations to total member reserves has fallen steadily. Although the Second Amendment of Articles of Agreement of the International Monetary Fund stipulated an increasing role for SDRs in the international monetary system, the failure to take any new decisions to make SDR allocations since then has tended to reduce the importance of SDRs in that system.

Although it is often contended that the reserve needs of the international monetary system are now met through international capital markets, there is a strong case for making a general allocation of SDRs in the near future. Many developing countries and countries in transition do not have access to international capital markets, and many of the countries that do have access to these markets can effect access only at a relatively high cost, with the marginal cost of borrowed reserves being higher owing to crowding-out effects. Moreover, even countries that do have access to international capital markets on reasonable terms face a need for larger reserves, arising from the very fact of the large capital inflows they receive.

SDRs provide a valuable and flexible instrument for dealing with international liquidity problems, for promoting sustainable growth in both developing and developed countries, and for dealing with emergencies. However, for SDRs to be able to perform these functions well, appropriate changes need to be made in the SDR system.

First, the list of permitted holders should be extended so as to include financial market institutions in order to increase the demand for SDRs and to promote their role in the international financial system. Second, developing country members should make voluntary commitments to hold SDRs up to specified proportions of SDRs to reserves, in accordance with a formula based on the reserve strength of the country and aggregate cumulative total allocations of SDRs. Third, there is a need for arrangements that would permit the Fund to make special allocations of SDRs to deal with crises. And finally, the procedures and practices relating to SDR transactions should be improved to allow SDRs to increasingly take on the characteristics of foreign exchange reserves.

* This is a shortened and revised version of a longer paper with the same title. My special thanks go to Jacques J. Polak, Aziz Ali Mohammed, Gerry Helleiner and members of the G-24 Technical Group for their valuable comments and suggestions regarding earlier drafts. I remain fully responsible, of course, for the views and the proposals contained in this paper.

I. Introduction

The international monetary system has changed dramatically since the introduction of Special Drawing Rights (SDRs). Convertibility of the dollar into gold has been eliminated. The system of fixed parity exchange rates that could be changed only by deliberate action by the authorities, usually under extreme pressure in exchange markets or in anticipation of such pressure when the balance of payments faces a structural disequilibrium, has given way to a system of floating exchange rates for the major currencies, with other currencies floating through links with major currencies or baskets of currencies. Currencies held in reserves have expanded to include the deutsche mark and the yen. From the viewpoint of reserve growth, the critical change has been the rapid growth of private international capital flows that has made it possible for countries to obtain reserves without having current account surpluses. They can do this through general capital inflows or by borrowing deliberately in the market for the purpose of increasing reserves.

The Amendment of the Fund's Articles of Agreement incorporating the SDR scheme was approved in 1969. Immediately following the adoption of the Amendment, the Fund approved the first allocation of SDRs - totalling SDR 9.3 billion. With the completion of the third instalment of this allocation on 1 January 1972, the aggregate cumulative total allocation of SDRs constituted 9.3 per cent of world non-gold international reserves.

In 1978, a further allocation of SDRs was approved, in the amount of SDR 4 billion per year. By January 1981, the aggregate cumulative total SDR allocations to all members amounted to 21.4 billion and constituted 6.7 per cent of the world's non-gold international reserves.

As agreement on the question of further SDR allocations could not be reached, no allocations of SDRs have been made since then. In April 1993, the Managing Director of the IMF proposed a new allocation of SDRs on the grounds that there was a long-term global need to supplement reserves and that the many countries that had joined the Fund since 1981 had never received an SDR allocation. While the proposal did not receive approval at the time, there was some support for an "equity" allocation of SDRs aimed at bringing into line the proportions of the cumulative total allocation of SDRs to quotas for all members. An allocation of this kind would, of course,

require an amendment of the Fund's Articles of Agreement. It was in the context of continuing disagreement on SDR issues, and at the request of the Interim Committee, that the Fund organized a seminar on the role of SDRs in the international financial system.

Although there was a considerable divergence of views amongst participants in the SDR seminar, important issues were raised. The views expressed and now published (Mussa, Boughton and Isard, 1996) will affect not only the more immediate prospects for SDR allocations but also the role of the SDR in the future. These divergent views, therefore, need to be carefully examined together with other issues relating to the functioning of the SDR system. This paper examines issues which are critical to the functioning of SDRs and the future of the international monetary system. It also makes some important proposals for strengthening the SDR and for expanding its role in the international monetary system.

II. International capital flows and reserve needs

Among the most important of the basic changes that have taken place in the international financial system since the late 1960s, when the SDR scheme was adopted by the IMF, are the liberalization and the vigourous expansion of private international capital markets. The growth of international capital markets and the increase in the access of many developing countries to those markets have undoubtedly changed the environment in which the international monetary system functions. As has been widely noted, there is increased scope now for developing countries to obtain borrowed reserves. It has even been argued that these developments have obviated the need for the deliberate creation of international liquidity through new allocations of SDRs (Corden, 1996; Hesse, 1996; Siebert, 1996).

In response, it has been pointed out, amongst others by Ahluwalia (1996), that not all developing countries have free and easy access to international capital markets. For some countries, the costs of raising capital in international markets are high; for others, there is no access at all. For all these countries, the need for reserves remains unsatisfied. Therefore, there is a case for the creation of international liquidity through SDRs. For an overall need to exist, not all countries have to face a need for reserves. Reserves created in this form would also have a much lower cost for countries that do have access to international capital markets.

In the discussion of the impact of capital market developments on international liquidity, too much may, in any case, have been made of the access that many developing countries now have to borrowed reserves. Such reserves clearly increase total reserves, but they increase external liabilities to the same extent. There are also several other features of borrowed reserves that should be noted:

• Borrowing for the sole purpose of adding to reserves necessarily takes place to some extent at the expense of other capital inflows that promote investment, employment and growth, as such borrowing produces a crowding-out effect;

• The direct cost of borrowed reserves - equal to the excess of the interest paid on those reserves over the interest earned on current-account-related reserves - is not likely to be very large, but it would not be insignificant;

• The marginal cost of borrowing for reserves would be much higher than the direct cost, because borrowing reserves would add to the total amount of funds raised in international financial markets and this would increase the cost of all external funds;

• Payment difficulties may arise because of the instability of funds borrowed for reserve purposes, as they may not be renewed for a variety of reasons, even when conditions in the country are reasonably good;

• Payment difficulties that borrowed reserves should have helped to handle may be worsened by the latter's unreliability in times of need - that is, by failures to renew them precisely when difficulties arise and they are most needed.

The balance-of-payments problem that developing countries may face in the new situation, with large capital inflows, is also quite different from that which prevailed earlier. Capital inflows are subject to fluctuations and borrowed reserves are unreliable. Capital flows into developing countries tend to be based on inadequate information and analysis, and are subject to swings that are often independent of conditions in the recipient country. Capital flows are also subject to contagion effects, with capital market institutions often following market leaders or other market institutions, whose decisions may be determined by factors unrelated to conditions in the particular countries or groups of countries concerned.

Once capital outflows begin, they tend to feed on themselves. Since the potential volume of outflows is related not to the size of annual inflows but to the size of the accumulated liabilities, they can become extremely large and may swamp the normal balance of payments. The external reserves of a developing country that has been receiving large inflows of capital no longer have to take care merely of abnormal deficits in the current account, but also of potential capital outflows that could be immense. Therefore, while the growth of international financial markets has created some access for developing countries to borrowed reserves, it has at the same time changed the nature and magnitude of the balance-of-payments problem the holders of these reserves have to deal with.

Large capital outflows can obviously be handled only by correspondingly large reserves. The total reserves of countries facing such outflows may no longer be sufficient, even if those reserves are much larger than in the past, because the need for reserves under the new system has become vastly greater.

The fact that large capital flows may create problems for recipient developing countries has been widely recognized (Camdessus, 1996; Mussa, 1996; Ahluwalia, 1996; and Buira, 1996). There has also been some discussion of measures, mostly of a restrictive nature, that developing countries may need to take to protect themselves from the potential disruptive effects of large capital flows under certain circumstances (see, for example, Helleiner, 1997).

The change in the nature of the liquidity problem resulting from the growth of international capital flows calls for larger reserves than ever before because of the growth of external liabilities, the instability and unreliability of capital flows, and the greater strains that the indirect effects of capital flows put on the current account.

The solution to this problem is to make new allocations of SDRs to increase both the total reserves and the proportion of allocated reserves in total reserves. This is also the solution for those countries that do not have satisfactory access to international financial markets. The growth of those markets has not met the need for international liquidity.

III. Holding of SDRs by financial market institutions

To enable SDRs to play an effective role in the international monetary system, it is important to strengthen the SDR system as much as possible. To this end, the market for SDRs should be enlarged by permitting commercial banks and other non-official financial institutions to hold SDRs or SDR Certificates and to carry out transactions in them with other authorized holders. Possible action along these lines was discussed at the SDR seminar organized by the IMF (Camdessus, 1996; Polak, 1996; and Yaqub, Mohammed and Zaidi, 1996). An early proposal that the right to hold SDRs be extended to non-official financial institutions had already been made by Polak in 1979.

At the present time, the demand from members and other authorized holders for SDRs to hold is greater than the supply of SDRs flowing from their use. As a result, the system of designation of members, under which the designated members would be required to accept SDRs when members wish to use them, has fallen into disuse. Although designation in the sense of compulsion to accept SDRs has now become unnecessary, the danger exists that at some time in the future the supply of SDRs arising from their use by members may exceed the demand for SDRs. This danger increases when new allocations of SDRs are made. If the danger were to materialize, designation would have to be brought back into use and some members would be compelled to hold more SDRs than they would otherwise be prepared to do.

The combined effect of the proposal made here and the proposal made in section IV below would be to increase the demand for SDRs to hold. These proposals would thus help to prevent the danger mentioned above from materializing.

The proposed change would help to meet one argument that has been advanced against making a new allocation of SDRs at this time - namely, that it might lead to an involuntary official transfer of resources from countries with balance-of-payments surpluses to SDR users. If market institutions are allowed to hold SDRs, any resulting transfer of resources will be market-determined. Acquisition by developing countries of resources from the market through the use of SDRs that have been allocated to them, rather than through the issue of their own liabilities, would enable these countries to secure control over resources that would be market-determined

but would be obtained more easily and on more favourable terms than at present.

Commercial banks and other financial institutions operating in international financial markets would be willing to hold SDRs, given their quality in terms of value and returns. These returns would be acceptable to them because there is no country risk attached to SDRs. It is this difference in the risks that distinguishes SDRs from "private SDRs"; the latter, though valued in SDRs and carrying interest rates determined in exactly the same manner as those for SDRs, would continue to be liabilities of the individual issuer and not of the system as a whole. That is why the unsatisfactory experience with "private SDRs" so far does not throw any light on the likelihood of success of market holdings of SDRs or SDR Certificates. For the relatively risk-free SDRs, the returns - themselves determined by the market - would be attractive. As a result, one could expect the market to be willing to provide substantial resources through this medium. For developing countries, the costs of obtaining resources through holdings of SDRs by financial institutions in the market would be (a) the same as for holdings by members and official institutions, (b) the same for all members, and (c) low compared with the costs of borrowed reserves.

When financial market institutions are allowed to hold SDRs or SDR Certificates, it would become possible for member countries to carry out direct operations in exchange markets by buying or selling SDRs or SDR Certificates in the market. They need not always go through the intermediate step of obtaining or providing foreign exchange. They may, of course, continue to use SDRs in the way they do at present, i.e. exchanging them for directly usable foreign exchange.

If the proposed change is made, some of the stronger developing countries could allow their own commercial banks or other financial institutions to be listed as approved holders of SDRs. They would then also be able to carry out domestic market operations through transactions with these financial institutions involving the purchase or sale of SDRs or SDR Certificates.

An amendment to the Fund's Articles of Agreement would be required in order to enable it to allow commercial banks and other non-official institutions to hold SDRs and carry out transactions in them. This would not be necessary, however, for the system of SDR Certificates suggested by Polak (1996). This system would require the Bank for International

Settlements or some other official institution, which is an authorized official holder of SDRs, to issue SDR Certificates against SDRs. These SDR Certificates could then be held and traded by financial market institutions on appropriate terms. The effects in terms of transfer of resources and market involvement would be the same as if SDRs were themselves held and traded by these institutions.

A clarification is necessary. Creating SDR Certificates would not increase the volume of international liquidity resulting from the allocation of SDRs. Total liquidity created through SDRs would remain the same because the SDR Certificates would replace the SDRs being held in trust by the Trustee institution. In effect, the total volume of liquidity that is created is equal either to the volume of SDRs in existence or to the sum of SDR Certificates and SDRs after the exclusion of the counterpart SDRs held by the Trustee institution. The creation of SDR Certificates does not increase the volume of liquidity, but it does improve the quality of SDRs by widening the scope for transactions in them and thus increasing the demand for them.

Adopting the SDR Certificate route would be easier because no amendment to the Fund's Articles of Agreement would be required. A scheme for the issue of SDR Certificates and trading in them could, therefore, be implemented with much less delay.

IV. Voluntary member commitments to hold SDRs

When the SDR scheme was adopted, it had four important features that have since undergone drastic changes. These relate to:

- the value of the SDR;

- the interest rate paid by members on their SDR allocations and received by them on their holdings;

- the system of compulsory designation requiring members designated by the Fund to accept SDRs used by other members;

- the reconstitution requirement to ensure minimum average holdings of SDRs over a period of time.

The value of the SDR was originally fixed at the then gold equivalent of the dollar. It is now equal to the value of a basket consisting of the five major currencies. The interest paid by members on SDR allocations and received by them on SDR holdings was originally fixed at an extremely low level and was quite independent of market interest rates. It is now fixed on the basis of the interest rates prevailing on selected short-term securities in the markets of the five countries whose currencies form the SDR basket. Compulsory designation, under which members designated by the Fund had to accept SDRs which other members wished to use, has fallen into disuse. This is because the initial fear of the new asset has probably disappeared and the SDR is now more attractive in terms of both value and return. Furthermore, the demand for SDRs has been augmented by the fact that some official holders other than Fund members are also permitted now to hold SDRs. The demand for SDRs to hold is now greater than the available supply. Designation is still used, but the object is to allocate the limited supply becoming available through use by members among those that wish to increase their holdings, rather than to force unwilling members to accept them. In view of this situation relating to SDR holdings, the reconstitution requirements have effectively been abandoned.

Despite these changes in the characteristics of SDRs, some analysts take the position that use of SDRs by developing countries can result in an unacceptable transfer of official resources to them from developed countries (Siebert, 1996). SDR rules make it possible to oblige countries in a surplus position - by their being designated - to buy and hold SDRs. Although countries are not forced at present to do so, large new allocations of SDRs may certainly create a situation in which designation may have to be used as an instrument of compulsion.

To address developed countries' concern that a new SDR allocation may once again create a situation in which designation and compulsion may be used against them, we offer a proposal. The proposal is for all developing country members of the Fund to commit themselves to hold more SDRs on a voluntary basis in accordance with a suitable formula for determining a minimum volume of SDR holdings to which all members agree to conform. This formula would be related to the strength of the member's external payments position, as reflected in the appropriately measured size of its external reserves. The application of this formula would result in most developing countries voluntarily expressing their willingness to hold more SDRs and SDR Certificates than they do at present. For those developing countries whose total reserves are relatively large, the volume of SDRs that they would commit themselves to hold would become larger than their cumulative total allocations.

As a counterpart to this commitment, these countries would also commit themselves, if SDRs are required by members for carrying out various transactions, to transfer SDRs from their holdings when these are above certain specified levels. These levels would be set by a formula that would be the counterpart of the formula for their voluntarily expressed willingness to hold SDRs and could of course be expressed simply as a percentage (less than 100) of their commitments to hold SDRs.

The object of the proposal for voluntary commitments to hold SDRs is to widen demand for the latter and to bring about the fullest support of developing countries for the SDR system. This support would extend not merely to limiting the use of SDRs to circumstances when the need for such use exists, but also to the holding of SDRs to the maximum extent possible when others use them. This voluntary commitment would express in concrete terms developing countries' faith in the system. Its effect would be to increase the confidence in the SDR system of all members, authorized official holders and financial market institutions.

Voluntary holding of SDRs in accordance with the proposed formula would not impose any real burden on most developing countries. The benefits derived from SDRs, like those derived from any other reserve asset, do not arise merely from their use but also from their availability for use when there is a need. When they are held, SDRs form a part of total external monetary assets. It is the form of these assets that would be different, not the volume.

The quality of SDRs is now much higher than before. The SDR now consists of a basket of five major currencies, and its interest rates are determined as the weighted average of short-term interest rates in the financial markets of the same five countries. As a result, the SDR or SDR Certificate undoubtedly offers an attractive return. As elaborated in section VI below, steps could be taken to improve procedures and practices in relation to their use so that they could be used more readily by Fund members needing to do so. Expanding the list of authorized holders to include institutions in international financial markets, as suggested in section III above, would make SDRs even more easily usable. Steps could also be taken in this connection to expand the list of official financial

institutions which are permitted to hold SDRs or SDR Certificates.

The proposal for voluntary holding of SDRs by developing country members would not in any way interfere with their ability to use SDRs when necessary. Weaker developing countries wishing to use SDRs would face no difficulties. Even countries with strong balance-of-payments positions and reserves would be free to use SDRs when circumstances require such action. However, the proposal would commit them to hold SDRs as a part of their reserves whenever their payments and reserve positions are strong enough to permit them to do so, and in normal circumstances to accept SDRs up to agreed levels from those using them.

The proposal presented here should be clearly distinguished from reconstitution requirements. The latter were punitive in nature and intended to ensure that countries using SDRs restored their holdings to a minimum extent within a prescribed period of time, without reference to the state of the country's balance of payments or reserves during that time. The proposal presented here calls upon many of the developing countries to commit themselves voluntarily to hold SDRs up to prescribed proportions of their reserves in normal circumstances even when this would result in their holding substantially more SDRs than their cumulative total allocations. These commitments, however, would be linked to the strength of their balance of payments and their total reserves.

Such a formula would not necessarily result in actual holdings of SDRs at the prescribed level since the total demand for SDRs to hold could, as it is now, be greater than the available supply of SDRs resulting from their use. A situation of excess demand would be likely to continue under the proposal set out here even after new allocations had been made. There is therefore little reason to fear the possible use of designation as an instrument of compulsion to make members accept more SDRs than they are willing to hold.

The proportions of reserves that developing countries commit themselves to hold under the agreed formula should also be related to the aggregate allocations that the Fund has made at any time. As new allocations are made, the formula should provide for an automatic increase in the proportions of reserves that should be held in the form of SDRs under the formula. A separate proposal is put forward in section V below for emergency allocations of SDRs to be made under certain circumstances. The formula for voluntary commitments to hold SDRs should provide for a corresponding increase in the proportions of SDR holdings to reserves when such emergency SDR allocations are made. These proportions should decrease when the emergency is over and the specially issued SDRs have been cancelled.

To the extent that developing countries commit themselves voluntarily to hold SDRs along the suggested lines, they will blunt the edge of the implicit criticism that they only want, through SDR allocations, to obtain official transfers of resources from developed countries. More broadly, they will strengthen the SDR system and therefore also the case for allocations when other circumstances are appropriate.

V. SDRs and international payments crises

Even if a payments crisis begins in a single country, it may spread to other countries belonging to the same category or the same region and very rapidly engulf the entire system. The IMF should be enabled to prevent this. Indeed, such action may be considered as part of the original IMF mandate - that is, to maintain a stable and orderly system of international payments.

Normally, when a member faces balance-of-payments difficulties that it is unable to handle with its own reserves (including gold, SDRs, its reserve position in the Fund and foreign currencies), it may receive assistance from the Fund through drawings on credit tranches. However, when capital outflows are involved, the crisis may become so great that the volume of assistance that the Fund can normally provide under all present arrangements may not be sufficient to bring the member's difficulties under control. The resources needed to deal with the Mexican crisis, for example, and to prevent it from spreading were huge. That crisis was ultimately contained only because the United States was willing to provide massive financial support to Mexico on a bilateral basis in addition to the support that was provided by the Fund. The resources that would be required if more than one country were involved in such a crisis at the same time would be even greater. Even if the Fund has these resources available or could raise them quickly under existing or extended arrangements, the effect might be to strain the capacity of the Fund to provide normal assistance to other members. Arrangements therefore need to be put in

place that would enable the IMF to have sufficient resources to deal with an emergency situation of this kind. It should not have to scramble at short notice in order to scrape together the resources needed.

Having drawn attention to the volatility and other weaknesses of capital markets, Buira (1996) proposes the creation of an emergency facility in the Fund to help members to deal with serious short-term balance-of-payments difficulties that may arise in a country, even when it is following basically sound economic policies but is not able to handle these difficulties out of its own resources. This facility would provide assistance to central banks of member countries that establish suitable arrangements in advance and provide permanent collateral. It could be used at their initiative in appropriate circumstances. The assistance would be in the form of short-term credit and would carry an interest rate that would be a couple of percentage points above the prevailing rate for SDRs.

De Cecco and Giavazzi (1996) presented a similar proposal for an emergency facility in the Fund. However, in their proposal, the facility is based on special SDR allocations to provide the resources that the special emergency facility would need. In one important respect, the proposal is more conservative than the scheme proposed by Buira, because its assistance is not automatic at the initiative of the member but requires action by the Fund. The latter would be authorized to issue any required quantity of SDRs when it decides that it is necessary to intervene in exchange markets to deal with speculative attacks. These SDRs would be issued temporarily and would be cancelled once they are no longer needed. The effectiveness of such a facility would require that the Fund be able to act with speed whenever such a situation arises (see also Williamson, 1996).

Some have expressed worries about moral hazard: the presence of such a facility might encourage members to follow less disciplined policies than they would do otherwise. One critic of these proposals goes so far as to suggest that in some cases even a default should be acceptable in the interests of discipline (Siebert, 1996). However, De Cecco and Giavazzi argue that the Fund would obviously act only when the underlying conditions do not justify prevailing market speculation against the currency; and they emphasize the immense harm that default, and the events leading up to it, could cause through the spread of speculation against other countries that could threaten the stability of the international monetary system.

It is proposed here that a special emergency facility based on SDRs should be set up in the Fund. Authority should be given to the Fund to make a special SDR allocation of the size needed to deal with severe balance-of-payments difficulties that have reached or are likely to reach crisis proportions.

Two possibilities may be envisaged for the proposed special allocation:

•   SDRs could be allocated to the member or members facing the crisis, with the allocated SDRs to be repurchased when the crisis is over;

•   SDRs could be allocated to a newly created special emergency account set up in advance, which would exchange the SDRs for the local currency of the member or members concerned, as required.

Both would require an amendment to the IMF Articles of Agreement.

If the system of commercial holding of SDRs or SDR Certificates, as separately proposed, is adopted, the member could also obtain foreign exchange by transferring these SDRs or specially issued SDR Certificates to commercial institutions rather than to other members, or provide the SDRs or SDR Certificates directly to commercial financial institutions willing to accept them in exchange for their claims against the country. The effect would be to meet the demand for conversion of these claims into foreign exchange or other acceptable assets, and thus to meet the crisis directly.

The emergency allocation of SDRs, whether directly to the member or to the emergency facility supporting the member, would be temporary in nature. Once the crisis is over, the SDR allocation would be cancelled as the member concerned would be able to return the SDRs or their foreign exchange equivalent to the Fund's special emergency account. The special SDR allocation could, of course, be made on the basis of agreement by the member or members to implement an agreed programme for dealing with the crisis.

Giving the IMF the authority to make such special SDR allocations, establishing a special emergency facility for that purpose and possibly making a large advance allocation of SDRs to it for use, when necessary, along the suggested lines would strengthen the international monetary system. One would expect that the mere availability of the SDRs to members would have a dampening effect on

speculation, and thus prevent or mitigate crises by generating confidence in the ability of the authorities to meet them. It would also expand the role of SDRs in the international monetary system, as laid down in the Second Amendment to the Articles of Agreement, even if the authority given to the Fund never has to be used.

VI. SDR procedures and practices

To make the SDR an effective reserve asset, it must be as easy to use as other reserve assets. Whatever other changes are made in the SDR system, including the changes proposed in this paper, it is clear that the ability to use SDRs freely and effectively will also depend on the procedures and practices followed by the IMF in dealing with SDR transactions. These procedures and practices need to be reviewed and changes made wherever necessary to increase the simplicity of the procedure and the speed at which transactions can be carried out. While all members of the Fund would benefit from the smooth working of the international monetary system that a fully developed SDR system would make possible, developing countries have a special interest in an improvement in the procedures and practices relating to the use of SDRs. This is not only because they are likely to be frequent users of SDRs but also because they benefit most from a general strengthening of the international monetary system. Many who take a pessimistic view of the role of SDRs in the future appear to have been influenced in their judgement by weaknesses in the way in which the SDR system is operated at the present time. But these weaknesses can be easily corrected, and improvements in procedures and practices relating to SDR use could have a strong positive influence on these judgements.

For these reasons, the Fund should assess present procedures and practices and improve them wherever possible and without delay. Developing countries may take the lead in this process, without necessarily waiting for other decisions to be taken or other more important modifications in the system to be made.

It is true that some procedural improvements can be brought about only when some of these other decisions have been taken or changes made. Appropriate systems will, for example, have to be set up when financial market institutions are allowed to hold SDRs or SDR Certificates. In fact, the systems that are required may be different, depending on whether it is SDRs or SDR Certificates that these institutions are allowed to hold. Many procedural changes are, however, independent of specific changes resulting from such proposals and these should be carried out without delay. Further changes should be made when new policies are adopted or new programmes set up. In any case, the objective in setting up improved systems must be to make transactions in SDRs smooth, effective and efficient.

The smoother the system for SDR use, the more holders will be willing to hold on to SDRs. If SDRs can be used as smoothly and directly as foreign exchange, there will be little reason for members to rush to use their SDRs and obtain foreign exchange as soon as difficulties appear on the horizon or even in anticipation of them. Use of SDRs merely to add to foreign exchange holdings will then decrease as more and more members continue to hold them as a part of reserves even when total reserves are falling. They would use them only when the need to do so became urgent.

With proper arrangements for the use of SDRs - particularly if financial market institutions are allowed to hold them - there will be few reasons for members holding SDRs to treat them as being very different from foreign exchange assets. Decision to use SDRs will then be limited to factors connected with their value and the return on them, in addition to the desire to strengthen them in the wider interests of the international monetary system.

VII. Conclusions and recommendations

Since the last allocation of SDRs over the period 1980-1982, the proportion of cumulative total SDR allocations to total member reserves has fallen steadily. Although the Second Amendment of the Fund's Articles of Agreement prescribed an increasing role for SDRs in the international monetary system, the failure to take any new decisions on new SDR allocations has tended to reduce the importance of SDRs in the international monetary system.

In response to the contention that the reserve needs of the international monetary system are now met through international capital markets, the following three points have been made:

(1) Many developing countries and countries in transition do not have access to international capital markets;

(2) Many of the countries that do have access to these markets can effect access only at a relatively high cost, with the marginal cost of borrowed reserves being even higher owing to crowding-out effects;

(3) Even countries that do have access to international capital markets on reasonable terms face a need for larger reserves, arising from the very fact of the large capital inflows they receive.

There is, therefore, a strong case for making a general allocation of SDRs in the near future.

SDRs provide a valuable and flexible instrument for dealing with international liquidity problems, for promoting sustainable growth in both developing and developed countries, and for dealing with emergencies. For SDRs to be able to perform these functions, appropriate changes need to be made in the SDR system.

A number of specific proposals have been made in this paper. These are:

• an expansion of the list of permitted holders to include financial market institutions in order to increase the demand for SDRs and to promote their increasing role in the international financial system, as stipulated by the Second Amendment of the Fund's Articles of Agreement;

• voluntary commitments by developing country members (with developed country members expected to follow suit) to hold SDRs up to specified proportions of SDRs to reserves, in accordance with a formula based on the reserve strength of the country and aggregate cumulative total allocations of SDRs;

• arrangements that would permit the Fund to make special allocations of SDRs to deal with crises;

• improvements in the procedures and practices relating to SDR transactions in order to make the use of SDRs simple and convenient so that they may increasingly take on the characteristics of foreign exchange assets held in reserves.

These proposed changes are all aimed at strengthening the role of SDRs in the international monetary system, and at strengthening this system itself. Amongst other benefits, they would enable the international monetary system to meet the problems created by large international capital flows, that are obviously otherwise desirable in themselves.

References

AHLUWALIA, Montek Singh (1996), "SDR Allocations and the Present Articles of Agreement", in Mussa, Boughton and Isard (eds.), chapter 4.

BUIRA, Ariel (1996), "Potential of the SDR for Improving the International Monetary System", in Mussa, Boughton and Isard (eds.), chapter 6.

CAMDESSUS, Michel (1996), "High Time for a Broad Review: Keynote Address", in Mussa, Boughton and Isard (eds.), chapter 1.

CORDEN, W. Max (1996), "The SDR: Conditional or Unconditional", in Mussa, Boughton and Isard (eds.), chapter 3.

DE CECCO, Marcello, and Francesco GIAVAZZI (1996), "Use of SDRs in the Financing of Official Safety Net Mechanisms", in Mussa, Boughton and Isard (eds.), chapter 6.

HELLEINER, G. K. (1997), "Capital Account Regimes and the Developing Countries", in UNCTAD, *International Monetary and Financial Issues for the 1990s*, Vol. VIII (UNCTAD/GDS/MDPB/1)(New York and Geneva: United Nations).

HESSE, Helmut (1996), "Is There Still a Rationale for the SDR in the Creation of Unconditional Liquidity in the International Monetary System?", in Mussa, Boughton and Isard (eds.), chapter 6.

MUSSA, Michael (1996), "The Rationale for SDR Allocation under the Present Articles of Agreement of the International Monetary Fund", in Mussa, Boughton and Isard (eds.), chapter 4.

MUSSA, Michael, James M. BOUGHTON, and Peter ISARD (eds.) (1996), *The Future of the SDR in Light of Changes in the International Financial System* (Washington, D.C.: International Monetary Fund).

POLAK, Jacques J. (1979), "Thoughts on an International Monetary Fund Based Fully on the SDR", *IMF Pamphlet Series*, No. 28 (Washington, D.C.: International Monetary Fund).

POLAK, Jacques J. (1996), "Should the SDR Become the Sole Financing Technique in the IMF?", in Mussa, Boughton and Isard (eds.), chapter 7.

SIEBERT, Horst (1996), "No Future for the SDR", in Mussa, Boughton and Isard (eds.), chapter 4.

WILLIAMSON, John (1996), "A New Facility for the IMF?" in UNCTAD, *International Monetary and Financial Issues for the 1990s*, Vol. VII (UNCTAD/GID/G.24/7) (New York and Geneva: United Nations).

YAQUB, Muhammad, Aziz Ali MOHAMMED, and Iqbal ZAIDI (1996), "A Focused SDR Allocation", in Mussa, Boughton and Isard (eds.), chapter 6.

GOVERNANCE IN INTERNATIONAL ORGANIZATIONS: THE CASE FOR REFORM IN THE BRETTON WOODS INSTITUTIONS

Ngaire Woods*

Abstract

"Good governance" is now a central item on the agenda of the IMF and the World Bank in their dealings with member States. Yet, the principles of accountability, participation and transparency that the institutions are applying to borrowing governments have not as yet been rigorously applied to the institutions' own governance. This paper attempts to do just that. In the first place, the paper defines "good governance" and examines the experiences of other international organizations which have attempted to balance principles of good governance with efficiency (including the regional development banks, the United Nations, GATT/WTO, the European Union, the International Fund for Agricultural Development, and the Global Environment Facility). The lessons drawn from this analysis are then applied to the IMF and the World Bank.

The research suggests that, while pressure for good governance has been magnified by the policy role of the Bretton Woods institutions, neither of them has adequately reformed core aspects of accountability and participation. In the first place, while both institutions rely ever more on their identities as universal institutions, this identity has been eroded by a gradual redistribution of membership rights which reflects neither power nor a coherent set of principles. In the second place, in both institutions there are formal and informal decision-making rules which work against the standards of governance they are urging on member governments. For example, the practice of consensus decision-making, which extends even to operational decisions, reduces transparency and accountability. The rather ad hoc categories of decision requiring special majorities do not reflect rational attempts to ensure accountability to major stakeholders (both donors and borrowers). Finally, "participation" in the definition of the core tasks of the agencies is confined to a small number of key actors. In each of these cases, both the IMF and the World Bank could better achieve good governance without unduly sacrificing efficiency.

*   I am indebted to Professor Gerry Helleiner for his incisive comments and suggestions on earlier versions of this paper. I should also like to thank members of the G-24 Technical Group and Frederick Van Bolhuis for their constructive input. I am very grateful for the assistance of many officials including: Leo Van Houtven, Joseph Gold, Karin Lissakers, David Knox, William Davey, Gabrielle Marceau, Graham Avery, Nigel Evans, Colin Keating, Charles Dallara, Eleanor Alesi and others who prefer to remain anonymous. Also gratefully acknowledged is the assistance of Zoe Young, Sam Daws and Robert Wade, as well as the research assistance of Mark Egan (University College, Oxford).

I. Introduction

The 1990s has seen a revival of thinking and questioning about global governance. A number of phenomena have accelerated this revival. Interdependence in the economic, environmental and social spheres has increased the need for global cooperation and institutions[1] for the management of an ever wider range of issues (Commission on Global Governance, 1995). At the same time, however, the intrusion of international organizations into domestic politics has sparked alarm about infringements of state sovereignty. As the IMF and World Bank embrace wider and deeper conditionalities in their lending (Kapur, 1997), and as the United Nations becomes involved in civil conflicts (Mayall, 1996), States are beginning to examine afresh whom these international agencies represent and whose policies they implement.

Furthering and guiding this new questioning is the recent wave of democratization across Latin America, Africa and Eastern Europe, and an ever wider debate about democratic standards and institutions. Notions of "good governance", "participation" and "ownership" have all entered the mainstream lexicon of institutions involved in development financing. As a result, international institutions have begun to urge democratic standards of greater representation, participation, accountability and transparency on their members. However, the institutions are finding that similar values are being urged on them in respect of their own governance (Boutros-Ghali, 1995; Commission on Global Governance, 1995; Held, 1995).

Some of the pressure for reforming governance in international institutions has come from non-governmental organizations (NGOs). The World Bank, for example, has come under heavy pressure from environmental groups. Such NGOs pose a thorny problem for international institutions which are, after all, structured on the premise that States are the building blocks on which global organizations are based. Yet, NGOs have become an important and recognized channel of representation and action in international fora, either because some "governments" are not trusted by major donors, or because some groups are simply not being represented or protected by their governments. For this reason, it has been argued that NGOs should "be mobilized in the interests of better governance" (Commission on Global Governance, 1995, p. 254). Indeed, NGOs already influence the agenda of international institutions (Weiss and Gordenker, 1996), and they have certainly

increased pressures for good governance to be urged on aid-receiving governments.

Against this backdrop of concerns for greater participation and representation within international organizations, it is not surprising to find that the voting structures of the IMF and the World Bank have come under fire. Voting power in each institution is heavily weighted in favour of its largest shareholders, which comprise a small group of industrialized countries. While supporters argue that this is one of the great strengths of these organizations (Lister, 1984), critics argue that it is time for them to be democratized. They highlight that today it is the developing and transition economies that are most affected by the policies of both the IMF and the World Bank, yet these countries are the least represented in the voting structure. Other critics argue that while the institutions need to reflect the realities of global economic power in order to be effective, they no longer do so.

These various critiques point to issues of governance that will be explored in this paper. It will be argued that reform of governance within the IMF and the World Bank is necessary. However, this does not mean simply a reform of the voting structure. Rather, the experience of other institutions examined in this paper reveals that different distributions of voting power do not translate automatically into greater ownership or participation. If good governance is to be achieved, then we need to look not just at voting but at the wider issues of decision-making, including participation, accountability and transparency. For this reason, the paper first examines what "good governance" means (section II). Section III explores how good governance might be applied to international organizations. The experiences of a number of organizations are drawn on to highlight possibilities and problems with core elements of governance, including representation, ownership, accountability and the role of decision-making rules. Section IV then applies the lessons and issues to the IMF and the World Bank. Section V addresses what this implies for reform of the institutions.

The paper does not deal with legal issues nor provide a detailed examination of the everyday workings of the institutions. Rather, it focuses on questions of governance and the relationship of voting structures to both formal and informal decision-making practices and procedures. The aim is to evaluate critically governance within the Bretton Woods institutions using lessons learnt from governance within other institutions, with an eye to informing arguments for the reform of the voting structures of the Fund and the Bank.

II. Defining governance and good governance

Governance has been defined as "the sum of the many ways individuals and institutions, public and private, manage their common affairs" (Commission on Global Governance, 1995). The term refers not to governments but rather to the "establishment and operation of ... the rules of the game that serve to define social practices, assign roles, and guide interactions" within a government or an institution (Young, 1994, p. 15).

In development thinking and research, it is now widely recognized that "good" governance plays a critical role in the implementation and results of development projects and strategies. A milestone in this thinking was the World Bank's 1989 report on sub-Saharan Africa, in which issues of governance were broached with an unprecedented frankness (World Bank, 1989). In this report the term "governance" encompassed the State's institutional arrangements, the processes for formulating policy, decision-making and implementation. It also included information flows within government, and the overall relationship between citizens and government. In each case an important distinction was made between the political commitment required in a government (as opposed to technical capacity) to achieve a particular standard in respect of each aspect of governance. The ground-breaking 1989 report on Africa has subsequently been expanded in several Bank documents on governance (World Bank, 1992, 1994a). According to these publications and other more general literature, governance has five core aspects. It is about "the formal and informal rules defining practices, assigning rules, and guiding behaviour" in respect of (a) policy formulation, (b) decision-making, (c) implementation, (d) information flows, and (e) the relations between rulers and ruled. "Good" governance is a value judgement about the nature of these formal and informal rules.

A basic prerequisite of good governance is an adequate level of competence and technical skill on the part of the actors. It is, however, important that the Fund and the Bank have now recognized core values such as political accountability, participation, an effective rule of law, transparency and adequate flows of information. Speaking in 1992, for example, the IMF's Managing Director voiced the need for "democratizing social decisions" in Latin America, and ensuring "for want of a better term, 'good governance' - that is, accountable and active govern-ments that enjoy the trust and support of their societies" (*IMF Survey*, 14 December 1992).

In some international institutions good governance is being urged on members with the broader objective of bolstering the promotion of democracy or certain basic human rights through development assistance. However, in the Fund and the Bank (in keeping with their constitutional mandates) the purpose of adopting standards of good governance has been to improve the effectiveness of members' use of resources.

A first element of good governance is "participation", the idea of which has been strongly developed within the World Bank and other development agencies. The *World Development Report 1994* (World Bank, 1994b), in analysing the development of infrastructure, highlighted the need for "user involvement" in project design and operation, as well as in decision-making and agreements concerning the sharing of benefits and costs. It is now accepted that participation is needed to foster "ownership" in projects - a greater sense of local commitment to the enterprise and a sense of local empowerment to overcome development problems. More strongly, the Wapenhans Report recommended the "mainstreaming" of participatory techniques in project design and implementation in order to improve project performance (World Bank, 1994c; Stevens and Gnanaselvam, 1995). The relevant techniques are now all outlined in the *World Bank Participation Source Book* (World Bank, 1996)

However, the concept of participation is not without ambiguity. In the words of two Bank officials describing some of the reasons for poor project performance: "Participation has often been equated with explaining the project to key stakeholders (individuals and groups who stand to gain or lose from the project), instead of involving them in decision-making. Borrowers are not committed to project goals. Their 'ownership' has been sought by making them responsible for preparation and implementation, instead of ensuring that the impetus for the project is local and that the process provides explicit opportunities for consensus building" (Piciotto and Weaving, 1994). We will see later in this paper that a similar set of problems and ambiguities besets ownership of policies within international organizations.

Within the Fund the notion of participation is also making headway in the operations and interpretation of the institution's work. As mentioned above, the IMF now communicates with a wider range of groups outside of government (such as with trade unions and business groups), consultations are now much broader, and more time and missions are used in order to negotiate programmes. More generally, participation is invoked as part of the rationale for privatization. The argument is made that privatization can ensure a higher level of public participation and commitment to economic adjustment and growth. On this view, the prime determinant of ownership is domestic financial inputs. For this reason, the argument for greater ownership is sometimes deployed by those who propound reducing external flows to developing countries. Finally, within the IMF, good governance is also seen as a way of strengthening the "institutional framework of government" and rooting out corruption and rent-seeking activities, as well as promoting the right kinds of economic reform (*IMF Survey*, 20 May 1996 and 12 August 1996).

We might summarize good governance as developed in the Fund and the Bank, and urged on member countries, in the following way:

(1) Political accountability
    (e.g., through elections or some direct link between those who rule and those who are ruled)

(2) Participation and ownership
    (of - or by - those most affected or at whom the benefit of any development project is ultimately aimed)

(3) Effective rule of law
    (predictability, and impartial and objective application and enforcement of the law)

(4) Transparency and information flows
    (the appropriate collection and release of data about the policies and performance of governing institutions so that citizens can monitor and scrutinize the management of public funds)

The inclusion of values such as participation and ownership has required international agencies to go some way towards rethinking their internal organization and procedures for identifying, preparing, approving, implementing and evaluating projects (Piciotto and Weaving, 1994). The emphasis has been to ensure that standards are met *within member governments*. Members are now pushing for the same standards to apply to governance *within the institutions* themselves, which poses a challenge of a

new order. To quote the Secretary General of the United Nations: "democracy has not featured in the history of the international system of States. Sovereignty, rather than democracy, has been its guiding principle". He argues that: "Today ... the democratization of the international system can be seen as both necessary and possible" (Boutros-Ghali, 1995). But if this is the case, we need first to ask what is the standard of good governance we should apply? Below we examine issues of governance that arise from the requirements of representation, accountability and decision-making rules within a range of international organizations, leaving an examination of governance within the IMF and the World Bank to the subsequent section.

III. Good governance within international organizations

A. *Governance and effectiveness*

Good governance within international institutions is often described as a balancing act between requirements of effectiveness and legitimacy. Yet the two are seldom separable. As Caron (1993) elegantly argues, international institutions need to enjoy a particular degree of legitimacy in order to be effective.

In the *short term*, the effectiveness of an organization might be defined as its capacity to carry out its mandate: to make the relevant or necessary decisions; to muster the necessary resources and capabilities; and to apply its resources to implementing and enforcing its decisions. Over the *longer term*, however, the qualities needed by an effective international organization include:[2]

• the capacity to prove that it is achieving its allotted role (i.e. to prove to its members that it is worthwhile);

• the capacity to adapt rather than to transform, i.e. to plan overall strategic directions and policy choices in conditions of stress and change, yet at the same time to ensure (through rigid transformation rules) a retention of its character and status (Clark, 1996; Young, 1992);

• a realistic view of what members can achieve; this requires sound procedures in the determination of policies which the membership can and will implement;

• a symmetry of power within the institution: for example, Young (1992) argues that "the more symmetrical the distribution of power, the harder it is to establish institutional arrangements initially but the more effective they are once formed" (since powerful States - or groups of States - will not be able simply to flout the rules of the institution);

- an ongoing *raison d'être* (recognized by the membership) for the institution (e.g. through the growth of interdependence in the issue area the institution deals with);

- a coherent underlying system of ideas (for defining problems and their solutions) which members perceive as valid, and a capacity to absorb new systems of ideas when its own are seen to be failing.

Overall, the effectiveness of an institution depends to a large degree on its members' perceptions as to how representative, inclusive and procedurally "fair" the institution is. This follows consistently from the findings of both the Fund and the Bank in their work in specific countries where the effectiveness of their programmes depends (more than they previously realized) on an appropriate level of country participation and commitment. Practically, this means that international organizations must constantly trade-off requirements of effectiveness and legitimacy. Below we examine this trade-off in respect of representation and voting structures, and then decision-making practices and rules.

B. *Alternative voting structures: the experience of the regional development banks*

Representation is difficult to achieve in an international system which is decentralized and comprises States of different sizes and capabilities. Yet representation is a cornerstone of democratic institutions because it reflects and implements the consent of those who are governed. If an institution aspires to a degree of democracy, its mandate and the question of who it affects cannot be separated from the question of who should enjoy representation within its executive. In other words, the core concern of democracy - the consent of the governed - implies that some form of consent of those who are affected by decisions of the institution is necessary.

Yet, as expressed above, representation has to balance concerns both for effectiveness and legitimacy. This was appreciated by the likes of United States Treasury Official Harry Dexter White in the early

stages of planning and discussion of the voting structure of the World Bank and the IMF (Lister, 1984, p. 38). The first definitive version of the White Plan, published in April 1942, argued:

> ... the real problem is how to distribute the voting power. If each member of the board were to be given an **equal vote**, then a small country that invested one million dollars would have as much power in making decisions as a country that has subscribed a hundred or a thousand times that amount. With the possibility that the number of small countries participating will be much greater than the large countries, a one-vote-one-member arrangement is palpably unwise. On the other hand, to accord voting power **strictly proportionate to the value of the subscription** would give the one or two powers control over the Fund. To do that would destroy the truly international character of the Fund, and seriously jeopardize its success. Indeed it is very doubtful if many countries would be willing to participate in an international organizations with wide powers if one or two countries were able to control its policies (Gold, 1972, p. 19; emphasis added).

At play here are two competing principles. The first focuses on the need to reflect power-political and economic realities in an institution. The second highlights the need to justify and legitimate an institution so that all countries agree to participate and comply with its rules.

The argument for "effectiveness" is age-old and assumes that international organizations must represent the powerful in order to preserve or create order effectively. This view underpinned the Council of the League of Nations, in which the most powerful took up permanent seats, and likewise it is reflected in the Security Council of the United Nations. A parallel in the Bretton Woods institutions is the principle that quotas need to reflect the realities of economic power in the world economy.

A different principle - that of equality of States - came to prominence in the aftermath of the Second World War (Broms, 1959), and was enshrined in the universal membership and voting of the United Nations General Assembly and the World Trade Organization. The principle is also reflected in the allocation of "basic votes" in the Fund and the Bank.

The moral basis for recognizing equality among States is that in doing so we protect individuals' rights to express their consent to be governed - by respecting their government and according it equal status with other governments. This reasoning is obviously imperfect in a world in which many States are governed without the consent of the people, and for this reason many NGOs now flourish in the international setting, claiming that they better represent grass-roots movements and organizations. Yet, as NGOs play an ever more important agenda-setting role, some governments point out that the democratic credentials of these organizations require some scrutiny: an issue raised, for example, by France in negotiations on the Global Environment Facility (Sjoeberg, 1994, p. 31). In the future, NGOs may well become subject to particular governance standards set by international organizations. In the meantime, however, they highlight a basic problem with the premise upon which "equality among States" proceeds.

"Equality" within international organizations also stumbles over a further problem - that of very differently sized States. One State-one vote gives a population of 200,000 the same vote as a population of over 200 million. For this reason it is sometimes argued that equality would be better served by equal representation of populations than by the representation of States, such as through basic votes in the Fund and the Bank (Lister, 1984, pp. 111-112). Today such proposals, however, are made with a strong caveat that any such scheme must be sure not to punish developing countries which have made headway in stabilizing their population.

In practice, arguments about effectiveness and equality have shaped the formation of most international organizations. Underpinning the case for equality has been an assumption, or at least a hope, that more equal voting power would ensure a greater level of ownership and participation by members in the institutions. Yet, the experience of the regional development banks does not bear this out.

The Inter-American Development Bank, the African Development Bank and the Asian Development Bank were all set up to provide a more regionally owned development bank which would ensure greater sensitivity to local needs, enhanced participation and a sense of ownership in the countries of the region. Unlike the IMF and the World Bank, the regional development banks would be primarily governed by regional members. The governance structure of each would embody a specific regional identity and ownership, reflected in their capital and voting structures. But has this worked? Has the voting structure of the institutions enhanced ownership and participation? Let us look at the experience of each in turn.

In the Inter-American Development Bank (IDB), the regional character is assured by several factors. Firstly, the regional members hold a majority of the bank's capital and votes (just over 50 per cent) and, indeed, the Articles of Agreement explicitly provide that the aggregate of the voting share of the borrowing regional countries cannot fall below 50.005 per cent (nor that of the largest shareholder - the United States - below 30 per cent). Second, the President of the IDB is always a Latin American and, until 1972, membership in the bank was confined to members of the Organization of American States.

The Latin American ownership of the bank has been said to have resulted in an institution which is more "in touch" with the region. It has a presence, in the form of field offices, throughout the region (although it has been criticized for under-utilizing them: Tussie, 1995, p. 10). Furthermore, it is the largest international lender to the smallest and the poorest countries of the region. At the same time, although regional developing country borrowers from the IDB enjoy a majority of votes, they have not used this voting power to push through loan agreements against the will of non-regional members. Tussie reports that there is no record of any loan having been approved through reliance solely on a Latin American majority (Tussie, 1995, p. 31).

Yet, while the above factors point to ownership of the IDB in a legal sense, they do not prove that there is ownership in the sense implied in standards of good governance, i.e. participation, commitment and a sense of responsibility for and to the organization. Looking more closely at the IDB, we find two less obvious aspects of its structure that strongly influence governance within it.

Firstly, in spite of the Latin American voting power within the bank, the United States enjoys enormous dominance. This is explained by both formal and informal decision-making practices within the institution. The United States has a veto on constitutional decisions which require either a three-fourths majority or a two-thirds majority of regional members, and until the Eighth Replenishment the Board's quorum required the presence of the United States Executive Director. Similarly, in the concessional window of the IDB (the Fund for Special Operations), where a two-thirds majority is required for all decisions, the United States retains a veto power even though its contributions have now dropped to 8.22 per cent. However, even in the ordinary capital account of the bank where the United States does not have a blocking minority (a simple majority is required), nevertheless it has negotiated a procedure to ensure it retains a power to delay loans that it disapproves. In practice, members of the Board say that United States influence is also magnified by the resources the United States mission to the bank has at its disposal - to present, argue and lobby for particular positions or policies. Furthermore, the United States enjoys a more diffuse influence from the fact that the IDB is based in Washington D.C., with one quarter of its top management, its Executive Vice-President and usually also the Financial Manager and General Counsel coming from the United States.

A second important factor of governance which emerges from the experience of the IDB is that while Latin American Governments enjoy a majority on the Board of the institution, this has not translated into real participation in, and responsibility for, determining overall policy directions and core objectives of the bank. Rather, due to a poor relationship between management and Board, the latter has suffered from what the 1993 Task Force on Portfolio Management called "culture of control" (IDB, 1993), constantly exercising a detailed control of loans and thereby neglecting crucial tasks such as re-examining the bank's core objectives, and articulating its broad policy direction.

These aspects of governance are not confined to the IDB. The African Development Bank (AfDB), more than the IDB, has expressed a determination to protect its "African character". This is reflected in its capital, voting and staffing structures. Located in Abidjan, Côte d'Ivoire, with an African President and mostly African staff, the AfDB did not admit non-regional members until 1982. Today twelve of the 18 seats on the Board of the bank are held by African countries. In the concessional window of the bank (the African Development Fund), which is 98 per cent funded by non-regionals, African members have retained a 50 per cent voting share.

Yet the "African character" of the bank, preserved by this formal structure of representation and voting, has not translated into African ownership as understood within the framework of good governance. Rather, three opposite tendencies stand out. In the first place, the AfDB has been very distant from its African membership. To cite the report of the 1994 Task Force on Project Quality (AfDB, 1994, p. 2), the bank had "no systematic relations" with the African countries which are its majority shareholders. In the field, they argued "the AfDB is absent when it should be present". Paradoxically, shortly after the completion of the Task Force's Report, the bank closed the few field offices that it had.

Secondly, in spite of majority representation on the Board, it is not the African members who have ended up defining the overall direction of the AfDB. A low level of engagement and concern on the part of African members with regard to questions of the institution's financial and operational strength, the quality of its work and its contribution to African development means that they have not controlled or influenced major policy decisions (AfDB, 1994, p. 29). By contrast, non-regional members of the AfDB who hold a minority of votes had "close relations and dealings with the bank", and involved themselves closely in analysing, monitoring and evaluating the bank's performance, as well as in defining new policies, directives, and budgetary and commitment objectives. By default, then, it is the minority vote-holders in this institution that ended up positively defining its directions and policies.

Magnifying the absence of African voices in charting the direction and policies of the AfDB have been the poor relations between management and Board. In 1994 the Task Force reported "paralysing mistrust, suspicion and resentment" within the bank and between its Board and management (AfDB, 1994, p. 26). Analysts argue that to work effectively, the institution needs a strong, effective and empowered management and staff (AfDB, 1994; English and Mule, 1996). The Task Force explained that the Board interfered too much in the wrong kind of issues, scrutinizing details in the budget process and sometimes even usurping the powers of the President (AfDB, 1994, p. 31). This repeats the story of relations between management and Board in the IDB. The result is that the Board, with its African majority, does not get to debate and define strategies for each borrower, nor the overall objectives of the institution.

Finally, the experience of the AfDB highlights the importance of a structure which builds restraints into an institution - restraints which ensure that no practices emerge which lead the institution away from its core purposes and goals. In financial institutions this usually involves a balancing between contributors and users of resources. The AfDB has not achieved this balance. Rather, it has often been depicted as an institution within which the majority shareholders compete for resources, making *quid pro quo* arrangements among themselves to gain access to funds. In doing so, they have shaped an institution which does not fulfil its creators' aspirations, i.e. it does not use its African character to promulgate research and a specialized understanding of Africa's development problems and their possible solutions.

Seen in overview, formal ownership in the IDB and the AfDB (through the holding of votes and shares) has not translated into the aspired levels of participation and responsibility for the institution. The Asian Development Bank (AsDB) is perhaps a happier example on this score. A minimum of 60 per cent of the its capital stock is held by regional members, who also occupy seven of the Board's ten seats. These regional members, however, are not all borrowers: they include Japan, Australia and New Zealand. Overall, donors (regional and non-regional) in the bank enjoy 59 per cent of the votes, while borrowers have 41 per cent of the votes. This structure represents a delicate balance, which was highly contested and debated when the institution was created. The small majority held by contributors to the AsDB is balanced by the allocation of 20 per cent of overall votes as "basic votes", equally distributed among all members, as well as by the maintenance of a minimum of 60 per cent of capital stock in the hands of regional members.

United States influence in the AsDB has played an important role, exercised both through financial leverage, such as that which the United States Congress applied in 1989 over suspending lending to China, and through its voting power, which it has maintained even while its contributions have diminished. However, the power of the United States within the bank is greatly diluted by Japan's influence (Watanabe, 1977; Sender, 1993). In the past, Japan's contributions have greatly exceeded its voting share. However, this imbalance is diminishing, so that in 1996 Japan held 16.52 per cent of total shares in the organization and 13.57 per cent of overall votes. Japan also exercises considerable influence through its contributions to the Asian Development Fund, through the personnel and research resources it puts behind its role in the bank, its occupancy of the presidency and the dominance of Japanese nationals among the staff (particularly in the higher echelons).

Unlike the IDB and the AfDB, developing countries in the AsDB do not have a controlling share of votes in the bank. However, governance of the institution has evolved in a way which does balance out concerns over regional representation and effectiveness. Although developing country regional members do not have a majority of votes, they have,

unlike in all other institutions, retained the advantage of basic votes which increase as the capital of the AsDB grows, so as to keep the proportion of basic votes at a constant 20 per cent of overall votes. Further enhancing the sense of participation and legitimacy in the bank is the balancing (against each other) of United States and Japanese influence.

The experience of the regional development banks shows that a majority share of capital and votes does not translate directly into greater participation in defining an organization's purpose and character, and in shaping its policies and direction. This kind of ownership (specified in standards of good governance) relies much more heavily on the commitment of members to the institution's core purposes, the institutional resources they make available to back their own participation, and the restraints built into the organization's structure. Such restraints ought to ensure that an institution focuses on achieving its core mandate, and that this focus shapes the evolution of its policies and decision-making practices.

Representation is the link between those who are governed and the institution which governs or makes decisions which affect them. However, representation is not the only means by which an institution is accountable to those it affects. Equally, if not more important, are the ways in which an institution makes decisions, including *how* members participate and according to which rules. Poor decision-making procedures carry risks, as one analyst puts it: "(a) that important minorities be alienated; (b) that decisions will not be respected and implemented at the national level; (c) that decisions will prove to have been ill-advised and lead to unanticipated, unfortunate results" (Lister, 1984, p. 80). In the section below, we examine decision-making and good governance, looking in particular at the impact of "consensus" on good governance.

C. *Voting versus consensus decision-making: the experience of the United Nations Security Council and the GATT*

International institutions make three different kinds of decisions: *declaratory decisions or statements*, both of which have an important symbolism and chart general directions and purposes for an institution without requiring implementation or enforcement; *policy decisions* setting down the general rules within which the institution operates; and *operational decisions* which decide whether specific uses of an institution's resources meet its overall policies and rules. Each of these kinds of decision is made according to a prescribed decision rule.

The most stringent decision rule in an international organization is the requirement of unanimity. In theory, in a world of sovereign States this is the only rule which fully protects the sovereignty of every government and ensures that "consent" (by States and thereby indirectly their populations) is explicit. Unanimity gives every State a veto. The problem with unanimity is that it makes effective action difficult and empowers even the smallest State to block a measure or to hold an action to ransom. In the end, the requirement of unanimity can disable an institution and force those who wish to act to do so in other fora. For these reasons, most organizations reserve the requirement of unanimity (if at all) for only the most fundamental of decisions and operate on most other issues under rules of majority or special majority, or by the practice of consensus.

Consensus decision-making is quite different to unanimity. While the latter requires every member of an institution to vote affirmatively (or to abstain where this is defined as a positive vote), consensus, in Joseph Gold's terms, is about the "avoidance of voting" (Gold, 1977). Consensus decision-making is said to give more voice to those with little voting power and to contribute to an atmosphere within institutions which is peaceable and constructive. For these reasons, it is often simply assumed that consensus decision-making contributes positively to good governance within an institution. In this section we will test this assumption, examining in particular the experience first of the United Nations Security Council and then of the World Trade Organization (WTO).

The experience of the United Nations Security Council is particularly relevant, since many who criticize the governance structures of the IMF and the World Bank have looked to this institution for an alternative model. An "economic security council", it has been argued, could lead to more representative and democratic management of the international economy (Bertrand, 1985; UNDP, 1994; Commission on Global Governance, 1995; Stewart and Daws, 1995; Ul Haq, 1995). Yet these arguments underplay some of the negative aspects of governance raised by the working practices of the Security Council and in particular the impact of consensus decision-making on governance within the United Nations.

Much of the Security Council's business today is conducted in "informal consultations of the whole",

in which voting is replaced by consensus decision-making. Such consultations, however, are always guided by the constraints of formal voting arrangements which require the concurring vote of the Permanent Five on the Security Council and a minimum of nine votes in total. Undoubtedly, the practice of consensus has improved the capacity of the Council to despatch its business. However, it has also had negative impacts on participation and transparency within the United Nations. These are worth highlighting.

In the first place, according to members of the Council, consensus decision-making has bred a much higher level of informal consultations, "private straw votes" and meetings of small groups. Key decisions, in other words, are taken outside of formal meetings. Even on procedural matters, when votes are taken they "are, so to speak, pre-cooked in informal consultations" (Wood, 1996). Whereas there used to be frequent votes on the adoption of the agenda, "nowadays agendas are always agreed in advance ... in informal consultations" (Wood, 1996). This means that only a restricted number of members get to participate in the process of real decision-making. And this is not the only adverse impact on governance.

A further, deeper problem with informal processes is that they are unrecorded. This means that the *reasoning* for a decision is not open to scrutiny by other States, and nor is the position taken by each member. In these ways the Council is not accountable to States who are not party to the informal processes, even if they are directly affected by the Council's decisions (e.g. for budgetary reasons). Obviously, the lack of any record also means that the business of the Council is also not open to wider public scrutiny.

The experience of the Security Council also highlights that reliance on informal negotiations "behind the scenes" magnifies the unequal resources available to members in order to work effectively to push their own preferences. Those with the greatest staffing and research capacities are much better placed to use the "informal negotiations", so that, in the words of one commentator, "delegations ... can simply be overwhelmed by delegations of members such as the United States" (Caron, 1993).

Consensus decision-making, then, can have adverse consequences on good governance. We find that the practices within the Security Council have not only sharpened the argument for a wider membership of the Council (to include Germany, Japan and developing countries), but have also catalyzed more insistent calls for greater transparency and accountability in the Council's procedures.

The Council has responded to calls for more openness in a number of ways. For example, in October 1994 the Council agreed that the President would give informal oral briefings to inform non-members of the Council about the informal consultations of the whole. Further to this, in February 1994 the Council members decided to make draft resolutions "in blue" (i.e. in near final-form) available to non-members of the Council. Additionally, a 1995 Presidential Statement (S/PRST/1995/234) sets out a list of "improvements to make the procedures of the Sanctions Committee more transparent" (Wood, 1996).

These (and other) changes have all been made in the name of improved access to information and consultation. However, upon closer inspection the reforms are all rather frail. They have not been formally institutionalized. Most have been undertaken by agreement among the members. This makes the new rules particularly weak since the Council can make and break its own Rules of Procedure at will - and does. What sceptical observers argue is that the permanent five members of the Council are "window-dressing" so as to close off any further attempts to force the Council to be more genuinely accountable or to undertake decision-making in a more transparent manner.

At the same time, the accountability of the Security Council has also been eroded in other ways. Within the United Nations an important channel of accountability from the Security Council to the General Assembly is the budget. According to Articles 17(1) and 18(2) of the Charter of the United Nations, approval of the United Nations budget requires a two-thirds majority of the General Assembly. However, this requirement has been altered, not by amendment of the Charter but less formally by Resolution of the General Assembly. This occurred after strong US lobbying for change in the 1980s which resulted in Resolution 41/213 calling for critical budget decisions to be adopted by consensus at the stage of the Committee for Programme and Coordination (Lyons, 1995). Crucially, the move gave the United States (and other individual States) the veto it sought over the United Nations budget (Rivlin, 1996).

The analysis of the Security Council highlights problems of transparency and participation which arise from consensus decision-making. It also underlines that members of any institution who wish to influence decisions must commit high levels of staff and resources in order to do so - i.e. effectively to generate proposals and lobby for them both outside and inside of formal meetings.

These findings are all strengthened by an analysis of decision-making within the GATT and its successor, the World Trade Organization (WTO). In the GATT, consensus decision-making played down the equal power of States to vote (on a one-State-one-vote basis, subject to special majorities for particular categories of decision) and enhanced informal powers of States to offer concessions or use retaliatory threats. Powerful countries, participants explain, could push negotiations behind the scenes, apply bilateral pressures and simply not hold meetings until a consensus had been reached. The effect was to concentrate negotiations among a small group of powerful members (usually the "Quad": United States, European Union, Japan and Canada), which tended to present decisions virtually as a *fait accompli* to the other (and particularly developing country) contracting parties.

An important change in governance has been made in the new WTO. While the GATT was always a "negotiating umbrella" under which States signed agreements, the WTO has a structure and enforcement mechanisms which make it a powerful international institution. It is now the administrator of all multilateral trade agreements, an overseer of national trade policies and has a dispute settlement procedure which, unlike that of the GATT, can make rulings which are automatically accepted by the organization unless there is a consensus against acceptance. This procedure has been dubbed "reverse consensus".

One of the strongest criticisms of the GATT's consensus procedure was that it made dispute resolution both unworkable and highly political. When consensus was required for the Council to accept panel rulings, the process was subject to delaying tactics by countries adversely affected by findings. Panel decisions were often seen as unfair and partial in their treatment of different countries. Such decisions were seen to reflect the desire to reach consensus rather than the application of rules. The outcome of disputes was seen more as a result of the relative power of the parties.

The WTO's new dispute settlement procedure requires that a consensus against a panel ruling be required in order to object to it. The procedure reflects the new relationship between effectiveness and legitimacy within the WTO. The institution was created as an equal-voting organization, contrary to the proposal, pushed by the United States during the Uruguay Round, for a weighted-voting Executive Board like those of the IMF and the World Bank. The resulting organization has succeeded in generating greater confidence, participation and use of the procedures by all of its membership. Whereas the GATT mechanisms tended to be used mainly by the Quad, in the WTO use has expanded: of all the requests before the WTO in mid-1996, about half were from developing countries. This effect has been strengthened by the fact that developing countries can now request legal assistance from the WTO - assistance which is provided independently of the legal office of the organization.

There are, however, residual problems with consensus decision-making within the GATT/WTO. In the first place, there is ambiguity about the precise scope and parameters of consensus, and in particular regarding the question as to whether a requirement for consensus should override other decision-making rules. For example, where decisions are being made in lower Councils which have rules of procedure of their own, some would argue that voting rules should apply where consensus is not reached. However, in practice, decisions are "bumped up" so that consensus may be reached at the next level and, if necessary, further "bumped up" until the decision reaches the General Council. Consensus, then, has become an all-pervasive practice which overrides other decision-making rules.

A further ambiguity relates to whether or not consensus may be used to take a decision to ignore a voting requirement. This nuance is important because consensus decisions reflect the mood of those present at the meeting. But many members of the GATT/WTO cannot be present at all meetings. Indeed in the GATT, in order to take up a place on the Council, contracting parties had to be "willing to establish responsibilities of membership therein", which included attendance by an appropriate representative at all Council meetings. Such commitments require substantial resources and personnel, and as a result a very large number of developing countries were unable to take up full membership of the GATT Council.[3] This continues to hold true for the WTO: in 1996 only 72 of the 124 members had delegations at the WTO.

The experience of both the Security Council and the GATT/WTO highlight several adverse consequences of consensus decision-making practices: members are excluded from the informal fora within

which core bargains are made; accountability is reduced by unrecorded meetings; formal decision-making rules are superseded; only those present are represented, and these members can even obviate a vote which could give voice to parties not in attendance at a particular meeting. In summary, consensus, while often applauded as a step towards good governance, can have the opposite effect, reducing transparency and accountability and thereby increasing the challenge of improving governance.

D. *Special voting arrangements and decision-making: the experience of the Council of the European Union, the International Fund for Agriculture Development, and the Global Environment Facility*

We have been examining the impact of decision-making rules which do not involve voting and it now remains to examine the impact of voting on governance. The different types of relevant voting requirements include: simple majorities (more than half the members); qualified majorities (support of a specified percentage, such as 70 or 85 per cent); and double majorities, which permit voting to be structured to ensure that both a majority of voting members and another category or group of members support a decision (such as a majority of the populations represented or of contributions to the institution). In the proceeding discussion, the impact of these various requirements on governance is examined in particular to ask whether they can be used to enhance accountability. The experience of the European Council (EUC), the International Fund for Agricultural Development (IFAD), and the Global Environment Facility (GEF) helps us to answer this question.

As the mandate of the Council of the European Union has widened, its members have urged the institution to become more effective as well as more representative, democratic and accountable. The Council has responded to these challenges in a number of ways. Effectiveness has been improved by a shift from unanimity to special or qualified majorities (effected by the Single European Act and the Maastricht Treaty). In practice, this shift has two effects.

The first is the move towards qualified majority voting (QMV) which tends to empower the Commission and smaller States within the Union. Under

QMV, no member of the Council can rely on being able to veto a measure; hence each must ensure that its interests are embodied (even if in a second best way) in whatever agreement emerges. This tends to dilute the power of larger States, as evidenced by the fact that where votes have been taken, Germany (the largest member State) is the country most often outvoted.[4] Furthermore, the fact that no single country can hold the rest to ransom tends to empower the Commission (and many would say the European Court of Justice too), as does the fact that the Commission is becoming more of a proposer and lobbyist of measures than merely a "broker of consensus". A stronger Commission within the European Union also strengthens the position of smaller States, both by containing the power of large States and because the smaller ones enjoy a disproportionate share of jobs within the Commission.[5]

A second impact of qualified majority voting is that it casts a new emphasis on blocking power and countries' various shares in the minimum "blocking" minority (30 per cent of Council votes). This was highlighted in the dispute which erupted in 1994 over how to reduce relative voting shares in the face of enlargement (Austria, Finland, Sweden, and - as was then expected - Norway). On United Kingdom insistence, the Council eventually agreed that the old blocking minority (in which the United Kingdom had a larger share) could postpone decisions, even when they did not have enough support to block them.

While empowering the Commission (and emphasizing the importance of blocking power), the advent of QMV does not resolve concerns about representation and democracy. In particular, larger States argue that the addition of more small States to the Union is exacerbating the under-representation of their populations. Several proposals for re-weighting votes have been made to reduce this problem (Commission of the European Union, 1996). In particular, several variants of double qualified majorities have been proposed which would require decisions to have the support not only of a (specified) majority of votes on the Council but also of an equal majority of the population (see also PMI, 1996; Hosli, 1995). The object of double-qualified majorities (DQMs) would be to enhance the representation of large, populous States, without touching the existing voting rights of States within the Union.

The likely impact of DQMs on voting power in the Council has been modelled in a number of ways. Overall, studies seem to show that while a double majority of 66 per cent would shift some voting power

to the larger members, a DQM of 50 per cent would simultaneously increase the power of both the largest and smallest members (Commission of the European Union, 1996; Hosli, 1995). Most scholars agree, however, that the most important impact of such changes will be on perceptions of the Union's representativeness and thereby its legitimacy.

Further to responding to calls for good governance, the European Union has also revised some of its procedural rules and practices. In the first place, some representation of regions within the Union (such as Germany's Laender) has been permitted by opening up the definition of who can sit on the Council.[6] In the second place, in order to stave off the criticisms of the lack of accountability of the non-directly elected executive, the Council has introduced procedures to include the Parliament more closely in decision-making. Under a new "co-decision" procedure, by mid-1996 some 49 instruments had been adopted, and members are now debating the possibility of simplifying and expanding the scope of the procedure (Commission of the European Union, 1995).

Overall, in the case of the European Council we can see that changes in voting rules and consultation procedures are being made (or debated) in order to improve the accountability and representativeness of the institution, not only of its member States but also of its population, elected representatives and regional governments. Two other institutions also demonstrate the ways in which voting rules and other procedures can be put to the service of concerns about governance: the International Fund for Agricultural Development (IFAD) and the Global Environment Facility (GEF).

IFAD has a pluralistic system of voting which reflects the balance of stakes and aims which existed in 1974, when governments agreed to create it. Finally established in 1977, its aim has been to combat hunger and rural poverty in the low-income food-deficient regions of the world. Its voting structure reflects its founders' hopes that it would channel "oil earnings" from OPEC countries to those most affected by the increase in oil prices. Votes (1800) were split among three groups of countries, giving 600 votes to each in category I (the developed countries), category II (OPEC countries) and category III (developing countries). Each group was then left to decide how it would allocate votes among its members. The way each did so reflects the different relationship of each group to the institution and its aims. Developed countries distributed 82.5 per cent of votes according to each member's contribution, and only 17.5 per cent equally among members. OPEC countries distributed

75 per cent of votes by contribution and the other 25 per cent equally. Developing countries distributed all votes equally among the members.

The main contributors to the Fund (developed countries) have had their influence in the institution protected not by a majority of votes but by special majorities and quorum requirements. Most major decisions (including lending policies, criteria and regulations regarding financing and approval of the budget) require a special majority of two thirds or more. This gives category I countries a veto power over the combined strength of OPEC and developing nations. Furthermore, there is a strict quorum requirement in both the Council and the Executive Board, requiring the pressure of members representing at least one half of the votes in each of the three categories and of all the votes.

In spite of its record (IFAD claims, in a 1996 Publicity Statement, that it has become "a symbol of North-South cooperation and South-South solidarity"), IFAD is now debating a major revision of its structure in the context of negotiations on the Fourth Replenishment of the Fund. On 25-27 January 1995 its Governing Council adopted a resolution to abolish the three-category system and introduce a new voting system upon the completion of the Fourth Replenishment. The new system will distribute votes among all members in part on the basis of membership (i.e. basic votes) and in (larger) part on the basis of contributions to the Fund. These changes reflect pressure from the developed countries (which are now the major donors) for a stronger voice within the institution. Pressure from these countries has already resulted in significant internal changes to improve accountability and efficiency in delivering projects.

IFAD faces internal changes owing to the changing stakes its membership groups have within the institution. Its voting structure reflects the balance of stakes which existed in the 1970s and the desire of each group (industrialized, OPEC and developing countries) to have its own preferred voting structure. Now that the contributions and positions of each group have changed, it is no surprise to find that the institution is being restructured to reflect a new balance. This is in keeping with a need for a voting structure which appropriately reflects changing stakes in an organization.

A more recent example of an alternative voting structure is the Global Environment Facility (GEF) launched as a pilot programme in 1991 and then restructured in 1994. The GEF is especially inter-esting since it was created self-consciously as a model of good governance: its new charter explicitly pledges "to ensure a governance that is transparent and democratic in nature, to promote universality in its participation and to provide for full cooperation in its implementation among the UNDP, UNEP and the World Bank" (Preamble of the Instrument for the Establishment of the Restructured Global Environment Facility). Today the institution attempts to embody equality, participation and commitment by all members, along with participation by grass-roots and non-governmental organizations at all levels (not just in projects but also in policy and programme development).

From the point of view of this paper, an interesting aspect of the restructured GEF is its voting system. Where decisions cannot be reached by consensus, formal votes must be supported by a 60 per cent majority of the total number of participants in the GEF (whose votes are placed by their repre-sentative members on the Council) as well as a majority representing 60 per cent of total contributions to the Fund. It is worth noting that the machinery for taking votes is rather cumbersome, requiring a written motion and notice of a formal vote prior to meetings, and so forth. However, the real import of the new voting structure, as we have seen elsewhere in this paper, is that it re-weights the structuring of "con-sensus" within a meeting. Even though votes will seldom, if ever, be taken within the GEF, consensual decisions will nevertheless be arrived at on the basis of informal tallies of "would-be" votes based on opinions expressed around the table. In this sense, the double voting structure adds an important note of equal accountability - to contributors to the Fund and to recipient countries that host projects - while not detracting from the basic membership rights of all (otherwise equal) participants.

One core difference between the GEF, the IMF and the World Bank is the perception, at the time of creation of each organization, as to what the stakes of its various members were. The Fund and Bank have governance structures which essentially reflect their mandates and the balance of stakes as at 1944. The GEF, created in the 1990s, reflects a trade-off between the interests of developing countries whose participation in the GEF was vital, and industrialized countries whose desire for environmental protection led to the creation of the institution. From the outset, it was clear that developing countries would not participate in the GEF if it were structured in the same way as the World Bank or the IMF (Sjoeberg, 1994). Further contributing to the structure of the GEF was the climate of the 1990s - including the focus on good governance and democracy discussed above in section II - which formed the backdrop to its creation.

In setting up the GEF, both donors and recipients had a stake in ensuring the success of the organization. Northern concerns about environmental degradation were the driving factor behind the creation of the Fund, yet all participants understood from the outset that action to moderate global environmental degradation emanating from the South could only proceed with the cooperation and participation of developing country members. Hence, the GEF was built from the start to an exacting standard of good governance. The argument for applying similar standards of good governance to the IMF and the World Bank is that these institutions now also rely (indeed, ever more heavily) on the commitment and cooperation of developing countries in order to fulfil their mandates. The next section elaborates this argument.

Overall, this section has examined three major aspects of governance: voting structure, decision-making practices, and formal decision-making rules. The experience of eight international organizations has been brought to bear to establish how these elements affect and help to define a standard of good governance for international institutions. The specific elements of good governance raised for international organizations are summarized in the box below.

Box

ELEMENTS OF GOOD GOVERNANCE WITHIN INTERNATIONAL ORGANIZATIONS

1. *Constitutional rules - representation and ownership:*

-   "Stakeholders" are adequately represented to ensure the continuing confidence of members who contribute financially and the continued cooperation and commitment by those members most affected by the institution's actions.
-   The mandate and overall goals of the institution are defined by all stakeholders.
-   The main fora of decision-making are open to all members at each stage of decision-making: setting the agenda, outlining possible alternatives, and excluding unviable options.

2. *Working practices - accountability and transparency*

-   Both the formal and informal working practices of the organization help it to achieve its mandate by ensuring core goals are prioritized and achieved.
-   Members have confidence that rules and practices are "fair" and applied impartially.
-   "Reasons" for decisions, and the positions taken by voting members, are available for the scrutiny of all members of the institution (and the public?).

3. *Adaptation and change*

-   The "mind-set" (or underlying system of ideas) and the role of the organization adapt to changing circumstances, and the evidence or research used in advancing or supporting particular policy positions is widely accepted by all members of the institution.
-   The constitutional structure evolves in a way which preserves the essential character of the institution.
-   The "rules of transformation" guiding changes in membership and rights are seen (by all members) as clear and fair.

IV. Voting and decision-making in the Bretton Woods institutions

In this section it will be argued that governance within the IMF and the World Bank today falls short of several of the elements of good governance identified in the preceding section. The allocation of quotas and the correlate membership rights in both institutions no longer reflect the application of a coherent, justifiable set of principles: quotas no longer reflect relative economic and political power, and the principle of equal representation, which was once implemented by the allocation of "basic votes", has been significantly eroded. Furthermore, decision-making practices have not adapted to the changed mandates of both institutions, whose work now takes them further and further into influencing domestic policy choices in developing countries. These changes pose several challenges of governance.

Before elaborating these challenges, it should be noted that the IMF and the World Bank (and other international organizations) have made some effort to respond to calls for more transparent, accountable and participatory governance. Regarding *transparency* for example, the World Bank (like the Inter-American Development Bank) has adopted a "disclosure of information" policy. The IMF too is publishing more, including background papers to bilateral negotiations, although not, as yet, country reports prepared in the context of Article IV negotiations. As regards *accountability*, the World Bank was the first multilateral organization to create an independent inspection panel for public accountability whereby affected parties in borrower countries can file complaints that the Bank has failed to follow its own policies, procedures and conditions in the context of a specific loan. In the IMF, "external evaluation" is being debated, although at present it is limited to those instances where the Board requests the views of outside experts (such as in recent discussions of ESAF). Finally, both the Bank and the Fund are advocating more local *participation* and *ownership* of their programmes. This was urged on the Bank by the Wapenhans Committee, and has been taken up in the Fund by the Managing Director, who is now making much greater use of the External Relations Department and speaking to business groups and trade unions in countries in which the Fund is working.

These changes have come about as a result of pressures (mentioned in the introduction) which other institutions have also faced. The response of the IMF and the World Bank, however, has had to be different and in a way more attentive because of the special position they enjoy in the world economy (as distinct from the G-7, G-3 or Bank for International Settlements). The Bretton Woods institutions are the only international financial institutions that have a universal membership and accountability to governments across the world. This special character is reflected in the structures of both institutions. To quote the former General Counsel of the Fund: "The principle implicit in the operation of the Fund is not only that the membership should be involved in the process of taking the decisions of the Fund but also that, to the maximum extent possible, the full membership should be involved". Alternative arrangements, he argues using examples, "that did not reflect the full membership of the Fund might not command the same confidence" (Gold, 1972, pp. 173-174).

At the core of membership arrangements in the Bank and Fund are quotas which set out drawing limits (in the Fund), the contributions or subscriptions of members, and their voting powers. Even where formal voting is not used to make decisions, formal powers have an underlying force of which all participants in meetings are aware; typically, a Board secretary will keep a running tally of votes on any particular decision which assists the chairman in formulating the "sense of the meeting". Votes also count in organizations as important symbols of status and commitment (Ogata, 1989). One board member of the Fund has referred to votes as a "badge of nationhood" (Clark, 1996, p. 23).

The debate about reforming the voting structures of the Fund and Bank has therefore never been just one between creditors wanting to limit their contributions and borrowers keen to extend their access to resources. Nor is it simply a scramble by members wishing to enhance their relative power, although certainly there is "a keen awareness [of members] that any significant change in the quota structure might affect their proportionate influence over the Fund's decision-taking and their ranking vis-à-vis other members" (Lister, 1984, p. 77). This point was underscored by British and French attempts to block Japan from increasing its Fund quota, the former fearing that it would fall from second to fifth position, and the latter refusing to be ranked lower than the United Kingdom (Rapkin and Strand, 1996). The debate on quotas is also one about the identity of the institutions and the legitimacy of their decisions and actions.

From the outset, the voting structure, including basic votes, of both the Fund and Bank was a core part of their identities as *universal* and *public* organizations. An equal number of "basic votes" (250) was allocated to every member.[7] As Joseph Gold explains: "The authors of the plans for the Fund and the negotiators felt that the bold step of weighting the voting power of members in a major international organization according to quotas, which in the main reflected economic and financial factors, should be combined with the political consideration of the traditional equality of States in international law. The basic votes were to serve the function of recognizing the doctrine of the equality of States. In addition, they were intended to avoid too close an adherence to the concept of a private business corporation" (Gold, 1972, p. 18). In a similar spirit, in 1955, when the quotas of small developing countries looked too small, the Fund decided to double their quotas and to set up a minimum quota, dubbed the "small quota policy". In 1963, there was a further revision of the quotas of the small countries (Lister, 1984, p. 56). Here we see in the establishment of the Fund a direct trade-off between the principles of effectiveness and equality, as discussed in section III.B.

However, the steps taken to ensure "universality" and "equality" in the IMF and the World Bank have since been significantly eroded. The small quota policies were adjusted back in the second half of the 1960s, when many very small countries applied for membership. The proportion of "basic votes" to total votes has diminished dramatically in the intervening years. While in 1946 basic votes in the IMF accounted for 11.3 per cent of total votes (Lister, 1984, p. 40), rising to a high of 14 per cent in 1955, 40 years later the proportion had slipped to around 3 per cent in both the Fund and the Bank. Following logically from the reasoning employed when the institutions were created, this erosion detracts from their universality as well as from the incentive for all members, both large and small, to participate fully in the work of the organizations.

The dominant voting structure in the organizations today is quota-based. Non-basic votes are allocated to each of the members of the Fund on the basis of quotas calculated using formulae which are supposed to reflect the relative economic strength of members. World Bank capital subscriptions roughly parallel these quotas, with some differences owing to the different weightings given to some variables, and the Bank's separate negotiations on capital increases. As mentioned above, quotas determine not only members' votes but also their level of contribution to resources and (in the Fund) their access to them.

While general reviews of quotas take place at intervals of not more than five years, adjustments of particular quotas may be made at any time (see Articles III [1] and [2]). The original formulae used to determine Fund quotas were drawn up in the United States in 1943 and were nominally based on measurements of national income, foreign reserves and international trade. However, political calculations played a very heavy role, as Raymond Mikesell, the man given the task of estimating the first quotas, describes: "White called me to his office and asked that I prepare a formula for the ... quotas that would be based on the members' gold and dollar holdings, national incomes, and foreign trade. He gave no instructions on the weights to be used, but I was to give the United States a quota of approximately $2.9 billion; the United Kingdom (including its colonies) about half the United States quota; the Soviet Union an amount just under that of the United Kingdom; and China somewhat less. White's major concern was that our military allies (President Roosevelt's Big Four) should have the largest quotas, with a ranking on which the President and the Secretary of State had agreed" (Mikesell, 1994).

The adjustment of quotas is just as political today as it was in 1943, and many commentators argue that it has not adequately reflected shifts in world economic power (see the reviews by Rapkin and Strand, 1996; and Buira, 1996). Of course, technical alterations in the formulae have been made. For example, in the Fund the growth of a country's trade was included in 1959; in 1964 the formulae were broadened and used to calculate a quota range; and in the 1975 Quota Review economies were categorized (for the purpose of quota determination) into four groups: industrial, more developed primary producers, oil-exporters and developing countries (Lister, 1984; Gold, 1977). The most important changes in quotas, however, have come about as the result of fierce and political negotiations. The means by which Japan increased its quota in the IBRD (Ogata, 1989) and subsequently in the IMF (Rapkin and Strand, 1996) offer good examples.

In the case of both the IMF and the World Bank, Japan wanted to increase its quota and had to overcome the objections of other States which were concerned that an increase in Japan's standing would necessarily entail a decrease in their own standing. Underpinning the Japanese strategy for increased representation in the World Bank was a strong feeling that the Bank's procedures for altering quotas was (and is) unfair. Ogata reports that the Japanese financial authorities working to increase their share likened their job to "the struggle over the revision of the unequal treaties in the Meiji period. To them it was a fight for the principle of equality that contributions brought recognition regardless of the donor" (Ogata, 1989).

Other groups today also argue that their representation in the Fund and the Bank is unfair. One complaint is that large and populous economies are left underrepresented by the existing calculations of quotas. A comparison is made between such countries as Brazil (1.47 per cent), Spain (1.32 per cent) and Mexico (1.19 per cent), and small economies such as Belgium (2.10 per cent), the Netherlands (2.33 per cent) and Switzerland (1.68 per cent) (Buira, 1996). To mitigate this problem a different basis for calculating quotas has been proposed: employing purchasing power parity (PPP) rates rather than official exchange rates in the measurement of GDP (Patel, 1996).

The adoption of PPP rates would not require a radical shift in analysis within the Bank or the Fund as both institutions have been using these rates in their analytical work for some time, the Fund, for example, in preparing its *World Economic Outlook* (May 1993) and the World Bank in preparing the *World Development Report* (1993). However, PPP calculations alter dramatically the picture of countries' proportions of world GDP: one Fund official has calculated that PPP values double developing countries' share (Wagner, 1995). If used in quota calculations, such values would significantly transform the distribution of contributions and votes among members. Indeed, developing countries have consistently called for comprehensive reviews of the economic criteria used in determining quotas (see G-24 Communiqué, in *IMF Survey*, 14 October 1996). However, there are yet more fundamental issues at stake here of which the issue of PPP calculations is just a symptom.

The criticisms discussed highlight the extent to which the institutions' "transformation rules" are vulnerable to the charge that they are not "sure", transparent or universally perceived as procedurally fair. Overall, the institutions' arrangements for change are highly politicized. One analyst describes the rules as applied both in the past and in the present: "the old formula was used when it could be used and set aside when its use produced embarrassing results", and "without any change of indicators, it would be easy, by small changes in weights, formulas and relationships between basic and weighted votes, to reflect any desired balance of influence among member States" (Lister, 1984, pp. 53 and 76). An awareness of the political bias behind the results of quota

calculations has "probably weakened the standing of the formula as an 'impartial' instrument for determining what a country's quota should be" (Lister, 1984, p. 48).

The Fund and Bank need rules of transformation which both bolster their identities as universal organizations and properly mirror the stakes and interests of their different members. Still more pertinent questions of governance are posed concerning the process whereby quotas and capital shares are altered: What kind of balance should quotas reflect? Which stakeholders should be represented and to what degree? How should the interests and stakes be represented of those who contribute the most, and of those most affected by the institution?

There is ambiguity in the present structure of representation. At its core it straddles an attempt to reflect economic weight, at the same time as an outdated configuration of political power and prestige in the world arena. Overlaid on these considerations are various political ones. It has been argued, for instance, that the shares of Japan and Germany in the IMF were suppressed in the late 1970s as a penalty for inadequate efforts to reduce their balance-of-payments surpluses (James, 1996, p. 601). Overall, the structure of quotas and shares is at best ambiguous and lacks a clear sense of whom the institutions represent and why. More critically, the structure is unfair in the sense that it cannot be justified in terms of the defined standards (economic or political) supposedly used as criteria.

Let us first consider the role of contributors within the institutions, an issue much debated when the institutions were established (Gianaris, 1991). On the one hand, as financial institutions, both the Fund and the Bank need some mechanism of restraint to ensure that resources are properly used and to assure the confidence of contributors. In this regard, commentators highlight not only the weakness of the regional development banks discussed above, but also the failure of the United Nations Capital Development Fund, set up by the United Nations General Assembly in 1966, attributing it to the fact that insufficient voting weight was given to the contributors. However, one also has to take into account the fact (in respect of the Bank and Fund) that several States have sought to *pay more* as well as to have *more voice*. Not all States have been permitted the level of quota they wanted: Australia, France, India and Iran, for example, insisted at the outset on recording their complaint of an inadequate quota (Lister, 1984, p. 51).

The Fund and Bank should rightly be concerned about adequately representing major contributors in their decision-making processes. However, levels of contributions do not depend upon members' choices; they depend upon the constitutional rules of each organization, as well as the rules which guide any changes in membership. We have already seen that in the case of the IMF and the World Bank these rules are flawed: quota calculations are not perceived as impartial or principled; rather, they reflect (and are seen to reflect) political compromises. For this reason, the question of contributors' rights can only be answered once clear and fair contribution rules have been established. On this basis one could then identify those types of decision on which contributors should have the most influence.

A second core issue of governance concerns the extent to which the mandates of the international financial institutions have altered in response to changes in the world economy (as mentioned in the introduction to this paper). Both the Fund and the Bank were originally fashioned explicitly to protect the sovereignty of member States and those who would draw on either organization's resources. As James (1996, p. 28) puts it: "The IMF's Articles of Agreement very deliberately protected national sovereignty and allowed States to formulate for themselves their own economic and political interests". Yet today the Fund exercises policy leverage through the use of its financial resources and transactions. The Bank, originally conceived as a vehicle for post-war reconstruction, is now also involved (since 1979) in policy-based conditional lending. These new mandates pose two new concerns for the organizations: how they can most effectively achieve their goals, and how they can reconcile their mandate with respect for members' sovereignty.

Both institutions have already found that to ensure agreement and implementation of "appropriate" policies, they need to elicit a very high level of cooperation and participation of governments as well as other groups within member countries. Hence, for the sake of efficiency as well as for reasons of principle, the institutions are embracing standards of good governance.[8] Yet, these standards have to be fully applied to policy-making within the IMF and the World Bank. In the first place, developing countries that are stakeholders of a new kind - not just as interest-paying borrowers but as parties whose co-operation is necessary for the institutions to achieve their purposes - should be better represented. Yet their voice has slipped, together with basic votes, and is underrepresented by GDP calculations, which do not take account of purchasing power. Furthermore, in the formulation of both general and specific policy decisions affecting them, developing countries should be major participants, yet they remain minority actors - both in the processes of formulating policy and in decision-making.

Here it is worth distinguishing decisions on general policy from those on specific operational matters. In the IMF and the World Bank both kinds of decision are made by the Board. Yet while general policy may well be most appropriately decided by the Board on the basis of the formal voting structure, this process is probably not the most appropriate for specific operational decisions. In making operational decisions, the highly political nature of decision-making by the Board - the compromises and trade-offs which underpin its decisions - is probably a hindrance to sound and consistent policy. This point was made some time ago in the Commonwealth Study Group's report (Helleiner, 1983), which suggested that "although weighted voting may be relevant when it comes to basic policy (size of quotas, SDR allocations, etc.), it has little relevance when deciding what are the appropriate policies for a country to follow in a particular situation". The group proposed that a better alternative would be a "self-denying ordinance simply to debate, discuss and advocate when conditionality in adjustment programmes is under consideration", a move which they argued "would do much to reduce political heat and bring the whole conditionality question back on to a mutually more responsive and constructive track" (Helleiner, 1983). The case for rethinking how operational decisions are made has not diminished since 1984. Indeed, in the ensuing decade "good governance" has taken a major place on the agenda of both institutions, providing both pragmatic and principled reasons for rethinking.

A further issue of decision-making which demands attention is the use of special majorities in the IMF. Originally there were very few categories of decision for which special majorities applied in the Fund. However, decisions taken in 1969 and 1978 increased the number of categories from 9 to 64 (Lister, 1984). The United States has since then successfully argued for a requirement of 85 per cent so as to ensure that it can exercise a veto over decisions, not just to adopt decisions to adjust quotas, establish a council, or allocate SDRs (see Art III.2.c), but also since 1977 over all "political" decisions (Gold, 1977). Yet another category of decisions requires a special majority of 70 per cent (Gold, 1996). The problem the Fund faces is one of incoherence in decision-making rules or, to quote Lister, "a lack of any strictly logical basis for determining which decisions should require a special majority" (Lister, 1984, p. 95).

Up to the present, the expansion of special majorities has been a *quid pro quo* in negotiations, and a way of off-setting declines in relative power in the organizations. When Japan increased its voting share in the IBRD (an increase which would reduce the relative power of the United States), special majorities provided a way to offset the United States loss of relative power (Ogata, 1989). Likewise in the IMF, the special majority required to adopt quota adjustments, to allocate further SDRs, and such like was raised to 85 per cent. The problem of special majorities is that they not only divert the accountability of the organization away from its broader membership but also from its other major contributors. There is surely a better way to enhance the voice of groups with a good case.

An alternative to the ad hoc re-adjustment of special majorities would be to introduce a form of double majority - such as those discussed above (in respect of the European Union and the Global Environment Facility). Double-majority voting in the Fund or the Bank could ensure that different stakeholders' claims are appropriately respected, including contributors without whom the institutions could not function and borrowers whose cooperation and participation is required to enable the institutions to achieve their objectives.

The argument against such a double-majority voting scheme is that it would make decision-making unwieldy and unworkable. Yet, it would not, in itself, alter the practice whereby votes on the Boards of both institutions are virtually never taken, both operating most of the time by consensus.[9] Undoubtedly, any form of double-majority voting would complicate the job of the Board secretary in keeping a tally of hypothetical votes. However, it is a clearer way to effect the changes in accountability and participation for which special majorities have been used and it might also improve the impartial and fair standing of the institutions' decision-making rules.

This brings us to the issue of consensus decision-making within the institutions. It has been said by some that the practice of consensus has diminished irritation over discrepancies in voting power (Southard, 1979). Others have argued that consensus ensures that the G-7 do not simply take all the decisions; rather, it permits developing countries to air their views and win arguments on the merits

(Bichsel, 1994, pp. 147-150). Yet, as we saw in the case of other international institutions, voting power is not suppressed by consensus decision-making. As Lister writes, "ultimately, the 'sense of the meeting' cannot but be reflective of the respective voting powers of those who favour and those who oppose a given proposal" and "voting power does determine each member's influence in each decision. The fact that this structure does not have to be externalized in formal voting on most occasions testified to its strength, not to its unimportance" (Lister, 1984, p. 108). Further to this, referring to a point made earlier in the paper: to "win on the merits" takes a lot of time and a lot of preparation, and for this reason the key to participation and influence in discussions is resources and high calibre staff. In many institutions, as we have seen, developing countries simply do not have the necessary institutional infrastructure and are "overwhelmed" by other better-resourced delegations.

Even though consensus is seen by some as a way to "open up" discussions, this is not its only effect. We found in the experiences of other organizations, such as the United Nations Security Council and the GATT/WTO, that consensus decision-making can reduce transparency and accountability within an organization. This is equally true in both the Fund and the Bank, where some argue that consensus simply masks United States dominance (on the IMF, see Kahler, 1990, and Southard, 1979). To counter such criticism, the Fund and the Bank have an interest in making their procedures transparent and accountable, and in examining where and how consensus adds to or detracts from these standards.

In some cases consensus is probably required for effectiveness; this is probably true of some kinds of general policy decisions which commit members to overall levels of contribution and of the parameters within which operations are undertaken. However, in the case of more specific and operational decisions, voting is a much more effective way to ensure accountability and transparency, since it records openly the support of or rejection by members of particular measures, and thus also gives some record of particular political or interest-based objections.

Thus far we have been discussing the membership and voting structure of the Boards of the Fund and the World Bank, while neglecting the role played in decision-making by the staff of each organization. The staff is crucial not only because they advise the Boards on the kinds of decision discussed above, but also because they make influential declaratory statements as to what types of policy are necessary and desirable in order to further development and economic stability in countries across the world, as expressed in their publications and by the heads of the organizations (the President of the World Bank and the Managing Director of the IMF). As such, the "culture" and predilections of the staff of each institution strongly influence the way they function (Clark, 1996).

The Fund and the Bank have very high calibre staff, which adds much to their prestige and standing. But, if principles of good governance are to be applied, we need also to ask whether the staff reflect the wide-ranging membership of the Fund and Bank, not just in terms of nationality but in terms of primary concerns, approach and outlook. In other words, just how "universal" and "participatory" are the institutions in their research and publications?

We saw earlier in this paper that each institution has accepted (for reasons of effectiveness) that programmes need to be designed with a high level of participation by those who are affected by them. This insight does not yet seem to have been reflected in staffing decisions within the institutions. What the figures show is an enormous homogeneity in the intellectual background of the staff. A study of the IMF shows that some 90 per cent of professionals with Ph.D.'s received them from universities in the United States or Canada (Clark, 1996, p. 9). Similarly, in the World Bank a 1991 study of the high-level staff in the Policy, Research and External Affairs Departments showed that some 80 per cent had been trained in economic and finance at institutions in the United States and the United Kingdom (Stern and Ferreira, 1993).

The notion of a broader range of staff poses a significant challenge to both institutions, which give pride of place to tight intellectual discipline (although comparing the Bank and the Fund, Professor Arnold Harberger has suggested that the Bank is "something like a travelling seminar", while the Fund operates more like a commercial bank with a "single corporate line in dealing with the outside world" - Clark, 1996, p. 25). Yet, if we follow the logic of the Bank's and Fund's publications on good governance, "participation for effectiveness" must start right back at the stage of defining the research agenda and policy parameters of the organizations. Recall from section II the complaint made by Bank staff that "participation" has too often meant explaining a project to a key stakeholder rather than having the stakeholder start and define the project. This same complaint must surely apply to the research of both Bretton Woods institutions. In their declaratory work, the Fund and the Bank need to reflect and underline more clearly the "universality" of their membership and therefore of their research.

V.   The case for reform in the Bretton Woods institutions

A first response to the argument for reforming the IMF and the World Bank might well be "don't fix it if it ain't broke". However, these institutions, while not "broke", have recognized that they need to refashion their modes of operation so as to fulfil more effectively mandates which are dramatically different from those envisaged when they were created. For the effectiveness of their work, each has come to accept the notion of good governance in the countries for which they work, and the need for local participation and widespread political support in order for economic reforms to be sustainable. But the institutions have been to slow to absorb what these principles mean for their own operations and for the trade-off between legitimacy and effectiveness which characterizes their decision-making processes.

The preceding section has opened up a number of specific problems which point to directions for reform. In the first place, the constitutional rules of the institutions need reinterpreting, specifically to ensure that membership and membership rights underline and reinforce the universal character and identity of the organizations. The IMF and the World Bank are not the only international institutions which regulate activities in the global economy. Others include the Bank for International Settlements (BIS), the G-7 and the WTO. Yet what sets the IMF and the World Bank apart (at least from the BIS and the G-7) is their universality and claim to represent nearly all countries in the world. At present this character is diminished by the erosion of basic votes, which are a symbol of equality within the organization, as well as by the methods used to calculate quotas (see table for a comparison of voting arrangements in different international organizations). The special character and legitimacy of the institutions is also diminished by the very slow way the institutions have adapted to a new climate of democracy and good governance. Others are adapting faster: the G-7 has permitted the international financial institutions to attend its summits; the BIS has begun expanding its membership; the WTO has begun life with equal membership (one country, one vote). The Fund and the Bank are still among the most international of organizations but

VOTING SHARES OF DEVELOPING COUNTRIES IN INTERNATIONAL ORGANIZATIONS [a]

(Per cent)

Institution	Developing and transitional countries' share of overall votes	Basic or membership votes (as a share of total votes)	Developing and transitional countries' share of basic votes
United Nations General Assembly	83	100	(as for total votes)
GEF	83[b]	100	-
World Trade Organization	76[b]	100	-
African Development Bank	67	None	-
African Development Fund	*53*		-
IFAD	66[c]	Category I: 17.5 Category II: 25 Category III: 100	-
Inter-American Development Bank	52	0.1	59
Asian Development Bank	40	20	62
IBRD	39	3	84
IDA	*39*	*0.8*	*83*
IMF[d]	38	3	83

Source: African Development Bank, *Annual Report 1993*; Inter-American Development Bank, *Annual Report 1995*; Asian Development Bank, *Annual Report 1995* and *web site*; World Bank, *Annual Report 1994*; IMF, *Annual Report 1995*.

a It is difficult to give precise comparable figures as the category of "developing countries" can be aggregated on a number of different measures. For the purposes of this table, unless otherwise specified, the category "developing countries" includes all those countries not defined as "developed countries" in the *World Development Report 1996*.

b Excluding Mexico (now an OECD country).

c Categories II (12 petroleum-exporting countries) and III (126 developing countries).

d Based on a membership of 175, i.e. excluding Brunei Darussalam (joined October 1995), Sudan and Zaire (suspended after June 1994), Somalia and South Africa (neither of which participated in the 1994 election of executive directors).

they need to reaffirm and to modernize their universal character. A revival of basic votes and a redrawing of the rules for allocating quotas is an obvious way to achieve this. These changes by themselves, however, will not translate automatically into better governance within the institutions.

A second problem in the IMF and the World Bank is that they need to balance more clearly stakeholders' rights within the organization: the rights of contributors (based on clearly defined rules as to who contributes what); and the rights of borrowers whose cooperation is required for the institutions to do their job. This balancing may well require a revitalization of basic votes, a rewriting of quotas, or at least a reapplication of quota formulae. The efficacy of any such alteration, however, will also depend upon decision-making rules and procedures.

In the preceding section, a number of criticisms of decision-making rules and practices were raised. The Fund and the Bank make at least three kinds of decisions: general policies, specific operational decisions and declaratory statements. The first two kinds of decision are taken by the Board of each organization and structured by the distribution of votes on it. Yet, there is no compelling reason why specific operational decisions should be taken in this way. Indeed, the experience of the regional development banks highlights the extent to which Board politics and trade-offs can lead to poor operational decisions. The distribution of votes on the Board should take into account concerns about representation and the participation of stakeholders. The Board would then be well placed to take general policy decisions. However, it does not follow that the same structure should underpin operational decisions. Here the new wisdom about good governance, participation and accountability should apply. This has a number of practical implications.

The practice of consensus decision-making may well be appropriate to general policies but it should not be applied to specific operational decisions. In preceding sections we have seen that consensus gives rise to decision-making which is seldom transparent and for which accountability is strictly limited: proceedings and voting are unrecorded, as are discussions prior to decisions. These strictures may well be less important in formulating general policy; however, given that operational decisions have a direct impact on particular countries and groups within countries, they should be made in as transparent and accountable a way as possible. This necessitates voting on operational decisions, with a voting structure which ensures participation, as required by standards of good governance.

Where special majorities exist for certain categories of decision, they should be part of a rational and well-defined set of decision-making rules. The rationale for a special majority requirement must be clear since it empowers large vote-holders with a capacity to block particular actions. In turn, this gives such vote-holders significant power to influence proposals before they are placed before the Board. If what is required is a special degree of accountability, then double majorities are probably a clearer, less partial remedy than special majorities.

Finally, important to the roles of the IMF and the World Bank is their capacity to make influential declaratory statements. The status of such statements reflects the reputation of both institutions as research

centres of excellence and as institutions which represent and research issues across the world from an international perspective. The staffing of the organizations, however, is not (and is not perceived as) representative of the different approaches and traditions of its member States.

Both the Fund and the Bank have moved positively towards enhancing the participation of member countries in which they work. There is now a strong case for precipitating and extending this trend to operations within the organizations, both in order to enhance good governance and to devolve responsibility for programmes upon developing and transitional countries as a group. Participation, it must be remembered, is a two-way street: more participation means more "ownership" of policies and, for affected members, less capacity to cast responsibility for programmes back on major contributors or the institutions themselves.

A change in the voting structures of the Fund and Bank may well seem like a panacea for the problems of governance which has grown out of their changing roles. Symbolically, a redistribution of votes would instantly alter the representativeness and accountability of these organizations. This paper has argued, however, that such a change (even if politically feasible) would not be sufficient to achieve the aims of good governance. For member States, greater ownership will require institutional resources and a commitment to participate fully and effectively in major policy decisions. For the institutions, the challenge is to reshape their practices so as to underline - through changes in staffing, voting rules and decision-making rules - their "universal" character, upon which rests their claim to a unique position in managing and advising countries throughout the world economy.

VI. Conclusions

This paper has argued that there are both practical and principled reasons for improving the standards of "good governance" within international organizations. If the IMF and the World Bank are to achieve the standard of good governance they themselves have defined for borrowing members, some reform of the constitutional rules, as well as of the decision-making procedures and practices within both institutions, is required. More specifically, in order to enhance their own accountability, transparency and members' participation, the institutions need to consider: redrawing quotas; revitalizing basic votes; ensuring that operational decisions are made in an open and recorded way (i.e. not by the practice of consensus on the Board); ensuring that clear and impartial rules govern the use of special majorities; and introducing double majorities where particular stakes or stakeholders need safeguarding. Also the staff within each organization needs to represent better the range of views of the membership, since participation requires not just "better explanations" but the full involvement of the membership in the definition of problems (and solutions) that the institutions need to address. At present the institutions are vulnerable to the critique that, rather than offering a genuinely "universal" approach to problems and solutions of economic policy, they reflect a narrow, predominantly Anglo-Saxon view. At the same time, increased participation places a heavier burden on groups such as developing countries to "come up with the goods". This means concentrating and deploying research and lobbying resources more efficiently in order to make a case for policies within the institutions.

Notes

1   The term "institutions" is used throughout this paper to refer to international organizations such as the IMF and the World Bank rather than to its more specialized meaning used by other political scientists and economists, i.e. "the rules of the game in a society, or, more formally, ... the humanly devised constraints that shape human interaction". On institutions defined in this way, see North (1990) and Keohane (1989).
2   In this paragraph I draw on the work of Young (1992). However, his own analysis concerns the effectiveness not of international organizations but of institutions, as defined in note 1.
3   A very large number of countries without membership held various types of "observer status". Other countries, with absolutely no membership in 1994, included: Angola, Benin, Botswana, Burkina Faso, Burundi, Chad, Cyprus, Fiji, Gambia, Grenada, Guinea-Bissau, Haiti, Honduras, Kenya, Lesotho, Liechtenstein, Malawi, Maldives, Mali, Mauritius, Mozambique, Namibia, Niger, Rwanda, Qatar, Saint Christopher and Nevis, Sierra Leone, Swaziland, Togo, Uganda, United Arab Emirates, and Yugoslavia.
4   See the figures in *Financial Times*, 22 June 1994.
5   The Philip Morris Institute (PMI, 1996) has calculated that Luxembourg enjoys a 31:1 ratio of nationals on the staff of the Commission to population, and Belgium 10:1, while Germany has 1:3 and the United Kingdom and France 1:2.
6   Articles 198a-198c of the Maastricht Treaty created a Committee of the Regions which the Council and Commission must consult in certain cases, and Article 146 now permits heads of regions to sit in the Council. The experience of the GEF (discussed below) also offers an example of how representation might be opened up

within constituent groups, such as when Indonesia (a Council member at the time) permitted members of its group (like the Pacific Islands) who would be particularly affected by climate change to speak when the issue arose. By contrast, in the United Nations Security Council, permanent members such as the United Kingdom and France (who, it must be said, do not formally represent any other countries) have made it clear that they will not use their position to represent "Europe" or other European States.
7   Although the issue of basic votes in the World Bank was not resolved until a few days before the end of the Bretton Woods Conference, since some delegations claimed that voting power should be determined exclusively by shareholding as it was in other banks and commercial enterprises (Gianaris, 1991, p. 919).
8   A recent extension of the argument for democracy is that non-State actors and sub-State groups should enjoy some form of representation within the institutions (Gerster, 1993, p. 127). However, in the IMF several Executive Directors have made it clear that they would not see the direct inclusion of NGOs as a way to enhance the legitimacy of the institution (Bichsel, 1994). Their argument is that NGOs are not in themselves necessarily democratic or accountable, and that the institution does (and should) represent governments. However, many countries' governments are not fully representative or accountable and NGOs provide an imperfect remedy. Recognition of this explains the support within both the IMF and the World Bank for responding to the demands of NGOs by alterations in decision-making procedures such as those taken by the World Bank, in creating an inspection panel, and through new standards of transparency permitting NGOs to monitor their work more closely and to assist affected individuals in bringing claims.
9   This is embodied in Rule C-10 of the IMF's Rules and Regulations: "The Chairman will ordinarily ascertain the sense of the meeting in lieu of a formal vote. Any Executive Director may require a formal vote to be taken with votes cast as prescribed in Article XII, Section 3(i)" (Gold, 1972, p. 197). Consensus decision-making was envisioned right from the start. In 1943 John Maynard Keynes wrote in a note to Jacob Viner: "in actual working voting power is not likely to prove important. If the organization begins voting about everything, it will not be long before it breaks down" (Gianaris, 1991, p. 920).

References

AfDB (1994), *The Question for Quality: Report of the Task Force on Project Quality for the African Development Bank* (Abidjan: African Development Bank).
BERTRAND, M. (1985), "Some Reflections on Reform of the United Nations", *JIU/REP/85/9* (Geneva: United Nations).
BICHSEL, A. (1994), "The World Bank and the International Monetary Fund from the Perspective of the Executive Directors from Developing Countries", *Journal of World Trade*, Vol. 28, pp. 141-167.
BOUTROS-GHALI, B. (1995), "Democracy: A newly recognized imperative", *Global Governance*, Vol. 1, pp. 3-11.
BROMS, B. (1959), *The Doctrine of Equality of States as Applied in International Organizations*, doctoral dissertation (Helsinki).

BUIRA, A. (1996), "The Governance of the International Monetary Fund", in R. Culpeper and C. Pestieau (eds.), *Development and Global Governance* (Ottawa: International Development Research Centre and North-South Institute).

CARON, D. (1993), "The Legitimacy of the Collective Authority of the Security Council", *American Journal of International Law*, Vol. 87, pp. 552-588.

CLARK, I.D. (1996), "Should the IMF Become More Adaptive?", *IMF Working Paper WP/96/17* (Washington, D.C.).

COMMISSION OF THE EUROPEAN UNION (1995), *Report by the Council and the Commission to the Reflection Group* (Brussels).

COMMISSION OF THE EUROPEAN UNION (1996), *Commission Opinion: Reinforcing Political Union and Preparing for Enlargement* (Brussels).

COMMISSION ON GLOBAL GOVERNANCE (1995), *Our Global Neighbourhood* (Oxford: Oxford University Press).

ENGLISH, E.P., and H.M. MULE (1996), *The African Development Bank* (Boulder, CO: Lynne Rienner).

GERSTER, R. (1993), "Proposals for Voting Reform within the International Monetary Fund", *Journal of World Trade*, Vol. 27, pp. 121-136.

GIANARIS, W.N. (1991), "Weighted Voting in the International Monetary Fund and the World Bank", *Fordham International Law Journal*, Vol. 14, pp. 910-945.

GOLD, J. (1972), *Voting and Decisions in the International Monetary Fund* (Washington, D.C.: IMF).

GOLD, J. (1977), "Voting Majorities in the Fund: Effects of the second amendment of the articles, *IMF Pamphlet Series* (Washington, D.C.: IMF).

GOLD, J. (1996), *Interpretation: The IMF and International Law* (Boston: Kluwer Law International).

HELD, D. (1995), "Democracy and the New International Order", in A. Daniele and D. Held (eds.), *Cosmopolitan Democracy: An Agenda for a New World Order* (London: Polity Press).

HELLEINER, G.K. (Report by Commonwealth Study Group) (1983), *Towards a New Bretton Woods: Challenges for the World Financial and Trading System* (London: Commonwealth Secretariat).

HOSLI, M. (1995), "The Balance Between Small and Large: Effects of a double-majority system of voting power in the European Union", *International Studies Quarterly*, Vol. 39, pp. 351-370.

IDB (1993), *Managing for Effective Development* (Washington, D.C.: Inter-American Development Bank).

JAMES, H. (1996), "The IMF in Competition with other International Institutions", paper presented at ISA Conference, San Diego, 16-20 April.

KAHLER, M. (1990), "The United States and the International Monetary Fund: Declining influence or declining interest?", in M. Karns and K. Mingst (eds.), *The United States and Multilateral Institutions: Patterns of Changing Instrumentality and Influence* (London: Routledge).

KAPUR, D. (1997), "The New Conditionalities of the International Financial Institutions", in UNCTAD, *International Monetary and Financial Issues for the 1990s*, Vol. VIII (United Nations publication, Sales No. E.97.II.D.5) (New York and Geneva: United Nations).

KEOHANE, R. (1989), *International Institutions and State Power: Essays in International Relations Theory* (Boulder, CO: Westview Press).

LISTER, F.K. (1984), *Decision-Making Strategies for International Organizations: The IMF Model*, Vol. 20, Book 4 (Denver, CO: Graduate School of International Studies, University of Denver).

LYONS, G.M. (1995), "Competing Visions: Proposals for UN Reform", in C. Alger et al. (eds.), *The United Nations System: The Policies of Member States* (Tokyo: United Nations University Press).

MAYALL, J. (ed.) (1996), *The New Interventionism 1991-1994: United Nations Experience in Cambodia, Former Yugoslavia and Somalia* (Cambridge: Cambridge University Press).

MIKESELL, R.F. (1994), "The Bretton Woods Debates: A memoir", *Essays in International Finance No. 192* (Princeton: Princeton University, Department of Economics).

NORTH, D.C. (1990), *Institutions, Institutional Change and Economic Performance* (New York: Cambridge University Press).

OGATA, S. (1989), "Shifting Power Relations in Multilateral Development Banks", *Journal of International Studies*, Vol. 22.

PATEL I.G. (1996), "Some Thoughts on Our Present Discontents", in R. Culpeper and C. Pestieau (eds.), *Development and Global Governance* (Ottawa: International Development Research Centre and the North-South Institute).

PICIOTTO, R., and R. WEAVING (1994), "A New Project Cycle for the World Bank?", *Finance and Development*, Vol. 31, No. 4 (December).

PMI (1996), *In a Larger EU, Can All Member States be Equal?* (Brussels: Philip Morris Institute for Public Policy Research).

RAPKIN, D., and J. STRAND (1996), "US-Japan Leadership Sharing in the IMF and the World Bank", paper presented at ISA Conference, San Diego, 16-20 April.

RIVLIN, B. (1996), "UN Reform from the Standpoint of the United States", *UN University Lectures*, No. 11 (Tokyo: The United Nations University).

SENDER, H. (1993), "More for Less: The Asian Development Bank is coming under increasing pressure to improve its performance: American's opposition to a capital increase sets it in direct conflict with Japan", *Far Eastern Economic Review*, 20 May.

SJOEBERG, H. (1994), "From Idea to Reality: The creation of the Global Environment Facility", *UNDP/UNEP/Working Paper*, No. 10.

SOUTHARD, F.A. (1979), "The Evolution of the International Monetary Fund", *Essays in International Finance*, No. 135 (Princeton: Dept. of Economics, Princeton University).

STERN, N., and F. FERREIRA (1993), "The World Bank as Intellectual Actor", *Development Economics Research Programme Discussion Paper DEP/50* (London: STICERD, London School of Economics).

STEVENS, M., and S. GNANASELVAM (1995), "The World Bank and Governance", *IDS Bulletin*, No. 26, pp. 97-105.

STEWART, F., and S. DAWS (1996), "Global Challenges: The case for a United Nations Economic and Social Security Council", *Viewpoint*, No. 10 (London: Christian Aid), January.

TUSSIE, D. (1995), *The Inter-American Development Bank* (Boulder, CO: Lynne Rienner).

UL HAQ, M. (1995), *The UN and the Bretton Woods Institutions: New Challenges for the Twenty-first Century* (London: Macmillan).

UNDP (1994), *Human Development Report* (New York: United Nations).

UNDP, UNEP, and WORLD BANK (1994), *Global Environment Facility: Independent Evaluation of the Pilot Phase* (Washington, D.C.: The World Bank).

WAGNER, N. (1995), "A Review of PPP-adjusted GDP Estimation and its Potential Use for the Fund's Operational Purposes", *IMF Working Paper* (Washington, D.C.: IMF).

WATANABE, T. (1977), *Towards a New Asia: Memoirs of the First President of the Asian Development Bank* (Singapore: Times Printers).

WEISS, T., and L. GORDENKER (1996), *NGOs, the UN, and Global Governance* (London: Lynne Rienner).

WOOD, M. (1996), "Security Council: Procedural developments", *International and Comparative Law Quarterly*, No. 45, pp. 150-161.

WORLD BANK (1989), *Sub-Saharan Africa: From Crisis to Sustainable Growth* (Washington, D.C.).

WORLD BANK (1992), *Governance and Development* (Washington, D.C.).

WORLD BANK (1994a), *Governance: The World Bank's Experience* (Washington, D.C.).

WORLD BANK (1994b), *World Development Report 1994 - Infrastructure for Development* (New York: Oxford University Press).

WORLD BANK (1994c), *Report of the Financial Reporting and Auditing Task Force* (Washington, D.C.).

WORLD BANK (1996), *The World Bank Participation Source Book* (Washington, D.C.).

YOUNG, O. (1992), "The Effectiveness of International Institutions: Hard cases and critical variables", in J. Rosenau and E.-O. Cziempel (eds.), *Governance without Government: Order and Change in World Politics* (Cambridge: Cambridge University Press).

YOUNG, O. (1994), *International Governance: Protecting the Environment in a Stateless Society* (Ithaca, NY: Cornell University Press, 1994).

NON-GOVERNMENTAL ORGANIZATIONS AND THE INTERNATIONAL MONETARY AND FINANCIAL SYSTEM

Charles Abugre
Nancy Alexander

Abstract

Globally, the population of non-governmental organizations (NGOs) has exploded. They are increasingly providing humanitarian and social services and advancing specific causes through advocacy. NGO movements are complicated and heterogeneous. It is useful to distinguish between operational and advocacy NGOs. Another important distinction, especially in the North, is that between environment and development NGOs. While the goals and tactics of these types of organizations overlap, they also have highly distinctive characteristics.

This paper describes the nature and the motivations of NGOs, in particular with respect to their activities related to the international financial institutions. Special attention is given to the orientation and motivations of Northern (especially Washington-based) operational and advocacy NGOs. Operational Northern NGOs channel approximately $7.7 billion in annual assistance to developing countries. Approximately 55 per cent of this total represents official grants. On an annual basis, NGOs channel at least 13 per cent of official development assistance. This represents more aid than either the entire United Nations system or the World Bank's International Development Association (IDA) provide.

The interaction between NGOs - especially Northern advocacy NGOs - and the international financial institutions has intensified since the mid-1980s. The paper identifies some considerations that drive analysis and action by these organizations on several issues, especially in relation to the World Bank. Northern NGOs have had some success in influencing the World Bank thanks to their capacity to affect public opinion, shape morally penetrating messages, gain access to their governments and utilize the machinery of power.

Whereas Southern governments are often forced to deal with Northern NGOs and the impact these have on the policies, programmes and projects of the international financial institutions, they often keep the indigenous NGOs at "arms length". Frequently, the relationships of Southern governments with their indigenous NGOs are characterized by rivalry for influence and resources. However, it is frequently in the interests of Southern governments to support their indigenous NGOs in ways that rectify the power imbalance between Northern and Southern NGOs.

The importance of the role of credible Southern NGOs is increasingly being seen, for instance, with respect to the implementation of the Initiative for the Heavily Indebted Poor Countries (HIPCs Initiative), and in regional and international trade and investment negotiations. It is recommended that developing country governments aim at building bridges with NGOs within their own countries and regional bodies. Many studies reveal that enhanced ownership of development activities by governmental and NGO actors and institutions is a key to their success.

Southern governments should also support NGO alliances which advance common development objectives in international, regional and national arenas.

I.   Non-governmental organizations - An overview of the movement

A.   *Definition and typology*

Many scholarly studies have sought to define the nature and activities of the non-governmental organizational world. Yet, precise definitions are elusive. Non-governmental organizations (NGOs) are actors in civil society.[1] They also include labour unions, cooperative societies, political parties, businesses and the media. The OECD Development Assistance Committee (DAC) employed the following definition for civil society:

> Civil society denotes a public space between the State and individual citizens where the latter can develop autonomous, organized and collective activities of the most varied nature (DAC, 1997, p. 7).

An NGO can be a two-person entity or a complex organization with a worldwide reach, and it can be secular or religious. Forms, structure and governance mechanisms differ widely. The common identity of NGOs is a claim to voluntarism, not-for-profit status, solidarity with a constituency, and operations outside the domain of the government. They may be human rights groups, professional research organizations, groups dedicated to promoting democracy and election monitoring, hunger relief organizations, women's groups and environmental campaigns. They may even be involved in quiet diplomacy and conflict resolution.[2] They may or may not include organized community-based groups, depending on the legal and regulatory framework under which they operate.

The NGO movement should not be romanticized. Some of these organizations advocate exclusion, supremacy of some groups over others, and violence. One should exercise care in classifying NGOs by certain criteria, such as:

- their effectiveness in terms of responding to the need of excluded groups for services and empowerment;

- their transnational or indigenous nature;

- operational and/or policy and advocacy-related activities (while operational and advocacy activities tend to be integrated in most regions of the world, United States organizations sometimes segregate these activities);

- the issue-focus (e.g. human rights, children, gender, environment, development or relief);

- type of constitution, as for instance, people's movements, support organizations, intermediary (professional) NGOs, or membership organizations;

- internal decision-making structure (one should ask: do the beneficiaries participate in decision-making? How does the NGO consult with the groups it claims to represent? Does the NGO build local capacity to dialogue while temporarily representing excluded voices?);

- the nature of the NGO membership, where it exists (for example, organizations of peasants, indigenous peoples or of the displaced may set up and register an NGO to provide support services to their members.);

- secular or religious character (religious NGOs may operate as secular bodies but draw the core of their membership and support from their respective church networks).

Among Northern NGOs, distinctions should also be made between those which operate in developing countries and those which tend to partner with, and work through, indigenous NGOs.

There is a small but growing number of NGOs devoted solely to the promotion of social justice and ecological issues by providing development education material to a constituency and mobilizing public opinion around specific issues which may be of local or international interest. Whereas there is little distinction between environment and development orientations among NGOs and the South, this does not hold true in the North. This paper draws sharp distinctions between the campaigning of Northern environment NGOs and Northern development NGOs since 1983, when the movement to reform the international financial institutions began. The environmental movement has been much more successful than the development movement in leveraging reforms (see section IV.A below). The agenda of the Northern environment and development movements has begun to converge in recent years, as evidenced by the Structural Adjustment Participatory Review Initiative Network (SAPRIN) and the "50 Years is Enough" campaign. The advocacy campaigns of the religious networks have also grown considerably.

While the capacity of operational Northern NGOs to leverage change in the international financial institutions has been weak, they dominate in other spheres. They lobby for money and reforms of bilateral agencies, on which they are dependent for resources[3] and, as material assistance providers, they have a high public profile and considerable resources. They may operate in a developing country, providing direct services (as is often the case in Africa) or work through local partner NGOs (as tends to be the case in much of Latin America and Asia). Increasingly, these NGOs incorporate social justice advocacy issues into their agenda.

B.   International reach of NGOs

The number of NGOs with consultative status in the United Nations system has quintupled over 25 years. NGOs engaged in advocacy with the United Nations system are both operational and non-operational in nature. One organization of the latter type, Amnesty International, has a budget larger than that of the United Nations Centre for Human Rights.

Since 1983, the number and type of NGOs relating to the Bretton Woods institutions have mushroomed. While these organizations are difficult to number, we know that some 14,000 transnational NGOs keep current with World Bank and IMF activities through reports of the Inter-Press Service. Increasingly, NGOs serve on government delegations and contribute to the processes which shape official decision-making, hammer out environmental treaties, monitor elections, use the media to mobilize public opinion, protest or promote policies and projects, and deliver services. They wield influence due to a variety of factors, such as size, the quality of analysis, moral stature among important publics, and their ability to achieve results.

The impact of the revolution in information technology on the NGO movement cannot be underestimated. To some extent, information is power. Consequently, access to information technology is accelerating coalition-building by enabling NGOs to share information among multiple nodes and networks and build strategies to achieve specific outcomes. "The most powerful engine of change in the relative decline of states and the rise of non-State actors is the computer and telecommunications revolution, whose deep political and social consequences have been almost completely ignored" (Mathews, 1997, p. 51). Because some regions lack access to information

technology, the existing concentration of power among Northern NGOs is exacerbated (see section II below).

Thousands of NGOs worked with governments to shape the outcome of United Nations Conferences, such as the Earth Summit, the World Summit for Social Development, and the Women's Conference. The preparatory process leading to the United Nations Earth Summit was precedent-setting insofar as it broke down barriers to collaboration between the United Nations and government officials on the one hand and NGOs on the other. It also provided a unique opportunity to construct new type of alliances - traversing traditional NGO boundaries - by bringing together environment, development, social justice, and religious and human rights organizations. This singular event may have been a decisive turning point in the growing movement to reform the international financial institutions.

NGOs are increasingly building coalitions, involving actors from a variety of movements: labour, environment, social justice, religious, community, human rights, media, etc. Section IV.C describes the complex and interlocking networks that have generated tremendous activism on the debt issue. The "50 Years is Enough" campaign also embraces many coalitions. Aimed at reforming the World Bank and the IMF, the campaign is comprised of over 200 groups in the United States and over 180 internationally. Their campaigns have become highly adept at working with the media to educate, mobilize and persuade. NGOs were able to influence the evolution of the HIPC Initiative through strategies which, among other things, involved simultaneous media work in many countries.

Many NGOs closely monitor and influence the various intergovernmental bodies established to follow up on the key United Nations conferences. The NGO movement to influence trade and investment regimes is growing rapidly in many developed countries[4] and environmental NGOs from the North and the South participate in the Global Environment Facility, the Montreal Protocol on Greenhouse Gases, the Biotech and Biosafety Protocols, etc. Such NGOs may carry more institutional memory of these events than some developing country governments. They generally have ready access to more information and invest quite heavily in preparing their positions. As a result, governments have often found NGO briefing sessions quite useful. G-77 governments consult some Southern NGOs on strategies and negotiating positions, and may even involve them in drafting official negotiating positions and background papers.

Often in collaboration with the South Centre, UNCTAD holds periodic consultations with select groups of NGOs, which have research and publications capability on relevant issues, including trade, finance and the environment. UNCTAD often relies substantially on NGO input in order to promote developing country goals related to issues, such as debt relief, development assistance and conditionality. NGO input was critical to shoring up support for UNCTAD at the institution's 1996 conference in South Africa.

A recent and growing phenomenon is the emergence of networks of Southern NGOs devoted to research and advocacy related to poverty, equity, political and social justice, and environmental degradation in the national, regional or global context. They link up with their partners in the North, including research institutions, to generate information for campaigns.

C.   The role of Southern NGOs in regional and international fora

It is in the fundamental, long-term interest of Southern governments to foster and expand democratic dialogue with their indigenous NGOs. Such dialogue can often advance their interests at home and abroad. At home, such dialogue, if successful, can help ensure that national development priorities are domestically determined and owned, rather than pre-determined and imposed by a donor. Abroad, this dialogue can be a powerful basis for transmitting more powerful and legitimate messages from Southern NGOs to their Northern counterparts and their campaigns to influence public opinion. More effective communication from South to North can help ensure that Northern publics are well informed about Southern negotiating positions.

Regional and international negotiations sometimes ask for more concessions by Southern governments than by Northern ones. Stronger Southern NGOs could do more to rectify this imbalance. For instance, when Southern governments are pressed to adopt certain labour and environmental standards, Southern NGOs call for reciprocal conditionality on Northern governments, for instance with respect to technology transfer, intellectual property rights, labour mobility, or environmental pollution.

In regional and international fora, Southern governments frequently miss the opportunity to draw upon the assets of these NGOs, which are their own "backyard".[5] These assets often include:

*   depositories of useful information which governments do not have;

*   institutional memories that, owing to the nature of many government bureaucracies, some governments do not possess;

*   capacity to mobilize significant media coverage of issues and events;

*   networks of contacts within and outside the countries which can be an asset to government officials.

In regional and global negotiating fora, Northern governments tend to maintain a close relationship with their NGOs and draw upon such assets. Southern governments, on the other hand, often avoid contacts with Southern NGOs. There are, however, important exceptions. For instance, the Secretary General of the Organization of African Unity (OAU) has an open door to NGOs, and he stimulated the launch of the Harare (Zimbabwe) Caucus of African NGO networks in August 1996. The OAU also draws substantially on NGOs in its conflict resolution role. Another example is the Southern Africa Development Committee (SADC); its energy committee relies on NGOs, and its ministerial meetings are open to official participation of NGOs, labour groups and businesses. In Asia, the Asian Coalition for Housing Rights was a lead actor in the run-up and follow-up to the Habitat Conference. Provision for parallel NGO meetings are made at Asia Pacific Economic Cooperation Group (APEC) and Association of South-East Asian Nations (ASEAN) fora. Moreover, throughout the "Summit of the Americas" process, NGOs have made important contributions. As a result of initiatives by the Inter-American Development Bank and recommendations made by the Uruguay NGO consultation to the 1996 Summit on Sustainable Development in Bolivia, case studies of national regulatory frameworks governing civil society organizations have been conducted.

Southern governments should expand support for indigenous dialogue as an essential part of the pluralistic process rather than as a reluctant response to externally-imposed conditionality. One does not have to adopt a "Western" view of democracy or human rights to note the clear linkage between strong and accountable States, on the one hand, and strong civil societies, on the other.

Box 1

> ## STRONG SOUTHERN NGOs EXERT IMPORTANT INFLUENCE OVER THEIR NORTHERN COUNTERPARTS
>
> **Southern governments play a critical role in determining whether their civil society organizations become sufficiently strong and consolidated to influence their Northern counterparts.** As appropriate in different circumstances, Southern governments can expand support of their NGOs to: build credible constituencies; improve their information and analytical capacities; develop coalitions across different sectors of society; and create effective linkages with domestic policy makers.
>
> **The IDA-10 debate has shown the way in which strong Southern NGOs can decisively influence Northern NGO positions.** During this debate, many Washington-based development groups supported IDA. However, African NGOs believed that the criticisms of the World Bank by some Washington-based environmental NGOs threatened IDA's replenishment. They challenged these groups and called their accountability into question. As a result, some environmental NGOs muted their criticism of the Bank. NGOs in other regions of the world have also contributed to support for IDA among Northern publics and decision makers. At the regional meetings of the World Bank-NGO Committee, NGOs have produced strong and influential statements of support for IDA.

D. *Sources of funding*

Operational Northern NGOs channel approximately $7.7 billion per year in assistance to developing countries, approximately 55 per cent representing official grants. This means that these NGOs provide at least 13 per cent of all official development assistance, more than either the entire United Nations system or IDA. These operational NGOs differ considerably in size; they include big transnational NGOs, such as CARE, Oxfam International and World Vision, as well as one-person organizations.

Membership-based Northern development NGOs and organizations representing people's movements usually require dues. The members of some Southern NGOs may be community-based organizations which do not pay dues but rather pool their labour and collective wisdom for community projects.

Significant funding for Southern NGOs comes from Northern NGOs, though an increasing number are also financed through Northern foundations and government contracts. Fewer are financed from direct bilateral or multilateral grants or from commercial activities.

The principal sources of funding for Northern NGOs are individual dues, private foundations, bilateral government allocations and some corporate contributions. Sometimes governments in a given region (e.g. the European Union) support NGO coalitions in that region. In addition, many NGOs are expanding their commercial activities; for instance, Oxfam of the United Kingdom and Ireland raises at least 55 per cent of its budget from its commercial activities (the Oxfam shops) and private donors. The media is an important fund-raising tool. Partly through a media blitz, Comic Relief in the United Kingdom raised $25 million in 1993 through a week of "funfare".

NGOs which specialize in policy analysis and advocacy are often dependent upon private foundations for support. The concentration of foundations in the United States has given NGOs based in the country a significant lead over their counterparts in Europe and the developing world. Increasingly, United States foundations have tried to rectify this imbalance by funding overseas NGOs. In addition, there are many efforts to foster philanthropic activities and institutions in developing countries.

The financial base of many Northern NGOs has eroded over the years because of factors such as insecurity arising from the prolonged recession of the late 1980s and early 1990s in much of the OECD; the absence of a cold-war rationale for assistance; an increasing sense that development problems are intractable and that aid is not sufficiently effective; growth in competing charities generating "compassion fatigue"; and the introduction of State lotteries which divert funds from charities in some countries. In some cases, funding has eroded due to NGO failures to address their own internal weaknesses. Especially during the past five years, the decline in bilateral official funding has forced many operational Northern NGOs to downsize, redefine their roles, and restructure their programmes and their relationships. This restructuring is creating both opportunities and threats. While some Northern NGOs are refocusing their programmes and developing a social base at home, others are "corporatizing" their image (changing titles of leaders, dress codes and centralizing decision-making even further) in order to be seen as credible by private donors.

There are instances in which NGOs have expanded in order to provide emergency assistance and disaster relief in trouble spots (in Somalia, the Great Lakes region and Liberia). Increasingly, governmental resources are channelled into relief efforts in conflict areas in Africa and elsewhere.[6] Some of these agencies have managed to expand their operations with integrity and effectiveness. Others have received stinging reviews by human rights groups as promoting "philanthropic imperialism".[7]

II. Power imbalances among Northern and Southern NGOs and Southern governments

A. *Relations among NGOs*

NGO agendas complement, intersect, compete and contradict one another. Accountability may be "downward" (to a membership base), "upward" (to a Board of Directors and funders), or "horizontal" (to NGO partners). In general, NGOs have multiple relationships of accountability.

There are instances when the power relationships between Northern and Southern NGOs are reasonably symmetrical, and Northern NGOs support and empower their Southern colleagues by means such as:

- providing information and rigorous analysis of developments in policies and practices of Northern governments and intergovernmental institutions;

- mobilizing concern about, and financial support for, sustainable development programmes among Northern constituencies; and

- providing financial, technical and political support for Southern NGO projects and programmes to promote social justice.

When power relations are symmetrical, NGO activities have a better chance of success; they are more likely to foster pluralism and influence development projects and programmes by giving voice to poor and minority groups and by efficiently channelling social services to poor populations. Northern NGOs which do not accept bilateral official aid sometimes have a stronger emphasis on empowering Southern NGOs than those which depend upon official aid. Asymmetrical power relationships between Northern and Southern NGOs mirror those between Northern and Southern governments in terms of financial dependence and conditionality. Southern NGOs are often forced to deal not only with conditions imposed by Northern NGOs, but also with those imposed by the agencies funding the Northern NGOs.

When the term "partnership" is applied to relations between Northern and Southern NGOs, it connotes equality and mutuality. Southern NGOs increasingly challenge their Northern counterparts when "partnership" rhetoric is misused, for instance, to make policies with little, if any, consultation with Southern NGOs. In a North-South NGO relationship, assessments of the accountability of a Northern NGO are often based upon the extent to which this organization supports Southern NGOs which in turn are accountable to a membership of community-based organizations. Such relationships have potential to strengthen Southern societies in certain circumstances - for instance, when there are decentralized and accountable decision-making mechanisms.

The revolution in information technology has accelerated information-sharing and coalition-building among some NGOs, while excluding many others. For instance, connectivity is far more prevalent in Latin America than in Africa. In developing their advocacy positions, Northern NGOs will be more adequately informed by the Southern NGOs as barriers to information technology are lowered. Greater symmetry in power and access to information technology is essential to tapping the reservoirs of expertise in the South in ways that build Southern capacity and self-reliance.

It is in the interest of Northern NGOs to support a stronger role for Southern NGOs in speaking to domestic and international issues on behalf of the South. But, there are cases (e.g. when a Southern government does not respect internationally accepted human rights) where it is important that Northern NGOs speak out in solidarity with their Southern counterparts or oppressed groups in the South. In general, it is not sufficient for Northern NGOs to speak on a country's behalf by virtue of the passions of its constituency (e.g. rain forest preservation) or of its capacity to deliver relief or social services. To effectively support their Southern counterparts, many Northern NGOs are reorienting and restructuring their activities to provide solidarity with those in the South, which have a legitimate role or social base from which to transform their own societies. For instance, they are strengthening their support for Southern NGOs through providing information dissemination services and links to Northern policy makers. Several NGOs are taking leadership by clarifying roles, relationships and responsibilities in ways that build accountability.[8]

B. Relations between NGOs and Southern governments

In general, Southern NGOs have not yet achieved the strength, acceptance and high profile of many of their Northern counterparts. While some governments still deny civil society organizations basic freedom, there are many examples of governments providing the political space necessary for such organizations to flourish. A strong civil society is increasingly seen as an essential attribute of a modernized and accountable State. The attitude that governments in the South have towards NGOs depends on numerous factors, including:

- historical and cultural experiences;

- the degree of social and political stability prevailing;

- the nature of the regime and experience of its leadership;

- the extent to which the government's development vision is understood and valued by citizens' groups;

- the nature and quality of the NGO activity;

- sources of funds;

- membership base;

- the way NGOs relate to government (including political orientation, transparency and accountability);

- the composition and respective roles of local and foreign NGOs; and

- the NGO's proximity to grassroots communities (NGOs may organize and articulate claims of grassroots communities which may not otherwise be heard by governments).

In some respects, civil society organizations are stronger in parts of Asia and Latin America than in Africa. However, South Africa not only tolerates NGOs, it also makes a budgetary provision to support their work. Other African governments such as Ghana, Malawi, Uganda, the United Republic of Tanzania and Zambia also have an open door to NGOs. In Kenya, the constitutional reform debate and civic actions are pioneered by NGOs and coordinated through the NGO Forum (comprised of Kenyan and international NGOs).

There are many examples of close and fruitful cooperation between Southern governments and their citizens' organizations. Often, however, the relationship between Southern governments and NGOs is one of mutual tolerance, at best. Social and political stability usually breed greater tolerance toward NGOs. NGOs engaged in service delivery tend to be tolerated more easily than those engaged in policy analysis and advocacy that might challenge the status quo. When NGOs engage in partisan politics, or campaign on sensitive issues, such as human rights, they are frequently treated with hostility. Friction between Southern governments and their indigenous NGOs is often caused by competition for aid. As noted earlier, when aid for social services is diverted from governments to NGOs, competition and hostility usually intensifies. Furthermore, donor pressure to downsize and roll back the functions of government often has serious implications for the management and leadership capacity of governments. Externally-funded NGO service provision should not displace services that governments should provide, given sufficient resources. However, this is happening, especially since growth in aid to NGOs sometimes outpaces growth in government revenue, including ODA.

The situation is even less tolerable in countries in emergency situations, which in numerous circumstances are quite literally taken over by relief agencies. Relief NGOs in Sierra Leone before the

Box 2

SUCCESSFUL COLLABORATION BETWEEN GOVERNMENT
AND NGOs IN SOUTH AFRICA

An example of productive collaboration between government and NGOs is that of the South African Women's Budget Initiative, which was initiated in 1995 as a joint project of NGOs (including the Institute for Development Alternatives in Southern Africa), the Parliamentary Joint Standing Committee of Finance and the Law, Race and Gender Project at the University of Cape Town. The project created a framework to analyse the gender impact of key budget expenditures, concentrating primarily on education, housing, welfare and work. The Ministry of Finance and the Central Statistical Department committed to creating a statistical data base disaggregated by gender in order to utilize the project framework. This collaboration is helping to ensure equitable development and contributing to harmonious relations between State and citizens.

June 1997 coup commanded over 50 per cent of official development assistance in emergency relief, leaving a young democratic government with pitifully few resources to accomplish basic functions, such as rehabilitation of a badly needed infrastructure. When expatriates or field representatives have lavish living habits and exorbitant salaries, they are a constant irritation to both governments and local NGOs. Actions by Northern and Southern governments to support responsible governance, even in times of acute crisis, can help prevent situations in which NGOs feel forced to take over governmental functions.

III. NGO opposition to asymmetry in decision-making

Many studies have found that development activities are most likely to succeed when the developing country government and affected communities have a sense of ownership and commitment to the activities. In particular, where Southern governments and NGOs maintain constructive relationships, they share an interest in ensuring that donors and creditors are not inappropriately intrusive in their affairs.

There is considerable donor rhetoric about the importance of ownership of development activities on the part of recipient governments. Such rhetoric can be found in the United Nations Special Initiative for Africa, the Partnership for Capacity-Building in Africa, the "Principles of Effective Aid" of the DAC, the work of the DAC Ad Hoc Working Group on Participatory Development and Good Governance,[9]

and guidelines for various bilateral donor governments. In practice, donors themselves have found that their modalities for relating to recipient governments can inadvertently undermine capacity-building. For instance, the Working Group sponsored by the Partnership for Capacity-Building in Africa issued a report in November 1996 which found that World Bank practices have sometimes undermined the capacity of African governments.[10]

The goals of ownership and capacity-building are undermined when donors identify the development priorities or problems in a country and then proceed to impose solutions. Donor accountability to sound country development strategies is a pre-condition for capacity-building. Yet donors sometimes have a cavalier disregard for such strategies, which are sometimes produced through consensus-building among governmental and non-governmental entities. In general, NGOs seek a less hierarchical donor system. As it is, various donors often vie for power and influence correlating to the amount and type of assistance provided. The IMF and the World Bank, as preferred creditors, sometimes dominate decision-making. The Fund has considerable influence over other official donors and commercial banks through its exclusive role in the Paris Club. Some types of domination, or leadership, are more appropriate than others. The World Bank often takes a lead because it manages most Consultative Groups, some Sector Investment Programmes, and projects and programmes in which other investors are often junior partners. Consultative Groups, usually chaired by the World Bank, bring all donors for a given country together (often in Paris) to identify development priorities and financing needs. These meetings are more useful for identifying the financial commitments which donors are willing to make than for fostering coordination in serving recipient governments' development priorities. The role of recipient governments should be much more substantial than it is at present.

The World Bank/UNDP aid coordination arrangements stipulate that the institutions will expand the use of borrowing country institutions and consultants, and implement common aid accountability and information processes, along with other donors. Developing country institutions, including NGOs, could monitor donor progress in such areas. There are only a handful of instances (e.g. Indonesia, Cambodia, Guatemala) in which organizations of civil society have participated in Consultative Groups. Many NGOs believe that these groups should meet in recipient countries and should encourage investments in the priorities designated by the country development strategy.[11]

Sector Investment Programmes coordinate the activities of all donors in a given sector (e.g. agriculture, health, education). While these programmes are donor-led, they usually involve actors within the recipient government and civil society to a greater degree than other donor-supported activities. Development strategies of individual donors/creditors identify the sectors and activities in which individual donors or creditors are willing to invest. Donors have different names for their development strategies (e.g. the World Bank's Country Assistance Strategy, the IMF-managed Policy Framework Paper, Germany's Country Profile, etc.). Too often, these documents identify investments without appropriate reference to the priorities embodied in the country's own development strategy and without sufficient input by relevant governmental and non-governmental actors. Certainly a division of labour is called for among donors. However, the interests of other parties (donors who are junior partners and, especially, recipient governments and their citizens) are not always taken seriously.

The Special Programme of Assistance to Africa provides a machinery for the donor community to channel adjustment assistance to the region. It is comprised of 17 bilateral and five multilateral donors, coordinates all non-project, economic adjustment grants and loans in the order of $5 to $7 billion for a given three-year cycle. African governments and civil society have little role in the workings of this Programme. There is a separate forum for Africans - the Global Coalition for Africa - which has no authority over, and little influence on, resource flows

or conditionality. Recipient governments can talk with donors in many fora, but usually not in the context of the Special Programme for Africa. The intellectual ferment and commitments of this Programme and the Consultative Groups are "upstream" of country-level policy development. These fora establish certain roles, principles and approaches that can only, with difficulty, be modified "downstream" by governments and organizations of civil society.

The Special Programme for Africa is now considering more open and transparent ways of doing business which could lead to "demand-driven" rather than "supply-driven" development. It could provide recipient government officials with the necessary incentives to take ownership and, thereby, shape their country's economic future. It could provide citizens with avenues for expressing their needs and aspirations. Alternatively, if donors play a central role in more open processes, it could confuse and undermine relationships between government and civil society. With few exceptions, donors should be on the sidelines of indigenous processes of consensus-building.

NGO campaigns to reform the international financial institutions sometimes lead to changes in the nature of operations in developing countries. However, NGOs have failed to foster greater ownership and capacity on the part of development-country governments and citizens. NGOs and developing-country governments could usefully work together to identify ways in which their concerted action could build the potential for greater ownership and capacity. As many studies show, indigenous ownership of development activities on the part of governmental and NGO actors is a key to sustaining the benefits of such activities.

IV. NGO advocacy and the international financial institutions

A. Background

Networks of academics and activists dealing with the international financial institutions include those relating to particular projects, countries and particular ecological or geopolitical regions of the world, particular institutions and issues: energy, environment/natural resource, indigenous people, poverty/development, human rights, gender, and the private sector. In general, operational NGOs are less knowledgeable about the international financial institutions and less hostile to them than groups specializing in policy analysis and advocacy.

NGOs are much less informed about the IMF than about the World Bank. There is burgeoning interest in the IMF - particularly with respect to the IMF's role in debt reduction and structural adjustment. There is also a growing sense among NGOs that the IMF is best-suited to managing short-term monetary transactions rather than longer-term development arrangements, such as those of the Enhanced Structural Adjustment Facility (ESAF). Whereas some groups are opposed to the ESAF, others are educating themselves with a genuine interest in a better understanding of how ESAF functions.

Over time, United States NGOs have worked with Southern NGOs to take positions with the United States Congress (with limited success) that legislatively enjoin the IMF to hire environmental scientists, increase access to information, create an independent audit and evaluation unit, and discourage military spending by active members. Activism by United States NGOs has probably expanded the already disproportionate role of the United States in the international financial institutions, especially the World Bank.

NGO movements criticizing the Bank gained momentum in the mid-1980s, spurred by reactions to structural adjustment and growing environmental activism. In 1982, the World Bank-NGO Committee was created with elected NGO representation from each region of the developing world. The World Bank had a strong hand in establishing and funding the Committee. Co-chaired by an NGO and a Bank official, the Committee has functioned as a vehicle for policy dialogue, particularly on structural adjustment and popular participation. In 1994, the Committee began to hold meetings in each region and has been especially influential in expanding the Bank's participatory work. The environmental movement to reform the Bank began in 1983 and focused on large-scale projects, usually involving resettlement. Environmental campaigners overturned support for the multilateral development banks in some quarters, as they publicized the devastating consequences for affected people and the environment of certain Bank-supported projects. In some cases, such as Polonoroeste (Brazil) and the Sardar Sardovar project (India), it was found that the operations carried out under such projects were not complying with the Bank's own policies.

The environmental movement is viewed as far more successful than the development movement in shifting the policies and practices of the development banks. Their success is usually attributed to their willingness to threaten funding, their large memberships and their singular focus on advocacy. To press for World Bank reform, the movement successfully allied with Republicans in the United States Senate in the mid-1980s and with the Democrats in the House of Representatives in the early 1990s. Big development organizations usually focus on operational services rather than on advocacy.

NGO calls for enhanced accountability on the part of the World Bank were fuelled by revelations by the Bank itself. The former President of the World Bank, Lewis Preston, commissioned an internal Bank Task Force to study the quality of the loan portfolio. Its findings showed that the quality of the portfolio was poor and declining. Portfolio assessments of the regional development banks also revealed profound quality problems.

In 1993 a few large shareholders convinced the Board to adopt a new information disclosure policy and to establish an inspection panel to investigate allegations of Bank non-compliance with its policies by directly affected groups. United States NGOs working closely with Southern NGOs asked the United States Congress to condition its support for IDA on compliance with these two reform objectives. These reforms have strengthened Bank accountability.

Declines in official development assistance are attributable to many factors enumerated above. In general, the post-cold-war era has led to increased inwardness on the part of industrialized country governments. To some extent, NGO critiques of the development banks have strengthened those government factions (often right-wing) which favour reduced involvement and contributions to the concessional arms of the development banks. However, that point is often overdrawn. Given the widespread agreement that reform by the multilateral development banks is essential to improving portfolio quality, NGOs which support full funding without calling for meaningful reforms can be viewed by decision makers as politically and pragmatically naive.[12] Many Northern development NGOs call for full funding of the concessional arms of the development banks if progress on institutional reform is to be made. During the last ten years, development and religious NGOs of the United States have been almost the only groups supporting full-funding of the institutions. Recently, the business community has been more active.

B. *Typical advocacy positions*

In general, NGOs seek to advance the goal of sustainable development, which is defined as equitable, environmentally sustainable and participatory development. This is sought through the promotion of:

- The principle of multilateralism

  Support for multilateralism has declined in the North, and in some countries, such as the United States, one can find significant hostility to the United Nations. While recognizing the weaknesses of the United Nations system, Northern environment and development movements generally advocate strong financial support of the United Nations system by their governments. NGOs call for enhanced collaboration between the international financial institutions and the United Nations system, including their accountability to a United Nations body, such as the Economic and Social Council.

- Openness and transparency of international financial institutions

  The agendas of Northern environment and development NGOs converge to support greater openness and transparency in the institutions. There are strong calls for improved implementation of the World Bank's information disclosure policy, and United States NGOs were highly instrumental in convincing the Congress to work with the United States Executive Branch to reform the World Bank information disclosure policy.

- Contributions to, and reform of, IDA

  Northern development NGOs constitute a small but significant lobby supporting the concessional arms of the development banks, especially IDA.[13] They have been almost the only groups supporting these institutions in the North. Despite the volume of contracting to United States firms through development bank-supported projects, United States businesses are only beginning to offer significant support for the institutions.

  Important support for IDA is also provided by the NGO Working Group of the World Bank-NGO Committee. The regional meetings of this Committee have produced clear statements of support for IDA by NGOs in Asia, Africa and Latin America. As noted above, African NGOs played a particularly important role in muting criticisms of Washington-based environmental NGOs, which were perceived as threatening United States Congressional support for IDA-10. In contrast to the parliamentary system in Europe, the Congress does not routinely honour financial commitments to IDA, and Congressional awareness and support for IDA has always been thin. Local NGOs have tried to raise awareness among members of Congress that the leadership role of the United States in the institution is undermined if it is in arrears and delinquent on current contributions.

  IDA proponents stress the importance of the institution, given the fact that private capital flows bypass the poorest IDA countries, where 80 per cent of all poor people live. In the North, advocacy positions often stress the value of concessional assistance to recipient countries with which the donor country has a historical relationship (e.g. the United States and Mexico or Liberia, France and Francophone Africa, etc.).

  At the same time, IDA proponents assert that reform is required to effectively support sustainable development, defined as poverty reduction in environmentally sound ways. In the United States, it is common to find support for IDA conditioned on progress with respect to development effectiveness (e.g. participation, poverty reduction, etc.). There is also widespread concern about analyses showing that approximately \$2 of every \$3 in IDA credits are needed to service debt owed to the World Bank.

- World Bank adherence to its operational policies

  Northern environmental NGOs have pushed for independent commissions to review controversial projects to determine, among other things, whether the Bank is adhering to its own policies. Environmental NGOs in the United States were highly instrumental in working with the United States Congress and Executive Branch to persuade the World Bank to establish the inspection panel, which is seen as promoting greater accountability to communities directly affected by Bank-supported activities. Environmental NGOs lead the call to extend the jurisdiction of the World Bank's inspection panel to the International Finance Corporation (IFC) and the Multilateral Investment Guarantee Agency (MIGA).

• Harmonization of information disclosure

NGOs urge the need for upward harmonization of information disclosure and other policies among the World Bank and its affiliate institutions and among various lending instruments (e.g. guarantees) in order to preclude one set of policies for private-sector-sponsored activities and another set for public-sector activities. Environmental NGOs are also sponsoring information programmes to help NGOs, commercial banks and investors become more familiar with the ways in which private financiers, development banks and private enterprises interface.

• Qualified World Bank support for private-sector activities

NGOs are concerned that the World Bank and its affiliates (IFC and MIGA) do not properly apply developmental criteria when taking equity positions or providing loans and guarantees. NGOs advocate screening all operations to ensure that they meet developmental criteria. They are also concerned that loans which support privatization processes do not roll back core State functions, establish private monopolies, or deprive poor populations of services. When the power of States is circumscribed in excessive or asymmetrical ways, the potential for sustainable development can be undermined.[14]

World Bank analysis and activities do not always give appropriate emphasis to risks of development strategies to borrowing governments and citizens. For instance, the World Bank's management has not given its Board a sufficiently balanced analysis of policy questions relating to its plans for expanding the provision of guarantees or the implications of providing adjustment support to subnational entities. The management's analyses and documentation thoroughly address the risks to the institution's credit status of such policy shifts. But little, if any, attention is given to certain risks to developing-country governments and citizens (e.g. premature competition with the indigenous private sector, contractual obligations which could erode sovereignty, environmental degradation, excessive growth in external debt).[15] Whether one supports the expanded use of such instruments or not, analyses provided by the World Bank Group should not be biased against the borrowers.

C.   NGOs and the external debt problem

1.   Recent developments

Until the early 1990s, multilateral debt was widely seen by many policy makers and the management of the international financial institutions as untouchable. Debt relief was limited to commercial bank and bilateral official debt. Decisive factors in changing this perspective included: academic work, analysis by the Non-Aligned Movement, receptive Northern governments, and internationally active NGO networks.

In 1992, EURODAD (the European Network on Debt and Development), with membership in 15 European countries, Oxfam International, which is a partnership of 10 NGOs with the same name around the world that fund development, relief, and advocacy in 70 countries, and other NGOs began systematic advocacy for comprehensive debt relief, and mobilized their membership to that end. They worked to achieve widespread acknowledgement of the seriousness of the multilateral component of the overall debt problem and then to seek solutions. Targets of advocacy include: the G-7 governments, the management of the international financial institutions, including their Boards and the major financial media. Advocacy by governments and NGOs culminated in acceptance of the Heavily Indebted Poor Country (HIPC) Initiative by creditors, including the World Bank and IMF.

Collaboration among Southern governments and NGOs from both the South[16] and the North has expanded significantly with positive results. Notably, the collaboration successfully used the media to influence decision makers and public opinion. The Government of Uganda even had its commitment to use debt resources for education published in the *Financial Times*, which made it difficult for the United States and other governments to say that the Ugandan Government would not use debt relief responsibly. The Ugandan, Mozambican and Nicaraguan press have all covered the HIPC Initiative through contacts with NGOs in their countries.

The staff of the Uganda Ministry of Finance went abroad to lobby Northern governments and attend NGO conferences but, even more crucially, the staff met with Ugandan NGOs and community groups to explain why the debt issue was so important.

NGO advocacy positions in the area of debt are based on a number of perceptions and beliefs:

- For many countries, debt burdens are too large relative to exports, national budgets and social expenditures, and constitute a barrier to development progress.

- Debt service more than offsets new resource flows because debt service payments have to be made in convertible foreign exchange, whereas aid is often tied to projects and procurement in the donor country.

- The burden of austerity is often borne disproportionately by vulnerable groups who have no voice in shaping policy.

- Austerity programmes sometimes result in cuts in essential services while leaving "non-productive" expenditures (e.g. the military) untouched.

- All creditors should take responsibility for debt reduction.

- The basic model of development is flawed to the extent that it puts a higher priority on servicing foreign debt than on meeting basic needs and rights of populations and protecting the environment.

2.   *NGOs and the HIPC framework*

The HIPC Initiative is the first debt initiative that is both comprehensive and concerted and aims at exiting from the endless rescheduling process by targeting the goal of debt sustainability. However, the framework of the Initiative has major flaws that need to be corrected (the extended timeframe, criteria for compliance, optimistic assumptions on aid and exports, and deficient thresholds and indicators). NGOs contend that the framework for assessing debt sustainability is inadequate and incomplete. The ranges are too high for the criteria currently employed - namely the ratios of the net present value of debt to exports (200 to 250 per cent); annual debt service to exports (20 to 25 per cent); and (at the insistence of the French Government) the annual fiscal burden of debt (fiscal revenue/debt of 280 per cent). For these criteria, NGOs recommend ratios of 150, 14 and 200 per cent, respectively. In addition, they assert that the HIPC framework should take outstanding nominal debt into account as well as the net present value of debt.

In addition, NGOs advocate the inclusion of a measurement relating to poverty or social development in the so-called "vulnerability analysis" that is an element of the debt sustainability analysis. Instead, creditors took what was intended to be a debt sustainability indicator as additional conditionality. Some major G-7 creditors (e.g. the United States and Germany) not only claim that the HIPCs need to perform adequately with respect to IMF and World Bank adjustment programmes, but also with respect to social development and poverty alleviation goals.

Most NGOs welcome the commitment of the Governments of Uganda and Bolivia to use the proceeds from debt relief for investment in the social sectors; however, they oppose requiring such a policy as a *sine qua non* for debt relief. Oxfam International recommends another approach to providing incentives to HIPC governments to reduce poverty. Specifically, they recommend that creditors reward HIPC countries which demonstrate a commitment to poverty with deeper and faster debt relief.

In the context of the HIPC Initiative there is a certain degree of division of labour among the various NGOs. EURODAD, Oxfam International and other NGOs are now able to lobby their governments and the international financial institutions for improvement of the framework. Conferences in Africa and Latin America enable NGOs to share information and build capacity for monitoring the implementation of the HIPC Initiative by the international financial institutions and local governments. It is intended to establish a division of labour in which networks and NGOs in the South monitor the implementation in their countries and inform the views of Northern NGOs and, where possible, their governments. For instance, local NGOs in Uganda and Bolivia, together with Oxfam International, allied closely with these governments to improve the terms of debt relief. Northern NGOs will continue to lobby governments in their countries, the G-7 and the international financial institutions, with the objective of improving the HIPC framework, in particular the following elements:

(1)   Paris Club members should implement the 1978 UNCTAD resolution to cancel all outstanding concessional debt. NGOs urge the United States and Japan to comply. Furthermore, the Paris Club should take steps to maximize debt relief (e.g. 90 to 100 per cent) and advance the cut-off date for eligible debt.

(2)   The IMF should increase its contribution through grants from appropriate accounts (e.g. Special Contingency Account and/or the sale of gold).

(3) The demands and obstacles posed by each creditor government need to be overcome (e.g. in the case of the United States, the Credit Reform Act; in the case of Germany and Italy, opposition to gold sales; in the case of Japan, opposition to debt reduction; calls for conditionality relating to social development; etc.).

Recently NGOs have launched another initiative on debt and development, the "Jubilee 2000" campaign, which aims at cancellation of all unpayable debt by the year 2000. It was started in the United Kingdom by a small group of concerned Christians, the United Kingdom "Debt Crisis Network". The effort was rapidly expanded through a vast network of churches, first in the United Kingdom, then in other European countries and elsewhere in the North and some parts of the South. Major Jubilee campaigns are being launched in the United States, Germany, Sweden and other European countries where churches, in particular catholic NGOs and EURODAD members, are becoming engaged. NGOs and governments could usefully collaborate to ensure that this initiative does not have unintended effects, including cutting flows of new resources or impairing the World Bank's capital base.

D. Structural adjustment and governance

Many anti-poverty NGOs oppose conventional structural adjustment policies because in their view such policies are promising short-term pain for long-term gains that often do not materialize. In other words, adjustment does not always produce economic growth and, if it does, the benefits do not always "trickle down" to poor people. In fact, many NGOs contend that groups of poor people and women are often disproportionately hurt by adjustment. Too few NGOs honour the role of adjustment in helping to overcome pre-existing economic problems and achieve macroeconomic stability, including balanced internal and external accounts.

Many anti-poverty NGOs also oppose roll-backs in State functions which should shape the distributive and ecological aspects of market activity. In particular, there is concern that privatization of State-owned enterprises can create private monopolies and disadvantage poor populations. For instance, when user fees are imposed to recoup costs of health and education services, there is evidence that some populations which were served by the public system go unserved by the private one. Environmental NGOs

oppose the reliance of some adjustment programmes on development strategies, which are seen as fostering the unsustainable extraction and exploitation of natural resources.

In general, structural adjustment is seen as contributing to the rise in inequality within many countries and between industrialized and developing countries. Sometimes, growing inequality can threaten the social fabric within a nations, and inequality between industrialized and developing countries put the latter at a competitive disadvantage in numerous ways. It is important that the World Trade Organization and the international financial institutions do not foster policies that reinforce asymmetries and double standards.

The international financial institutions should identify and correct problems related to the failure of many industrialized countries to adjust, which shifts undue adjustment burdens onto Southern governments and citizens. They should weigh in against Northern countries maintaining protectionist regimes, even while supporting stricter trade liberalization conditionalities for economically weaker countries. They should also call into account industrialized countries with profligate military spending (e.g. the United States) that exert pressure through the institutions to cut military expenditures in selected countries. The international financial institutions should not bias their policy advice on non-productive expenditures against developing-country members, nor should they be channels for advice urging Southern governments to accept a pace or sequence of adjustment measures that exposes indigenous enterprises to competitive pressures in imprudent ways. While competitiveness is a worthy value, it is important that the structural advantages of transnational corporations are not systematically reinforced at the expense of indigenous enterprises.

Many NGOs view some activities of the World Bank Group as providing benefits and subsidies to Northern transnational corporations in ways that risk putting indigenous private enterprises at a structural disadvantage.

The unwieldy proliferation of conditionality is unhealthy for many reasons, including: the demonstrated ineffectiveness of most conditions; the ways in which conditionality undermines ownership of policies by recipient country governmental and non-governmental institutions; the tension among various types of conditions; the transaction costs involved; the ways in which conditionality distorts donor-recipient relations; and the near-certainty of uneven and unequal treatment of countries (to the detriment of weak countries).

The international financial institutions have partly acknowledged shortcomings of adjustment programmes, and this has led to so-called "second generation" adjustment programmes, many of which take on governance conditionalities. The rationale for certain components of the governance agenda (e.g. transparency) is undermined when the international financial institutions do not apply pressures uniformly across all member governments. Governance concerns are raised more frequently with respect to sub-Saharan African countries than with respect to certain Asian ones (e.g. China, Indonesia).

Intentionally or unintentionally, the individual and collective strategies of NGO advocates can lead to additional, and new forms of, conditionality relating to governance. There is no consensus on governance conditionality, but those NGOs that are in favour of it advance the following arguments:

(1) The international financial institutions are insufficiently accountable and cannot be trusted to achieve certain development outcomes, therefore assurances must be sought from the borrowing governments. For example, while the Bank asserts that its goal is poverty reduction, it has acquiesced when borrower governments have cut social services that are required to achieve that goal. Therefore, the onus is on the borrower to prove that its fiscal priorities support the goal of poverty reduction.

(2) Certain Southern governments are not sufficiently accountable to certain groups of citizens (e.g. poor people, tribal peoples, ethnic minorities), and there are inadequate channels for such groups to express their views and seek legal or financial redress in the event that damages are incurred as a result of Bank-support activities (Northern governments are not paragons of excellence in this regard either).

(3) Certain aspects of development (e.g. climate change) affect the "global commons". Unfortunately, international institutions have established many points of leverage over Southern governments and few points of leverage over Northern governments and transnational corporations. The production and consumption patterns of industrialized countries have put the "global commons" at risk, yet the burden of-

adjustment increasingly falls upon Southern countries. For instance, after many Northern countries have significantly destroyed their forests, they are taking a proprietary interest in the preservation of Southern forests.

(4) Where there are clear, objective and widely adopted international standards with respect to a particular concern, such as human rights, the international financial institutions should take them into account in activities which they support. While the international financial institutions are precluded from engagement in political activities, the distinction between economic and political activities cannot be drawn clearly and is not useful.

The debt crisis in the early 1980s galvanized NGO concern about adjustment programmes. This concern has grown over time, the latest initiative to force a rethinking in this area being the Structural Adjustment Participatory Review Initiative (SAPRI), which engages some 500 NGOs and other organizations of civil society in working with the World Bank to review the impact of adjustment lending and policy advice in selected countries.[17] The SAPRI exercise is potentially important because it is tripartite, involving governments, organizations of civil society and the World Bank. Its success largely rests upon the extent to which meaningful in-country dialogue occurs.

E.   Stakeholder participation

NGOs generally support popular participation in formulation, implementation, monitoring and evaluation of projects, programmes and country-wide strategies. Participation is seen as a way to reduce poverty, foster sustainable development, improve portfolio quality, and enhance accountability of international financial institutions to affected populations and communities. The Development Committee Task Force on multilateral development banks stated:

> ...there is a relationship between the attainment of good public sector policy and economic efficiency. Good policy includes the rule of law, protection of legitimate economic activities and interests, a government's accountability to its citizens, effective measures to curb corruption, a participatory approach to development, easy access to important information and services, and sound decision-making reflecting the actual needs of people. (World Bank, 1996, p. 8)

The Wapenhans Report called for enhanced ownership of Bank-supported operations by client governments as well as enhanced participation by stakeholders, including NGOs. Numerous analyses since the Report's release in 1992 have confirmed the importance of stakeholder participation to operational viability and sustainability.[18] The Bank's typology of popular participation levels includes: information-sharing, consultation, collaboration and empower-ment. The locus of decision-making shifts from official to non-governmental entities as one proceeds through these four levels.

In the World Bank, enhanced participation was triggered by factors including discussion with the Bank-NGO Committee in 1987; consultation re-quirements related to the environmental impact assessment and resettlement processes initiated in 1991; the NGO role in the Global Environmental Facility; the NGO role in the microfinance facility - Consultative Group to Assist the Poorest; and the creation of Social Investment Funds[19] to mitigate the social impacts of structural adjustment. The Bank's approach to "mainstreaming" participation is spelled out in an action programme entitled "The World Bank and Participation", which was approved by the Board in September 1994.

According to the World Bank's 14th annual report on participation (World Bank, 1996a) 48 per cent of projects approved by the Bank's Board in fiscal year 1996 included some provision for NGO involvement. Participation activities are concentrated in: (a) certain regions, especially the African and South Asian regions; (b) certain sectors, especially agri-culture and social sector projects; and (c) certain stages of the project cycle, especially implementation. Participation activities are expanding owing to factors such as the incentive system, the presence of NGO liaison specialists in Resident Missions, the design of new learning and innovation loans, a more flexible, "alternative" project cycle, and the importance placed on participatory approaches to developing the Country Assistance Strategies.

The participation rhetoric of the World Bank often leads to confusion since its use of the terms - particularly "participation" and "stakeholder" - is imprecise. The Bank needs to work with stakeholders to build consensus about the roles and responsibilities of different stakeholders (including the Bank, itself) in different circumstances. It should also more adequately define various types of participation and the preconditions for effective participation. Box 3 illustrates different types of stakeholders as summarized by Fowler.[20]

The participation initiatives of the World Bank may support the relationships of Southern govern-ments with their NGOs but they can also undermine them. The Bank is investing in strengthening its own capacity to relate directly to NGOs in borrowing countries. There is no reason why NGOs and in-terested Southern governments could not encourage the World Bank to invest significant resources in strengthening the capacity of borrower governments to enlist effective local participation in lending and non-lending operations. For instance, governments and civil society organizations could work together to ensure that Country Assistance Strategies do not undermine national ownership and local consensus-building by pre-empting or supplanting national development strategies.

At the 1996 Africa Regional Meeting of the World Bank-NGO Committee, it was argued that by sidelining the governments and putting itself at the centre of communication concerning the Country Assistance Strategy, the Bank can undermine actual or potential democratic processes. It is usually preferable for the World Bank and other donors to be on the sidelines supporting interaction among govern-mental and civil society entities. Such interaction can lead to indigenously owned development priorities and strategies. Donor strategies, such as the Country Assistance Strategies, should serve these priorities.

Where governments are able and willing to provide political space for indigenous dialogue, governments and civil society organizations can work together to help maintain ownership of development activities and to build institutions capable of creating a better future.

V. Conclusion

The points of conflict between Southern govern-ments and their indigenous NGOs and between Southern governments and Northern NGOs are better known and understood than the areas of actual and potential convergence.

Governments of developing countries should aim at building bridges with NGOs within their own countries. Many studies reveal that enhanced ownership of development activities by governmental and NGO actors and institutions is a key to their success. Improved and expanded dialogue among Southern governmental and NGO actors is an essential step toward building ownership and consensus around

Box 3

STAKEHOLDER CATEGORIES

CATEGORY Determined by:	STAKEHOLDER	CHARACTERISTICS
1. Bank obligation	The disadvantaged	Primary clients
	Borrower governments	Partners and clients
	Governors	Owners with formal oversight
	Funders	Shareholders and capital markets
2. Bank effectiveness	Official aid agencies	Complementary inter-governmental activity
	Technical organizations	Provide additional competence
	Intermediary organizations	Provide additional linkages
3. Bank as public entity	Public interest bodies	Critical, reform or oppositional agenda

NGO claims derive from all three categories. For instance, NGOs address international financial institution issues as public interest bodies, as intermediaries providing linkages to affected communities, as technical organizations providing expertise, as taxpayers assenting to direct or indirect financial support for the international financial institutions by their government, or as representatives of disadvantaged communities affected by operations of these institutions. It can be argued that disadvantaged communities have particularly strong claims on the World Bank - not only because they represent a constituency of the client government, but also because reducing the poverty of such communities is the avowed purpose of the Bank.

---

policy positions taken at home and abroad. Southern governments may also be well advised in taking a proactive stance to support NGO alliances that advance NGO and government development objectives in international, regional and national arenas. Indigenous NGOs from some regions are weak or absent in regional and international fora.

Southern governments can influence NGO agendas by supporting Southern NGOs that can be effective interlocutors with their Northern counterparts and in interaction with the international financial institutions. Whereas Northern NGOs have no accountability to Southern governments, they do profess accountability to Southern NGOs.

124   *Abugre and Alexander: NGOs and the International Monetary and Financial System*

Notes

1   Civil society organizations are organized parties that fall anywhere between the family unit and the government, including traditional associations, religious groups, professional associations, trade unions, women's movements, human rights organizations, political parties, media and non-governmental organizations.

2   Examples include the Inter-Africa Group (IAG) in Ethiopia and the Institute for Development and Electoral Assistance (IDEA) in Stockholm. IAG has spearheaded election observation processes, constitutional formation, and demobilization strategies in Ethiopia. In the region, it has hosted a humanitarian summit and managed relief and conflict resolution processes. IDEA organizes and provides support to civil society groups for election monitoring. It also offers a neutral forum for feuding parties to talk. IDEA recently signed an agreement with the United Nations to provide election-monitoring support.

3   Not only operational NGOs lobby for bilateral official aid. There is a broad base of support for aid among research, education and advocacy NGOs as well.

4   A growing number of NGOs are monitoring the World Trade Organization closely, including the International Council of Voluntary Agencies (ICVA), Third World Network, the Swiss Coalition, the WTO Network in Canada, FIELD and the World Development Movement in the United Kingdom.

5   NGO publications and analyses are often highly influential. For instance, publications of the Third World Network (including *Third World Resurgence, African Agenda, Third World Economics*) are important sources of information and perspectives for governments and international NGOs.

6   The DAC estimated that, in 1994, 6 per cent of ODA was devoted to relief, but many observers estimate a level in the 10 per cent to 12 per cent range.

7   De Waal and Rakiya have extensively documented harrowing stories of the waste and plunder by relief NGOs in Somalia, Angola, Rwanda and Bosnia.

8   The efforts of the Asian NGO Coalition, the International Centre for Voluntary Action, FOCUS on the Global South, and the Bank Information Centre are notable in this regard.

9   See *Final Report of the DAC Ad Hoc Working Group on Participatory Development and Good Governance* (Part I) and *Lessons from Experience in Selected Areas of Support for Participatory Development and Good Governance* (Part II), OECD DAC, 1997.

10   At the meeting of the Bank/Fund Development Committee in April 1997, President Wolfensohn of the World Bank pledged to retrofit the Africa Region loan portfolio to strengthen capacity-building, but there has been little discussion of how that could be accomplished.

11   Guatemalan NGOs have documented this process. Their case study has been published by the Centre for Democratic Education (Silver Spring, Maryland, USA).

12   During 1997, Bread for the World's work with members of the United States Congress on World Bank reform issues positioned it effectively to call for a recommendation by the United States Senate for a fiscal year 1998 contribution of $1.035 billion for IDA. A House-Senate conference committee will now work out the difference between that Senate recommendation and the House recommendation of $606 million.

13   IDA proponents include many Southern NGOs, including those represented on the NGO Working Group of the World Bank-NGO Committee; InterAction (a coalition of 160 private voluntary organizations based in the United States) and many of its individual member organization, such as Oxfam America and Bread for the World; Faith Action for People-Centered Development (including the United States Catholic Conference, Mennonites, Friends Committee on National Legislation, Church World Service/Lutheran World Relief); and the United States Coalition for multilateral development banks (headed up by the Bretton Woods Committee and the Overseas Development Council).

14   Widespread NGO opposition to the Multilateral Agreement on Investment is due to, among other things, the belief that the power of States would be inappropriately constrained by the agreement.

15   The shortcomings of Bank analysis are especially noteworthy with respect to the proposal to use IBRD resources for guarantees to private lenders for enclave projects in IDA-only countries. Enclave projects have had a high failure rate and, given their size and the duration of contractual obligations on the part of borrowing governments, serious questions arise with respect to how the sovereign rights of these governments might be constrained and with respect to the magnitude of economic, environmental and social risks involved.

16   African Network and Campaign on Debt and Development (AFRODAD) promoted the formation of debt and development coalitions in several countries, including Mozambique, Uganda, the United Republic of Tanzania and Zambia. The Inter-Africa Group (Ethiopia) and Third World Network (Ghana) are also influential. In Latin America, the Latin American Network on Debt and Development (LATINDAD) is of key importance. Among the active groups in Asia are the Freedom from Debt Coalition (FDC) in the Philippines, FOCUS on the Global South (Thailand), Public Interest Research Group (PIRG), and Delhi Forum in India.

17   The SAPRI initiative will initially be carried out in seven countries: Bangladesh, Ecuador, Ghana, Hungary, Mali, Uganda and Zimbabwe.

18   The 1996 World Bank Social Development Task Force Report cites evaluation data showing the important contribution that participation makes to operational success.

19   During fiscal year 1995, the World Bank channelled some $1.2 billion through the governments of 24 countries to a total of 30 Social Investment Funds, which provided grants to local NGOs.

20   Fowler, Alan, "The World Bank and Its Stakeholders: Who are They and Why?", unpublished, undated paper presented to a seminar at the World Bank.

References

BREAD FOR THE WORLD INSTITUTE, "News & Notices for World Bank Watchers", various issues.

DE WALLE, Alex, and Omar RAKIYA (1996), *Africa World Review Magazine* (London: Africa Research and Information Bureau), December.

DEVELOPMENT ASSISTANCE COMMITTEE (1997), *Lessons from Experience in Selected Areas of Support for Participatory Development and Good Governance,* Part II of the Final Report (Paris: OECD).

EDWARDS, Michael, and David HULME (eds.) (1996), *Beyond the Magic Bullet: NGO Performance and Accountability in the Post-Cold War World* (West Hartford, CT: Kumarian Press).

FOWLER, Alan (1995), "Strengthening the Role of Voluntary Development Organizations: Nine Policy Issues Facing Official Aid Agencies", in *Strengthening Civil Society's Contribution to Development: The Role of Official Development Assistance,* conference papers of the Overseas Development Council and the Synergos Institute, Pocantico Hills, New York, 26-28 September.

IMF and WORLD BANK, Development Committee Task Force on Multilateral Development Banks (1996), "Serving a Changing World" (Washington, D.C.), 15 March.

JORDAN, Lisa, and Peter van TUILE (1997), "Political Responsibility in NGO Advocacy - Exploring Emerging Shapes of Global Democracy", mimeo, June.

KAPUR, Devesh (1997), "The New Conditionalities of the International Financial Institutions", in UNCTAD, *International Monetary and Financial Issues for the 1990s,* Vol. VIII (UNCTAD/GDS/MDPB/1) (New York and Geneva: United Nations).

MATHEWS, Jessica T. (1997), "Power Shift", *Foreign Affairs,* January/February.

MOHAMMED, Aziz Ali (1997), "Notes on MDB Conditionality on Governance", in UNCTAD, *International Monetary and Financial Issues for the 1990s,* Vol. VIII (UNCTAD/GDS/MDPB/1) (New York and Geneva: United Nations).

WATKINS, Kevin (1995), *Oxfam Poverty Report* (Oxfam).

WORLD BANK (1996a), "Cooperation between the World Bank and NGOs: FY96 Progress Report" (Washington, D.C.: NGO Group, Social Development Department), August, 1997.

WORLD BANK (1996b), Social Development Task Force Report (Washington, D.C.).

THE STATE IN A CHANGING WORLD: A CRITIQUE OF THE WORLD DEVELOPMENT REPORT 1997

Devesh Kapur*

Ideas efficacious at some times and in some human surroundings
are not so at other times and elsewhere.

William James

Abstract

The first part of the World Development Report (WDR) *seeks to refocus attention on roles and capabilities that enhance State effectiveness. The next two parts lay out a two-part scheme to achieve this goal. First, roles must focus on social and economic fundamentals, but should always be tailored to capabilities. The second set of solutions, aimed at reinvigorating institutional capabilities, puts the onus on competition, decentralization and participation, and international collective action. Finally, the* Report *examines options for removing obstacles that could derail the reform process.*

The WDR *is generally successful as a didactic device calling attention to the continuing significance of the State in developing countries. It is broadly successful in making the subject matter accessible and understandable to a broad audience. On several issues where the World Bank had adopted a strong position just a few years ago,* WDR 1997 *takes a more nuanced approach, these include the analyses of decentralization, central bank independence and social insurance. On several other controversial issues, such as the presumed virtues of electoral democracy, the* Report's *analysis is also reasonably balanced, and its principal recommendations concern improving efficiency and effectiveness in the public sector.*

However, by trying to accommodate most current fashions and addressing contentious issues quite superficially, the value-added it provides is limited. In particular, it overemphasizes the importance of State "credibility" and the myriad exercises at quantification to "prove" its case in this regard are often misplaced.

By failing to examine contentious issues and tradeoffs inherent in many of the choices that the State has to make and the numerous value judgments inherent in such choices, the Report *abounds in bromides and generalities. Even though the State is an inherently political creature, there is a virtual absence of politics in the* WDR. *In examining issues such as corruption, participation, transparency and agencies of restraint, it indirectly touches upon certain aspects of power but avoids any explicit examination of this crucial issue, whether in the domestic or international context.*

The Report *is stronger in its diagnosis of what does not work rather than of what does work, and in recommendations are on "what" rather than on "how".*

* The author is indebted to Professor Gerry Helleiner and Dr. Aziz Ali Mohammed for their comments on a previous draft.

I.   Introduction

"*Why* and *how* some States have been more effective than others at playing a catalytic and sustainable role in economic development and the eradication of poverty?" This vexing question is at the heart of the World Bank's *World Development Report 1997* on the theme "The State in a Changing World". The search for better government has been one of the central quests of the modern era - a quest that is both as necessary as it is difficult. The sheer range of tasks that States undertake means that any global analysis of the role of the State in today's world is likely to be either so general as to be uninteresting, or so specific as to carry few general implications. Given the potential pitfalls, the World Bank should be commended for at least making the attempt.

Half a century of continuous and sustained engagement with governments of all ideological hues, with widely varying capacities and commitment to economic development, would seem to confer upon the Bank a strong comparative advantage to address this difficult issue. A considerable part of its analytical and operational work is addressed to the institutions and functions of the State. And in their role as the World Bank's annual intellectual flagship publication, the *World Development Reports (WDRs)* have examined the role of the State more broadly (for instance, *WDR 1991*, "The Challenge of Development") as well as particular aspects of the State's functions and its effectiveness - for example in the areas of poverty alleviation, public finance and the provision of infrastructure. Moreover, in recent years several regional studies (such as the *Long-Term Perspective Study on Africa and the East Asian Miracle*) as well as functional analysis (in particular *Bureaucrats in Business*) have also examined various facets of this subject.

If the Bank seems perched at a particularly advantageous vantage point to address the issue of the changing role of the State, several other factors would appear to militate against it. At its core the "State" is fundamentally a political entity; its role is a political issue. And, largely because of its Articles (and over time its functional expertise), the Bank has been uncomfortable about engaging political issues explicitly, although much of its work has political determinants and consequences.

With the State much maligned of late, being held responsible at one end for egregious acts of commission and omission, and at the other derided for its irrelevance in the face of pressures from a variety of forces, both supranational and subnational, the question arises why the Bank chose such a topic at this point of time. The *Report* itself lists four factors that have given "the rethink [about the State's role] particular impetus":

- the collapse of the command and control economies of the former Soviet Union and the countries of Eastern Europe;

- the important role of the State in the "miracle" economies of East Asia;

- the fiscal crisis of the welfare State in most OECD countries;

- the collapse of States and the explosion of humanitarian crisis in several other parts of the world.

There may have been two additional reasons. First, a closer scrutiny of supranational and subnational forces that have been both cause and consequence of the weakness of States and were deemed to hold unbounded promise for the human prospect - for instance global capital markets and non-governmental organizations - has led to some sobering reassessments (Edwards and Hulme, 1996; Soros, 1997). Particularly troubling to some observers is a sense that the growing dominance of the market metaphor is resulting in a seemingly inexorable trend towards universal commodification. For these observers the underlying assumptions of human nature in the rhetoric of the market metaphor are exacerbating the difficulties in inspiring more humane visions of the "good society" (Radin, 1996; Kuttner, 1997). But for the Bank there is a second reason closer to home. As a creature of nation-States and enjoined to work with them, the Bank's own effectiveness mirrors that of the State. If the State faces a predicament today, so does the Bank, which may explain the empathy the *Report* shares with the State more than at any time in recent years.

II.   Structure and approach of the *WDR 1997*

Beginning with the emphatic statement that "Development - economic, social, and sustainable - without an effective State is impossible" (p. 18),[1] the *Report* lays out the principal questions for its inquiry (p. 29): "What institutional arrangements best allow markets to flourish? What is the role of the State both as a direct agent (mostly in the provisions of services) and as a shaper of the institutional context in which markets function? How do policies and institutions interact in development?" Answers to these questions have long been seen to be central to understanding the process of economic development, but the complexity of these issues has also often been underestimated.

The *Report* is divided into four parts. The first part attempts to provide a conceptual framework in which to understand the State and the rationale for rethinking its role in today's world. In particular, it calls for refocusing attention on State effectiveness and the roles and capabilities that enhance State effectiveness.

This basic message is translated into a two-part scheme. The first, elaborated in the second part of the *Report*, strongly cautions States against biting off more than they can chew. The role attributed to the State must match its capability: the less its capability, the more limited should be its role, according to the *Report*. The State must first focus on economic and social fundamentals, which the *Report* defines as a "foundation of law and property rights", a "benign policy environment, including macroeconomic stability", "investment in people and infrastructure" and "protection of the vulnerable". The more limited the capabilities of the State, the more important become liberalization and deregulation. While industrial policy is not ruled out, only States with a strong capacity are advised to consider it.

The second element of improving State effectiveness is specified in the third part of the *Report*, which examines options for "reinvigorating institutional capability". The *Report* puts the onus for building an effective public sector on rule-based public institutions and policy-making that curbs arbitrary State action and corruption. In order to achieve this firstly, State institutions should be subject to greater competition and organizational reforms, encompassing pecuniary and non-pecuniary incentives; secondly, the State should be made more responsive to people's needs by enhancing participation and decentralization; and thirdly, there is a need for international collective action in providing global public goods that benefit all States, but especially weaker ones.

The fourth and concluding section of *WDR 1997* revisits the agenda for change and examines options for removing obstacles that could derail the process.

Given the vastness of the subject, it is almost inevitable that *WDR 1997* is more noteworthy for its breadth than for its depth. It strives to be a consensus document providing balanced analysis. The *Report* succeeds in making the subject matter accessible to a broad audience, helped undoubtedly by a dazzling presentation of colourful graphics.

On several issues where the World Bank had adopted a strong position just a few years ago, *WDR 1997* takes a more nuanced approach. These include the analyses of decentralization (chapter 7), central bank independence and social insurance. On several other controversial issues, such as the presumed virtues of electoral democracy, the analysis is also reasonably balanced. The *Report's* principal recommendations on improving the efficiency and effectiveness in the public sector - greater decentralization of functions and responsibilities, greater competition, more transparent procedures, and meritocratic recruitment processes - are neither dogmatic nor novel. These ingredients of the "new" public management have been around for a while now (Foster and Plowden, 1996). The *Report* at least attempts to eschew the blueprint approach and leaves room for diversity of State response.

Unfortunately, for the most part the *Report* fails to examine contentious trade-offs inherent in many of the choices that States make and the numerous value judgments inherent in these choices. Such analysis would have been essential to understanding the diversity of State response. For example, while stress is laid on transparency and speed for successful privatization, the extreme difficulties of achieving both simultaneously are glossed over. Similarly, decentralization and pluralism are put forth as important ingredients of improving the effectiveness of the State, but there is no discussion of how this may be achieved without the excessive contractualization that seems to be an inevitable concomitant of this shift. Moreover, the importance of local solutions and traditional institutions is recognized (chapter 7), but there is no analysis of how poor countries can deal with the threat posed to these very traditions and local approaches from the global market juggernaut. Finally, the transmission of global changes to fragile local cultures, accelerated by the increased pace of technical change and "openness", necessarily forces socially and culturally vulnerable groups (especially tribal groups) to adapt willy-nilly at a rapid pace, which almost inevitably appears to fracture their social institutions. The dilemma defies simple solutions, as evidenced by the social conditions of tribal groups in North America and Australia, countries with vastly superior resources to come to grips with this conflict. It has to be faced, not avoided.

As a result of avoiding contentious issues, the *Report* abounds in bromides and generalities (e.g. "reliable institutions make credible States"). This is unavoidable in some cases. For instance, the *WDR* takes the juridical status of the international system of States as a given. As a multilateral institution, the World Bank cannot question the sanctity and viability of some States as independent political entities, no matter how artificial and weak they may be and despite serious doubts whether some States can ever be "effective" in the sense defined by the *WDR*, in the absence of a shared sense of nationhood among their citizens.

The remarks that follow have been grouped under three categories: the Bank's conception of the State, important issues that have been either underplayed or avoided in the *Report*, and the quality of evidence the *Report* provides to make its case.

III. The World Bank's conception of the State

A most curious aspect of the *WDR's* conception of the State is the virtual absence of politics in the analysis of an entity which is political at its very essence. One could have expected the analysis to squarely confront issues of power and, in examining such issues as corruption, participation, transparency and agencies of restraint, the *WDR* does touch indirectly upon the one or the other such aspect. But the absence of a more forthright examination of "power" is puzzling. Explicit political analysis has never been the World Bank's strength, stemming no doubt from its Articles' proscription against political considerations in lending decisions (even though this fig-leaf has been wearing thin in recent years). Consequently, it is not surprising that the *WDR's* implicit model of the ideal State is a modified Weberian State: a happy marriage of Singapore with a New England small town - a technocratic ruling class wedded to a communitarian ideal with the result of swift, well-informed decision-making, that does not pander to populism or get driven by personal enrichment but is marked by transparency and participation.

As an expression of governance of, by and for human beings, the State embodies all the frailties and contradictions of its progenitors. Conflicts between

human interests are inevitable even in a world of perfect information. In the real world, plagued as it is with chronic difficulties in understanding what human beings are doing, the problem is worse. Consequently the State is inherently a somewhat chaotic institution, no matter how orderly the analysis thereof, a feature well recognized by James Wilson in his sweeping study of bureaucracies: "All complex organizations display bureaucratic problems of confusion, red tape, and the avoidance of responsibility. These problems are much greater in government bureaucracies, because government itself is the institutionalizing of confusion (arising from the need to moderate competing demands); of red tape (arising out of the need to satisfy demands that cannot be moderated): and of avoided responsibility (arising out of the desire to retain power by minimizing criticism)" (Wilson, 1989). To expect otherwise (the example of Singapore notwithstanding), is a will-o'-the-wisp.

Understanding organizational behaviour and dynamics has not been the strong suit of the World Bank, with its own poorly conceived reorganizations providing ample testimony in this regard. One reason is that the literature on public administration - the traditional bastion of analysis of the functioning of State bureaucracy - has occupied a low position in the intellectual pecking order of the social sciences, and this is true within the Bank as well (admittedly its rigour and insights have been often limited). Consequently, the organizational aspects of State behaviour are poorly understood. Compounding the problem is the extreme difficulty (if not impossibility) of designing systems of public choice that simultaneously combine fairness and basic standards of justice in economic distribution with simplicity of design that preserves efficiency in economic processes. Freedom of political choice is certainly compatible with a wide variety of social and political orders, but it necessarily carries with it the power to disrupt. Perfectly informed (and even perfectly rational) human agents can choose to impair the economic prosperity of future generations, and indeed even to diminish their own future prospects of consumption. As the political philosopher John Dunn has argued, "Political freedom in fact entails the opportunity to impair the future real wealth of a community" (Dunn, 1990). All this is to emphasize that the reality that States may engage in such behaviour is not simply a pathological condition intrinsic to them; rather, it reflects the frailties of its creators and constituents.

In focusing on State capacity and how to augment it, the *WDR* is preoccupied with the technocratic ingredients of State capability. It does not dwell on the more intangible (and analytically difficult) social foundations that determine State legitimacy and authority, without which the best of designs for improving its capability are bound to flounder. Nor does it dwell on another intangible, but crucial, variable: political judgment on the part of a country's leadership (Berlin, 1996) without which any project to improve the effectiveness of the State is perhaps predestined to flounder. Machiavelli's dictum that "a ruler who is not himself wise cannot be given good advice" points to a chronic dilemma that has confronted all States: how does one get people of good political judgment into positions of political power? A reader of *WDR 1997* will not be enlightened on this score.

States today are suffering from an authority crisis stemming from a multitude of factors: reduced capacity to provide satisfactory solutions to the major issues on their political agendas, partly because the new issues are not wholly within their jurisdiction, partly because older issues have significantly greater international components (from labour rights to land resettlement, from taxation to trade), and partly because the compliance of their citizens can be taken even less for granted. The range of issues within which the authority and legitimacy of States is operative has narrowed and, although the composition of demands has changed, they have scarcely diminished in the aggregate. One consequence of ignoring issues of legitimacy is that the symbolic role of the State in redistribution is downplayed. Although State interventions in the pursuit of redistribution have only too often reduced efficiency while doing little for equity either, the need to be *seen* to be doing something in this sphere is typically essential to its retention of a modicum of political legitimacy - a powerful driving force behind seemingly irrational State actions. There is a widespread sense (although hard data are difficult to come by) that the recent liberalization efforts have exacerbated inequities. The political implications and constraints this reality imposes on States would have been worth examining.

There are many other issues that are fundamental to understanding the effective functioning of States which the *Report* skirts, either by the manner in which it defines the issues in some cases or by simply avoiding them in others. Space constraints do not explain these lacunae since the *Report* dwells at length on several issues that do little to deepen our understanding of the State.

IV. Underexplored issues

A. *State capability*

The *Report* repeatedly emphasizes the importance of the capability of the State, which it defines as "the ability to undertake and promote collective actions efficiently" (p. 3). This definition is simple and seemingly elegant. But does efficient collective action imply greater good for the greater number? What does efficiency for society mean? Is it defined in terms of costs and, if so, how are financial, human and environmental costs to be reconciled, and over what time horizon? How are these to be distributed amongst the citizenry? How are individual rights to be balanced against group rights? Are the answers to these questions *sui generis* to individual countries? Disputes on "sustainable development" - attempting to reconcile the views of those who place emphasis on the "sustainable" end of the spectrum with those who emphasize the "development" aspect - illustrate the difficulties. Reconciling means and ends has always posed thorny dilemmas with which all societies and States have to struggle. They cannot be wished away by definitional simplicity. This does not mean that the definition is incorrect - any alternative definition of State capability would face its own problems. Rather, the seemingly straightforward, technocratic and almost axiomatic character of the definition fails to alert the reader as to its normative implications.

B. *Property rights*

The *Report* strongly emphasizes the benefits of a sound property rights regime (chapter 3), especially for private property. It is now well recognized that poorly defined property rights can (and do) hurt the poor. At the same time, property rights have acquired an almost hallowed status in the World Bank's thinking in recent years. *WDR 1997* recognizes that in certain settings strengthening communally based property rights may be the better option (p. 45). Others have stressed that, particularly in rural settings, non-market institutions rooted in traditional social norms may be a more suitable response to the problem of scarce resource allocation (Sjaastad and Bromley, 1997). When property rights are established rapidly - for instance during periods of transition - conflicts are not removed but settled in a particular way. The particular legal configuration and the modes of enforcement of newly established property rights could also create problems if the prior absence of property rights reflected prevailing power relationships.

The last is as true in the international sphere as in domestic contexts. For the developing countries this is most apparent in the domain of intellectual property rights (IPRs). If, as the *WDR* seems to argue, knowledge is important for development, what are the consequences of an aggressive IPR regime with exclusionary and monopolistic characteristics? A specific example for such consequences is more expensive medical products for the poor. Another one is the rents accruing to private firms in the rich countries which arise from their patents on plant genetic material sourced from developing countries. These rents result from the inability of poor countries to organize and protect their common resources. While the aggregate welfare consequences are not well understood, at least one study has demonstrated that a policy of tighter intellectual property rights does *not* benefit poorer countries (Helpman, 1993). Therefore, the question arises as to whether developing countries should support a more aggressive IPR regime.

C.   *Industrial policy*

The discussion of "industrial policy" in chapter 4 of the *WDR* is somewhat elusive since the term is not explained. Is "industry" in "industrial policy" narrowly defined or does it refer to a more "strategic" element in economic statecraft? The discussion in this section seems to indicate the former. Thus, given that services are a dynamic part of many developing economies (as well as the increasing blurring of boundaries between services and "industry", especially in the informatics sector) and with agriculture continuing to play a major role in poorer countries, the treatment is especially disappointing. In services, for instance, a government could champion the higher education sector not simply to improve domestic human capital, but also as an export activity in a sector that is labour-intensive. Is that "industrial" policy?

Elsewhere the *Report* emphasizes that effective public sectors have been characterized by a strong central capacity for "strategic policy formulation" (p. 81). But is this not at the heart of "industrial policy" broadly defined? The *Report* is replete with references to the word "strategy", whether in its call for a more "strategic selection" of collective goods and services by the State or in its laying out "strategic options" at the end of various chapters. But it is never

made clear what "strategic" means, and one wonders if it is an elliptical way to signal industrial policy without explicitly acknowledging that term.

D.   *Corruption*

The *Report* takes the position that all corruption has negative effects, but it is most concerned with "unpredictable" corruption, the effects of which it finds to be most pernicious (chapter 6). Unfortunately it straitjackets itself by viewing corruption entirely through the lens of property rights. More curious is the *Report*'s definition of corruption as "the abuse of *public power* for private gain" (p. 102, emphasis added). It is clear that, for the World Bank, "public power" means public *office* rather than the arbitrary exercise of power by any actor, public or private, but in the public *domain*.[2] By definition, the role of markets and the private sector in corruption is wished away. At one point the *WDR* States that "the briber has as much responsibility as the bribed; effective penalties on domestic and international business must be part of the solution" (p. 9, "Overview"). However, it does not elaborate what this might entail.

Having locked itself into a property rights perspective, the *Report* does not examine other aspects of corruption. The abuse of power may not necessarily be driven by considerations of personal gain. By the definition of the *WDR*, public officials engaging in torture or ethnic cleansing would not be corrupt if they were not doing it for personal gain. Moreover, often it is not abuse of power *per se*, but a more human "keep the head down" behavioural pattern stemming from a desire to minimize the downside (for instance a transfer to a less desirable location) that leaches away a bureaucracy and whose cumulative effects can be as negative as those resulting from the aforementioned definition of "corruption". Is unethical behaviour that has public consequences a phenomenon that is distinct from corruption?

The analysis is also wanting in explaining why it has been so difficult to stem corruption not only during but also after the privatization process. In several countries, both developing and developed, that have been at the vanguard of privatization, the "sleaze" factor continues to haunt the political landscape, while in others privatization has indeed contributed to reducing corruption. What explains these differences? Could it be that in more traditional societies the rapid monetization of the human experience in the absence of the evolution of a parallel set of norms, creates the climate for corruption? It would seem reasonable to believe that if corrupt officials could not hide their money they might well plunder less. What is the role of the lack of transparency in overseas accounts, many of them held in OECD countries, in nurturing money laundering and tax evasion? The absence of potent anticorruption laws in OECD countries (until very recently) regulating their companies doing business abroad is surely important in this regard. This is in contrast to OECD pressures on developing countries with respect to the control of money laundering arising from drug-related activities.

E.   Civil society and participation

The term "civil society", having moved from its cottage industry status a few years ago to a robust growth industry, finds an important place in this *WDR* (chapter 7).[3] It is worth noting that, other than the business group constituent of civil society, the World Bank did not regard it as a significant variable in its analysis of the "East Asian miracle", just a few years ago. The *Report* documents well the positive contributions of this "third sector" and the importance of partnerships between the State, the private sector and the constituents of civil society to a country's development efforts.

However, the *WDR* for the most part equates civil society with non-governmental organizations (NGOs); this is perhaps an indication of the pressures the Bank faces. There is little discussion of the accountability and legitimacy of NGOs - the fact that the State in many cases lacks one or the other attribute does not *ipso facto* imply that NGOs necessarily posses them. There is also no acknowledgment that, philosophically, "civil society" also embodies the politics of "difference". Many formations that constitute civil society - religious, ethnic or caste groups, unions, business associations - can be quite parochial and exclusionary in character. Like "common sense", which is often less than common, civil society can be less than civil. The *Report* does not address this issue - or whether these formations are good in themselves, or rather for their instrumentality. The lacuna in the analysis reflects the Bank's preoccupation with the relationship between civil society and the State, with little understanding of the relationship of civil society with the "nation" or with religion, which can unleash forces that can derail the State (Hann and Dunn, 1996). The last is a particularly salient omission, since dominant Western views of civil society have historically had strong

religious roots - whether the Anglo-Saxon tradition of civil society as the vision of the ethical life within a Protestant congregation or the French tradition based on the Catholic vision of the role of a religious community within a strong secular State (Seligman, 1992).

"Participation", like "civil society", is now broadly acknowledged to be an essential ingredient of sustainable development. But, as with the treatment of "civil society", the *WDR* does not seriously examine the limits of participation as a constraint on State actions. This is all the more curious since barely a stone's throw away from where the *Report* was drafted a casual observer can find very visible manifestations of the often limited political fruit that participation can provide, even in societies that have a hospitable climate for participatory action.

F.   International collective action

The analysis makes a sound case for increasing the supply of global public goods, from research to the global environment, from making international development assistance more effective to protecting global economic stability (chapter 8). There is little to dispute in this, but what is missing is equally interesting. Thus, while the welfare-improving effects of greater openness to the movement of trade and capital is stressed, nothing is said about the movement of people (except in the case of refugees). Similarly, while much is made of the importance of the rule of law within countries, little is said regarding its importance in the international context, as for instance the implications of extraterritorial application of a country's laws when they run counter to international mechanisms to promote global economic stability, or geopolitical and commercial interests that frequently override the high-sounding rhetoric on the rule of law (p. 107-108). The *Report* (as a large part of the development community) also sidesteps a dilemma: the bottom line is supposedly "people", but the numeraire for allocations and analysis is done in terms of States.

G.   Anglo-Saxon legal norms

The *Report's* emphasis on formal institutions for reinvigorating State effectiveness - well-functioning legal institutions that enforce the "rules of the game" and property rights - did not get much play in the

East Asian Miracle study (World Bank, 1993). In the East Asian case, formal legal systems have been (until very recently) quite limited. To a considerable extent, commercial arrangements in East Asia have not been based on formal, explicit, contractual relationships. The emphasis on formal mechanisms neglects an important point. The development of a complete set of formal institutions is costly. Historically, social norms have served as a surrogate mechanism to lower transaction costs. The process of economic development is accompanied by a breakdown of informal institutions or social norms and a corresponding rise of formal institutions. But the latter seldom rise concurrently to take their place. How societies manage this transitional lag is crucial. Consequently, the importance of formal legal institutions is perhaps more in their *ex ante* effects on behaviour by their mere existence than in their use. In the latter mode, they serve principally in a fire-fighting capacity, a use that itself frequently signifies a failure of informal institutions developed by societies to resolve disputes.

Although the *WDR* acknowledges informal institutions, its heart is understandably in formal institutions. Management theorists wax eloquent on the effects of "corporate culture" on corporate performance. Similarly, there is now a vigorous debate on the social conditions upon which the viability and efficiency of the market system rests (Platteau, 1994; Moore, 1994; Murshid, 1997). Does national culture have similar implications for the nation? Are some configurations of society more conducive to effective States? Again, the document tiptoes around this analytical quagmire, choosing implicitly to attribute cultural "flaws" with *sui generis* origins to common attitudes and behavioural patterns, a consequence of systems where power has been concentrated and used arbitrarily. Such an approach, while undoubtedly often valid, is not without limitations. East Asia has not been characterized by any less concentration of power than less "successful" countries. Culture encompasses understandings of obligations and rights among various actors in a given cultural system, as well as self-enforcing norms for a broad range of transactions, including those in markets. Moreover, variables rooted in culture, such as patterns of ethnic ties, trust and cooperation both within and between societal groups, may affect transaction costs, and mitigate free-rider problems.[4]

Finally, it is interesting to note that the recent stress on enforcing property rights, whether through law and order or through contract enforcement, places almost the entire analytical emphasis on the judiciary with scarcely any mention of the role of executive investigative agencies and the police - a case of putting the cart before the horse.

H.   Credibility versus flexibility

The dilemma of rules versus discretion is inherent to all decision-making bodies. In a more volatile world what are the trade-offs between credibility and flexibility? Amidst increasing demands for a more agile State, the dilemma of checking arbitrary decision-making without building rigidities (p. 108) is a tricky one. The *WDR* recommends "lock-in" rules using mechanisms that make it costly to reverse course (privatization or signing on to international agreements being good examples). However, there are also cases where the credibility arising from "lock-in" rules is outweighed by the lack of flexibility in a volatile world, as recent problems with regimes of fixed exchange rates have indicated. But flexibility creates its own problems. The dilemma is especially pronounced in cases where long-term contracts may be required, such as in infrastructure. Thus, recent exchange-rate depreciations in South-East Asia, while emphasizing the importance of flexible-exchange-rate regimes, also show how these might exacerbate problems in infrastructure financing. Rapid changes in policies, by pointing to a government's commitment to reform, may signal credibility. However, what can be done quickly can often be undone quickly. On the other hand, gradualism may simply be a cover for foot-dragging, whose costs can also be highly detrimental. Unfortunately, the *WDR* does not provide a framework that may help elucidate these choices.

I.   Population

While providing new rationales for regulation in finance, utilities and the environment, the analysis is weak with regard to countries with weak institutions (see Table 4.2). Even in the better endowed countries, bank supervisors have to run ever faster merely to keep abreast of rapidly changing instruments and risks in financial markets. The mushrooming of non-banking financial institutions and the growth of electronic money add to the already difficult task facing many poor countries in the financial sector. The *WDR's* homilies ("given an appropriate and enforceable legal framework" for financial-sector development) appear more like linguistic sophistry than practical advice, given the sharp asymmetries in the time periods required to institute policy changes on the one hand and to develop corresponding institutional structures on the other. The virtues of economic openness are now taken as axiomatic by the Bretton Woods institutions. It would be worthwhile to more closely scrutinize whether in countries where institutions are particularly weak there are perhaps some areas, such as the financial sector or the capital account, where the degree of deregulation and the form of economic openness, and not just the role of the State, may need to be matched to capability.

V. Misplaced quantification

One of the weaknesses of the *Report* is its misplaced emphasis on quantification. In some cases problems arise from comparing apples and oranges. In documenting the growth of the State as measured by government expenditure as a share of GDP (Figure 1), data for OECD countries include all government expenditure, central as well as local. Data for developing countries, however, only include central government expenditure. Consequently, the decline of government expenditure to GDP may be simply a result of fiscal decentralization occurring in the same period (indeed, Table 7.1 on subnational finance appears to indicate this). All that can be said is that one measure of the size of the State - central government expenditure - appears to have stopped growing in the mid-1980s.

More troubling is the myriad of regressions, many based on an ambitious private-sector survey that tries to buttress support for the importance of "credibility" - a problematic measure as it is highly subjective. For instance, how sensitive are responses by the domestic private sector to expectations or the degree of political openness in their countries? Another question is whether an elaborate survey was required to "prove" the point that "credibility" matters, since no one had argued otherwise. The results of this survey will certainty be widely quoted. However, while one would expect a survey on credibility to be credible itself, the strong conclusions drawn from it unfortunately lack such credibility, plagued as they are with technical problems of sample bias, endogeneity, simultaneity and collinearity.

The survey covers domestic private-sector firms in 69 countries. This is an ambitious undertaking. One territory, the West Bank and Gaza, is not a country (at least not yet) and does not have the presumed autonomy of an independent nation-State. In Asia,

firms from only three countries responded (Fiji, India and Malaysia). Only 4 per cent of all the firms surveyed in developing countries were from Asia (Table TN7 in the Technical Note). China did not allow the survey, while in other cases firms did not respond (e.g. Singapore) because they were uninterested or simply unwilling to put down on paper anything that could be construed as critical of their government. This is not a minor sampling bias. With the exception of Malaysia, no country from the economically most dynamic region of the world is included in the survey results. Rather than use that reality to inquire as to what the lack of response may mean, the three countries that did respond have been included to comprise the "South-South East Asia" group of countries. In the interest of transparency the *Report* simply stated which countries did not participate. In fact, while maintaining confidentiality of the precise nature of individual country responses, the World Bank could (and should) have listed the percentage of firms responding by country as well as those countries that declined to participate in the survey.

The use of indexes to rank countries on a variety of criteria has been in vogue in recent years as country "beauty contests" have soared in popularity. These criteria, whether the UNDP's Human Development Index, Transparency International's Corruption Index, the competitiveness indexes of the World Economic Forum or the International Institute for Management Development, all suffer from a variety of conceptual and statistical problems - a reflection of the difficulties of constructing indexes with unambiguous rankings.[5] The *WDR's* extensive use of indexes (social capital, corruption, school quality, budget institution quality, credibility, institutional capability, and policy distortions) conveys a pseudo-scientific basis to the conclusions drawn. All these factors, as the *Report* points out, affect the effectiveness of governments. Since in many cases these are subjective indicators, qualitative judgments have to be arrived at. But the manner of presentation appears to give a sense of "hard" reality without any caution or discussion as to the limitations of these indexes and hence the robustness of results. For instance the index for political liberties is one formulated by Freedom House. There is no discussion of why this is the appropriate indicator rather than one developed in, say, Accra or Singapore, if requested. The choice of index is a revealed preference for certain political values and one should not be coy about it. A separate question is whether these indicators accurately reflect reality. Recent detailed analysis of a somewhat similar indicator - quantitative measures of democracy -

suggest that these measures contain substantial inaccuracies (McHenry, 1997). Similarly the "Quality of bureaucracy" is derived as a composite index from sources whose principal evaluation criteria are variables that are of importance to foreign investors.[6] There may well be quite practical reasons why these second-best indices have been used. But there are no caveats as to what biases may thereby have been introduced. Under the circumstances the *Report* should have restricted itself to ordinal rankings as much as possible (as in Box 3.1).

But there are also analytical problems, and the results can be interpreted quite differently. For instance, the rankings of the 15 obstacles to doing business (in declining order of importance) are tax regulations/and or higher taxes, corruption, financing, crime and theft, and infrastructure. In fact, it is clear from the background paper (Brunetti, Kisunko and Weder, 1997, Appendix Table 8), though less evident from the latest *WDR* (Box 3.1), that domestic firms ranked policy variables frequently cited by the Bank as major obstacles to business quite low: these include regulations on foreign trade, labour regulations, foreign currency regulations and price controls (ranked 9, 10, 11 and 14 respectively). For domestic private business, regulation is much less important than issues related to law and order. Foreign businesses, because they are usually larger, have the muscle to deal with law and order problems more easily. But issues related to trade and foreign exchange are clearly of much greater importance to foreign business - a message which the Bank invariably supports.

In reality, the indices used provide at best only indicative results, given that the methodological terrain is a veritable minefield. For instance, Figure 5 (in the "Overview" chapter) examines the relative effects of policies and capabilities, each measured by an index, on economic growth. For any country, policies and capabilities change with time. Are these being measured at the beginning of the period, at the end or somewhere in between? The index of policy distortions is a composite of inflation, black-market premium and openness (as measured by trade to GDP ratio). Even if we leave aside the well-recognized problems in the measurement of these variables,[7] why these three variables? A vast literature has examined the effects of a myriad of country policies on growth, including policies affecting investment in physical capital, human capital, equipment investment, and research and development; government spending, tax policy, and financial policies; trade policies defined in different ways; policies affecting income distribution; and macroeconomic policies. Policy "distortions" can

(and surely do) occur in most of them and the policy variables constituting "distortions" can be measured and weighted in different ways. Furthermore, just a few years ago a World Bank research publication concluded that luck, especially in the forms of shocks to the terms of trade, plays as much of a role in explaining the variance of growth rates as policies (Easterly et al., 1993). But here no such qualifications seem warranted, and only policies and bureaucratic capabilities seem to matter.

Policy distortions themselves undermine capability - some more than others. Poor capabilities may themselves result in policy distortions. There are serious questions of endogeneity and simultaneity in the analysis of these relationships, and it is unclear how, or whether, these have been addressed. Consequently, peculiar conclusions can be drawn if the numbers (which are never ranges) are taken literally. Based on Figure 5, the *Report* argues that "good policies by themselves can improve overall results. But the benefits are magnified where institutional capability is also higher" (p. 33). In fact, as Annex I shows, the results when initially computed indicated that capabilities mattered more than policies. When "capability" changed from "low" to "high", growth increased by 1.7 per cent a year for a given degree of policy distortion. However, when policy distortions improved from "high" to "low", growth increased by just 1.0 per cent for a given level of "capability".[8] This would suggest that, at the margin, States should focus on improving capability rather than policies. But since such a message would have constituted quite a departure from the Bank's usual recommendations, the offending column was simply dropped from the published version.

Similarly, the desired message is driving the analysis in Figure 5.6, which attempts to show that a better bureaucracy requires relatively better paid public servants (Annex II). The published version compares Philippines with "other East Asia" and shows that bureaucratic capability and the ratio of public to private wages are correlated. Originally the comparison was between the Philippines and the Republic of Korea. There, although the relative salaries of public officials in the Republic of Korea (compared to their private sector counterparts) were two-and-a-half times that of their Philippines counterparts, their "capability index" was only one-and-a-half times as good. One could therefore draw the (contrary) conclusion that the system in the Republic of Korea was more inefficient - it got much less "bang for the buck" than the Philippines! Using different comparators (a particular group of East

Asian countries, and wages and salaries of senior civil servants only) embarrassment is avoided: the "other East Asia" capability index is three times that of the Philippines, while the corresponding wage ratio is only two-and-a-half. Honour and results have been saved!

These comments do not imply that the *WDR's* conclusions are invalid or wrong. Many make common sense, but are not always underpinned by rigorous analysis. Moreover, many of the issues identified in the *Report* as important are precisely those that critics contend have not been important in the East Asia experience. One may conclude that what is at issue here is not so much the credibility of the analysis as the credulity of the readers.

VI. Conclusion

Academia and policy circles have demonstrated remarkable fecundity in their analysis of the State. Given this analytical abundance, what is the value-added provided by *WDR 1997*? Writing a *WDR* on "The State in a Changing World" is certainly a difficult task, and there is little doubt that, at least as a consciousness-raising device, *WDR 1997* succeeds in sensitizing opinion with regard to the significance of the State. Consequently, one could argue that the role of the *WDR* is mainly a didactic one, so that the various results should be seen as merely illustrative. The World Bank is not a university and the *WDR* should not be seen as a research document *per se* to which more rigorous standards of proof can be applied. Indeed, the *Report* is more convincing when it sticks to sound common sense advice. And, as with most other analysis of the State, the *Report* is stronger in its diagnosis of what does not work rather than of what does work, and it is stronger in its recommendations on "what" rather than "how".

However, the *WDR's* "nouvelle cuisine" like character makes for a rather unsatisfying intellectual meal, with high cost and low nutritional value. In part this is a reflection of the very nature of the *WDR* as an excellent public relations instrument for the Bank. But it also reflects the fact that the Bank has become an insecure and besieged institution, as well as increasingly intellectually risk-averse. One conse-quence is a tendency to downplay the dilemmas and complexities that are inherent in the changing role of the State and the institution's analysis, borne on a strong updraft of "win-win" and "feel-good" argot. Thus, the *Report* glides over hard and unpleasant realities.

Multilateral institutions are circumscribed in the degree to which they can be candid on issues that are inherently political, such as the "role of the State". Such efforts are apt to slip into the realm of subtle institutional public relations, especially when support for these institutions is lukewarm. It is therefore worthwhile to ponder for a moment over the com-position of resources spent by multilateral institutions on research and on whether these resources could be better deployed elsewhere. The opportunity costs of the approximately $4 million spent on a *WDR* are not insignificant. If, for instance, instead of preparing an annual *WDR*, the World Bank were to deploy this sum to support research on malaria, would global human welfare be any worse? It is not just multilateral development bank projects to developing countries that require sound cost-benefit analysis. The internal deployment of resources by these institutions could benefit from such scrutiny as well.

Notes

1   The Overview (p. 1) is similarly emphatic: "An effective State is vital for the provision of the goods and services - and the rules and institutions - that allow markets to flourish and people to lead healthier, happier lives". The basis of the leap from flourishing markets to "happier lives" is unclear.

2   Indeed, a later issues paper on combating corruption, prepared for the September 1997 meetings of the Development Committee by the staffs of the Bank and IMF, defined corruption as "the abuse of public *office* for private gain" (emphasis added).

3   The term "civil society" has its roots in the Scottish enlightenment. Its current rediscovery owes much to East European dissident movements in the 1970s and 1980s.

4   For long the attitude amongst development analysts to the role of informal institutions was perhaps best illustrated by Arthur Lewis's comments when it was suggested to him that a set of Indian institutional norms, the caste system, constituted a powerful barrier to economic development: "The love of money is a powerful institutional solvent" (Arthur Lewis, 1962).

5   Transparency International's Corruption Index, has been criticized as being "subjective" and "misleading" because it fails to distinguish between the type and scale of corruption (*Financial Times*, August 13, 1997). Similarly, even the Human Development Index, following its revision, continues to be plagued by statistical artifacts (Luchters and Menkhoff, 1996).

6   BERI's (Business Environmental Risk Intelligence) Index of Bureaucratic Delays; the International Country Risk Guide's Index of Quality of Bureaucracy; and the Business International/Economist Intelligence Unit's Index of Bureaucracy and Red Tape.

7   For instance, the black market premium and openness are correlated. The black market premium may simply be picking up the thinness of the foreign-exchange market. It is affected both by interest rates and by penalties for dealing in the black market. Trade openness, as measured by the trade to GDP ratio, is sensitive to

country size and is particularly dubious if openness is broadly conceived to apply to more than merchandise trade.

8 These figures are from an earlier - unpublished - draft of the WDR, the *Report No. 16376*, March 1997, Figure 2.2.

References

ARTHUR LEWIS, W. (1962), "Foreword", in T.S. Epstein (ed.), *Economic Development and Social Change in South India* (Manchester: Manchester University Press).

BERLIN, I. (1996), "On Political Judgment", *New York Review of Books*, 3 October 1996.

BRUNETTI, A., G. KISUNKO, and B. WEDER (1997), "Institutional Obstacles to Doing Business: Region-by-Region Results from a Worldwide Survey of the Private Sector", *World Bank Policy Research Paper*, No. 1759 (Washington, D.C.).

DUNN, J. (1990), *The Economic Limits to Modern Politics* (Cambridge, U.K.: Cambridge University Press).

EASTERLY, W., M. KREMER, L. PRITCHETT, and L. SUMMERS (1993), "Good Policy or Good Luck? Country Growth Performance and Temporary Shocks", *Journal of Monetary Economics*, Vol. 3, No. 32, pp. 459-484.

EDWARDS, M., and D. HULME (1996), "Too Close for Comfort? The Impact of Official Aid on Nongovernmental Organizations", *World Development*, Vol. 24, No. 6, pp. 961-973.

FOSTER, C.D., and F.J. PLOWDEN (1996), *The State Under Stress: Can the Hollow State be Good Government* (Bristol, Pennsylvania: Open University Press).

HANN, C., and E. DUNN (eds.) (1996), *Civil Society: Challenging Western Models* (London: Routledge).

HELPMAN, E. (1993), "Innovation, Imitation, and Intellectual Property Rights", *Econometrica*, Vol. 61, No. 6 (November), pp. 1247-1280.

KUTTNER, R. (1997), *Everything for Sale: the Virtues and Limits of Markets* (New York: Alfred Knof).

LUCHTERS, G., and L. MENKHOFF (1996), "Human Development as Statistical Artifact", *World Development*, Vol. 24, No. 8 (August).

McHENRY, D. (1997), "The Measurement of Democracy in Africa: An Assessment of the Utility of Quantitative Indices", paper presented at the 1997 Annual Meeting of the American Political Science Association.

MOORE, M. (1994), "How Difficult is it to Construct Market Relations? A Commentary on Platteau", *Journal of Development Studies*, Vol. 30, No. 3 (April), pp. 818-830.

MURSHID, K.A.S. (1997), "Generalized Morality and the Problem of Transition to an Impersonal Exchange Regime: A Response to Platteau", *Journal of Development Studies*, Vol. 33, No. 5 (June), pp. 693-713.

PLATTEAU, J.-Ph. (1994), "Behind the Market Stage Where Real Societies Exist. Part I: The Role of Public and Private Institutions; Part II: The Role of Moral Norms", *Journal of Development Studies*, Vol. 30, No. 3 (April).

RADIN, M.J. (1996), *Contested Commodities* (Cambridge, MA: Harvard University Press).

SELIGMAN, A. (1992), *The Idea of Civil Society* (New York: Free Press).

SJAASTAD, E., and D. Bromley (1997), "Indigenous Land Rights in Sub-Saharan Africa: Appropriation, Security and Investment Demand", *World Development*, Vol. 25, No. 4, pp. 549-562.

SOROS, G. (1997), "The Capitalist Threat", *The Atlantic Monthly*, February, pp. 45-58.

WILSON, J.Q. (1989), *Bureaucracy: What Government Agencies Do and Why They Do It* (New York: Basic Books).

WORLD BANK (1993), *The East Asian Miracle: Economic Growth and Public Policy* (New York: Oxford University Press).

WORLD BANK (1997), *World Development Report, 1997* (New York: Oxford University Press).

Annex I

ORIGINAL:

"Countries with stronger institutional capability and good policies grow faster"

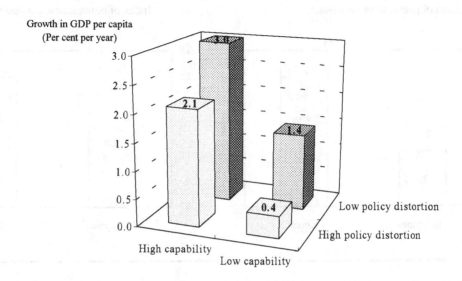

Source: World Bank, *Report No. 16376*, March 1997, Figure 2.2.

FINAL:

"Countries with good economic policies and stronger institutional capability grow faster"

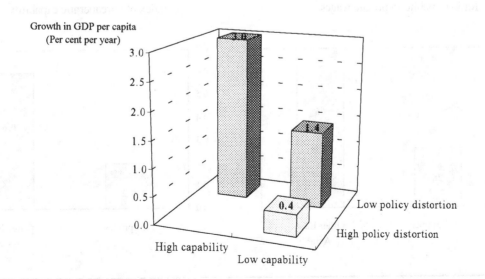

Source: *World Development Report 1997*, Figure 5.

Annex II

ORIGINAL:

"Figure 5.6   Meritocracy in Korea's civil service has raised its capability"

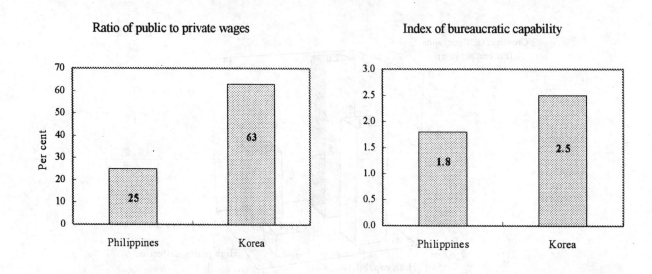

Ratio of public to private wages   Index of bureaucratic capability

Source: World Bank, *Report No. 16376*, March 1997.

FINAL:

"Figure 5.6   Lack of meritocracy and poor pay in the Philippines' civil service
have lowered capability"

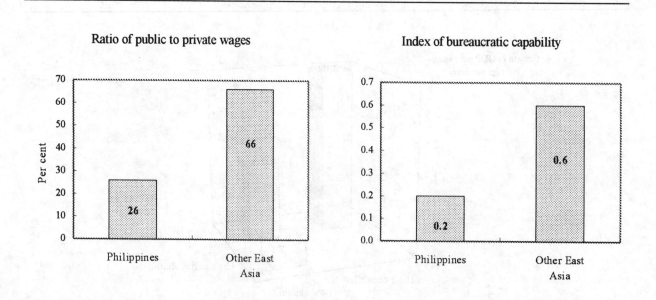

Ratio of public to private wages   Index of bureaucratic capability

Source: *World Development Report 1997.*

UNITED NATIONS CONFERENCE ON TRADE AND DEVELOPMENT

Palais des Nations
CH-1211 GENEVE 10
Switzerland

International Monetary and Financial Issues for the 1990s

Volume V (1995)

United Nations Publication, Sales No. E.95.II.D.3
ISBN 92-1-112371-2

Göran Ohlin
  The Negative Net Transfers of the World Bank
Louis Emmerij
  A Critical Review of the World Bank's Approach to Social-Sector Lending and Poverty Alleviation
Nguyuru H.I. Lipumba
  Structural Adjustment Policies and Economic Performance of African Countries
Robert Wade
  The East Asian Miracle: Why the Controversy Continues
Alfred Maizels
  The Functioning of International Markets for Primary Commodities: Key Policy Issues for Developing Countries
Donald R. Lessard
  Effective Use of Financial Markets for Risk Management by Developing Countries: An Overview

Volume VI (1995)

United Nations Publication, Sales No. E.95.II.D.7
ISBN 92-1-112375-5

Manuel R. Agosin, Diana Tussie and Gustavo Crespi
  Developing Countries and the Uruguay Round: An Evaluation and Issues for the Future
Dani Rodrik
  Developing Countries After the Uruguay Round
Ann Weston
  The Uruguay Round: Unravelling the Implications for the Least Developed and Low-Income Countries

Volume VII (1996)

United Nations Publication, Sales No. E.96.II.D.2
ISBN 92-1-112394-1

John Williamson
  A New Facility for the IMF?
Ariel Buira and Roberto Marino
  Allocation of Special Drawing Rights: The Current Debate
Chandra Hardy
  The Case for Multilateral Debt Relief for Severely Indebted Countries
Azizali F. Mohammed
  Global Financial System Reform and the C-20 Process
Raisuddin Ahmed
  A Critique of the World Development Report 1994: Infrastructure for Development
Dipak Mazumdar
  Labour issues in the World Development Report: A Critical Assessment
Ann Weston
  The Uruguay Round: Costs and Compensation for Developing Countries

Volume VIII (1997)

United Nations publication, Sales No. E.97.II.D.5
ISBN 92-1-112409-3

G. K. Helleiner
  Capital Account Regimes and the Developing Countries
Rudi Dornbusch
  Cross-Border Payments Taxes and Alternative Capital-Account Regimes
Guillermo Le Fort V. and Carlos Budnevich L.
  Capital-Account Regulations and Macroeconomic Policy: Two Latin American Experiences
Louis Kasekende, Damoni Kitabire and Matthew Martin
  Capital Inflows and Macroeconomic Policy in Sub-Saharan Africa
Yung Chul Park and Chi-Young Song
  Managing Foreign Capital Flows: The Experiences of the Republic of Korea, Thailand, Malaysia and Indonesia
Devesh Kapur
  The New Conditionalities of the International Financial Institutions
Aziz Ali Mohammed
  Notes on MDB Conditionality on Governance
Matthew Martin
  A Multilateral Debt Facility - Global and National
Peter Murrell
  From Plan to Market: The World Development Report 1996 - An Assessment

Other selected UNCTAD publications

Trade and Development Report, 1996 United Nations Publication, Sales No. E.96.II.D.6
ISBN 92-1-112399-2

Part One Global Trends
I The World Economy: Performance and Prospects
II International Capital Markets and the External Debt of Developing Countries

Part Two Rethinking Development Strategies: Some Lessons from the East Asian Experience

I Integration and Industrialization in East Asia
II Exports, Capital Formation and Growth
III Responding to the New Global Environment

Annex Macroeconomic Management, Financial Governance, and Development: Selected
Policy Issues

Trade and Development Report, 1997 United Nations Publication, Sales No. E.97.II.D.8
ISBN 92-1-112411-5

Part One Global Trends

I The World Economy: Performance and Prospects
II International Financial Markets and the External Debt of Developing Countries
Annex Issues Involved in Trade Disputes that Have Arisen Concerning the National Treatment
Provision of the WTO Agreement

Part Two Globalization, Distribution and Growth

I The Issues at Stake
II Globalization and Economic Convergence
III Income Inequality and Development
Annex: Trends in Personal Income Distribution in Selected Developing Countries
IV Liberalization, Integration and Distribution
V Income Distribution, Capital Accumulation and Growth
VI Promoting Investment: Some Lessons from East Asia

****

These publications may be obtained from bookstores and distributors throughout the world. Consult your bookstore
or write to United Nations Publications/Sales Section, Palais des Nations, CH-1211 Geneva 10, Switzerland, fax:
+41-22-917.0027, e-mail: unpubli@un.org, Internet: http://www.un.org/publications; or from United Nations
Publications, Two UN Plaza, Room DC2-853, Dept. PERS, New York, N.Y. 10017, U.S.A., telephone:+1-212-963.8302
or +1-800-253.9646; fax: +1-212-963.3489, e-mail: publications@un.org.

Proceedings of the International Conference on East Asian Development: Lessons for a New Global Environment, Kuala Lumpur, Malaysia, 29 February - 1 March 1996,

UNCTAD/GDS/MDPB/2

United Nations Conference on Trade and Development, Geneva
and Institute of Strategic and International Studies, Kuala Lumpur

Session 1	Regional and National Dimensions of East Asian Development
Session 2	Government-Business Relationship and Industrialization
Session 3	Policy Initiatives for Marginalized Sectors
Session 4	Policy Options in a Globalizing Environment
Session 5	Policy Lessons

UNCTAD Discussion Papers

No. 94, January 1995	XIE Ping	Financial services in China
No. 95, January 1995	William W.F. CHOA	The derivation of trade matrices by commodity groups in current and constant prices
No. 96, February 1995	Alexandre R. BARROS	The role of wage stickiness in economic growth
No. 97, February 1995	Ajit SINGH	How did East Asia grow so fast? Slow progress towards an analytical consensus
No. 98, April 1995	Z. KOZUL-WRIGHT	The role of the firm in the innovation process
No. 99, May 1995	Juan A. DE CASTRO	Trade and labour standards: Using the wrong instruments for the right cause
No. 100, August 1995	Roberto FRENKEL	Macroeconomic sustainability and development prospects: Latin American performance in the 1990s
No. 101, August 1995	R. KOZUL-WRIGHT & Paul RAYMENT	Walking on two legs: Strengthening democracy and productive entrepreneurship in the transition economies
No. 102, August 1995	J.C. DE SOUZA BRAGA M.A. MACEDO CINTRA & Sulamis DAIN	Financing the public sector in Latin America
No. 103, September 1995	Toni HANIOTIS & Sebastian SCHICH	Should governments subsidize exports through export credit insurance agencies?
No. 104, September 1995	Robert ROWTHORN	A simulation model of North-South trade
No. 105, October 1995	Giovanni N. DE VITO	Market distortions and competition: The particular case of Malaysia
No. 106, October 1995	John EATWELL	Disguised unemployment: The G7 experience
No. 107, November 1995	Luisa E. SABATER	Multilateral debt of least developed countries
No. 108, November 1995	David FELIX	Financial globalization versus free trade: The case for the Tobin Tax
No. 109, December 1995	Urvashi ZUTSHI	Aspects of the final outcome of the negotiations on financial services of the Uruguay Round
No. 110, January 1996	H.A.C. PRASAD	Bilateral terms of trade of selected countries from the South with the North and the South

No. 111, January 1996	Charles GORE	Methodological nationalism and the misunderstanding of East Asian industrialization
No. 112, March 1996	Djidiack FAYE	Aide publique au développement et dette extérieure: Quelles mesures opportunes pour le financement du secteur privé en Afrique?
No. 113, March 1996	Paul BAIROCH & Richard KOZUL-WRIGHT	Globalization myths: Some historical reflections on integration, industrialization and growth in the world economy
No. 114, April 1996	Rameshwar TANDON	Japanese financial deregulation since 1984
No. 115, April 1996	E.V.K. FITZGERALD	Intervention versus regulation: The role of the IMF in crisis prevention and management
No. 116, June 1996	Jussi LANKOSKI	Controlling agricultural nonpoint source pollution: The case of mineral balances
No. 117, August 1996	José RIPOLL	Domestic insurance markets in developing countries: Is there any life after GATS?
No. 118, September 1996	Sunanda SEN	Growth centres in South East Asia in the era of globalization
No. 119, September 1996	Leena ALANEN	The impact of environmental cost internalization on sectoral competitiveness: A new conceptual framework
No. 120, October 1996	Sinan AL-SHABIBI	Structural adjustment for the transition to disarmament: An assessment of the role of the market
No. 121, October 1996	J.F. OUTREVILLE	Reinsurance in developing countries: Market structure and comparative advantage
No. 122, December 1996	Jörg MAYER	Implications of new trade and endogenous growth theories for diversification policies of commodity-dependent countries
No. 123, December 1996	L. RUTTEN & L. SANTANA-BOADO	Collateralized commodity financing, with special reference to the use of warehouse receipts
No. 124, March 1997	Jörg MAYER	Is having a rich natural-resource endowment detrimental to export diversification?
No. 125, April 1997	Brigitte BOCOUM	The new mining legislation of Côte d'Ivoire: Some comparative features
No. 126, April 1997	Jussi LANKOSKI	Environmental effects of agricultural trade liberalization and domestic agricultural policy reforms
No. 127, May 1997	Raju Jan SINGH	Banks, growth and geography
No. 128, September 1997	Enrique COSIO-PASCAL	Debt sustainability and social and human development
No. 129, September 1997	Andrew J. CORNFORD	Selected features of financial sectors in Asia and their implications for services trade

****

Copies of *Proceedings of the International Conference on East Asian Development: Lessons for a New Global Environment, UNCTAD Discussion Papers* and *Reprint Series* may be obtained from the Editorial Assistant, Macroeconomic and Development Policies, GDS, UNCTAD, Palais des Nations, CH-1211 Geneva 10, Switzerland (telephone: +41-22-907.5733; fax +41-22-907.0274; e-mail: nicole.winch@unctad.org).